the
COMPLETE
ILLUSTRATED
ENCYCLOPEDIA
OF

Magical Plants

revised

THE
COMPLETE
ILLUSTRATED
ENCYCLOPEDIA
OF

Magical Plants

revised

SUSAN GREGG

FAIR WINDS
PRESS
BEVERLY, MASSACHUSETTS

© 2014 Fair Winds Press
Text © 2008, 2014 Susan Gregg

First published in the USA in 2014 by
Fair Winds Press, a member of
Quarto Publishing Group USA Inc.
100 Cummings Center
Suite 406-L
Beverly, MA 01915-6101
www.fairwindspress.com

18 17 16 15   2 3 4 5

ISBN: 978-1-59233-583-1
Digital edition published in 2014
eISBN: 978-1-61058-869-0

Originally found under the following Library of Congress Cataloging-in-Publication Data

Library of Congress Cataloging-in-Publication Data
Gregg, Susan, 1949-
The complete illustrated encyclopedia of magical plants / Susan Gregg.
    p. cm.
  Includes index.
  ISBN-10: 1-59233-364-8
  ISBN-13: 978-1-59233-364-6
  1. Herbs--Miscellanea--Encyclopedias. 2. Plants--Miscellanea--Encyclopedias.
  3. Flowers--Miscellanea--Encyclopedias. 4. Magic--Encyclopedias. I. Title.
  BF1623.P5G74 2008
  133'.258--dc22

                                                        2008008834

Cover and book design: Kathie Alexander

The information in this book is for educational purposes only. It is not intended to
replace the advice of a physician or medical practitioner. Please see your health care
provider before beginning any new health program, including using any herb, plant,
or flower for medicinal purposes. It is important to remember that they are drugs and
should be used only under the supervision of a qualified health care provider.

Printed and bound in China

Contents

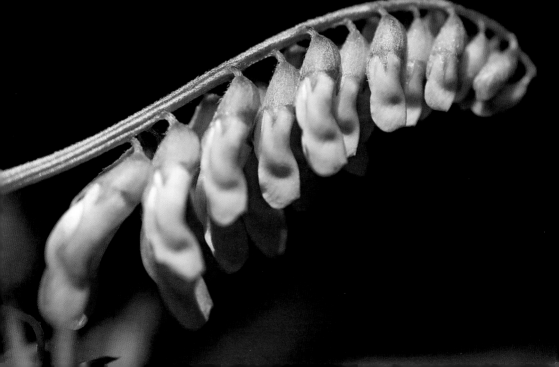

Introduction

A garden is truly a place of enchantment. From a simple mixture of sun, water, soil, and air come massive Banyan trees and dainty Lilies of the Valley. Plants provide everything we need to survive on this planet, from food to healing remedies to the raw materials for the clothing we wear and the homes we live in to the air we breathe.

What is more magical than a seed? Wrapped within each tiny seed is the potential of a new life. Every majestic Oak tree was once a tiny acorn. Likewise, within you lie endless possibilities. Nearly anything you can dream up in your imagination you can create in your life as long as you are willing to take the necessary actions.

This book is about harnessing the magical properties of the plant world. There is nothing quite as satisfying as connecting with the magical nature of life. Once you do, your life is never really the same. We live in a universe of endless possibilities, and the only real limit is how far we are willing to go in the pursuit of our happiness.

Does magic really work? Can plants help you find love and create abundance? The answer to those questions is a resounding yes, but there is a but. Think of it this way: Your car certainly can't get you where you want to go by itself, but you can use it to get you where you want to go. Your car will transport you to any destination you desire if you simply get into it, start the engine, and steer it in the correct direction, following the appropriate roads and highways. The same is true of using herbs, flowers, and plants. Once you learn how to harness their energy, they are wonderful "vehicles" for helping you get where you want to go in life. You can use them as tools to create whatever you want.

Plants are alive and full of their own unique energy. As you learn to align yourself with their energy, anything is possible. Planting a seed, watching it grow, seeing it flower, and watching a small blossom turn into a delicious piece of fruit is magical in and of itself. With a little practice, you can harness the magic of the plant kingdom to help you create what you want when you want it. You can use plants to heal your mind, your heart, and your body. They will definitely help you connect with your spirit and deepen your appreciation of the Divine. They will also help you learn to listen to your intuition and tap into your own inner strength and wisdom.

I suggest starting your exploration of the magical properties of herbs by browsing through this book, picking out a few of your favorite herbs, and working with them for a while. Once you've invited herbs into your life, I think you'll be inspired to deepen your knowledge and expand your awareness of just what plants can do. They are nature's pharmacy and can help you manifest your deepest dreams and desires.

I love the smell of fresh herbs. When I first moved to Honolulu, I went to Chinatown for an acupuncture treatment. The woman was also an herbalist. As I was lying on the table full of needles, I could hear her talking in Chinese while she was chopping herbs and making up various mixtures for her patients. The sounds and the smells were intriguing. I had always been fascinated by nature, magic, and wishcraft (yes wish, not witch), our inherent ability to manifest our reality. The sights and sounds of that Chinese herb shop reminded me just how healing and magical herbs can be.

"In All Things Of Nature
There Is Something Marvelous."

—ARISTOTLE

Indeed, the practice of using herbs, plants, and flowers to nurture and heal our minds, bodies, and spirits is a time-honored tradition. Indigenous healers have used herbs for hundreds of years. Even in the twenty-first century, nature continues to be our pharmacist, as many of today's pharmaceutical drugs are derived from herbs. Yet there is so much more the plant world can teach us. Connecting with nature, with the magic, and with the amazing universe that exists just beyond our everyday awareness can become an exciting way of life.

This book will give you a wonderful introduction into the world of enchanted herbs, plants, and flowers. They resonate with me; Mother Nature touches my soul in such a profound manner when I use them. I hope you also allow your heart and mind to be open to their endless possibilities and the magic that is always present in them. If you'd like to go further in your exploration, there are many wonderful teachers who can assist you. There is much to be said for finding a mentor who can guide you and direct you on your path toward happiness, freedom, and joy. There is an old saying, "When the student is ready, the teacher appears." If you want to explore herbs or your spiritual nature further, the bulletin board at your local health food store or New Age bookstore is a good place to begin your search. Finding a mentor is a wonderful opportunity for you to practice following your intuition. Listen to your inner wisdom and follow your heart, and they will take you to places you never imagined possible.

It is important to note that the medicinal uses of the herbs, plants, and flowers listed in this book are for your information only and are in no way meant to be a substitute for professional medical care. They are very powerful drugs; before you use any of them, be sure to consult your medical doctor and/or an experienced herbalist. If you read within these pages about an herb, a plant, or a flower that sounds like it might be of benefit to you medically, I encourage you to bring this encyclopedia along with you the next time you visit your doctor. Then, together, the two of you can come up with a treatment plan that harnesses the healing energy of these amazing plants. And who knows? You might actually be enlightening your doctor to some of these plants' amazing healing capabilities.

Herbs, plants, and flowers are fascinating creatures with spirits and wisdom. I hope you enjoy getting to know them as much as I do. When we aren't fully connected to the wisdom of the Earth and the wonder of the plant kingdom, we are depriving ourselves of an incredible gift.

May this book open your mind, your heart, and your spirit to the loving gifts so generously offered to all human beings by the plant kingdom and Mother Earth.

A Brief History of Magical Plants

PREHISTORY

The history of using plants for healing and magic goes back more than a millennia. The earliest human beings were primarily hunters and gatherers. Most of their spiritual beliefs were earth-based. Earth was seen as the great mother and the goddess was greatly revered.

In prehistoric communities, the priestess was in charge of the tribe's health. They knew the magical and healing properties of plants, herbs, and roots. They would pray, perform ceremonies, expel what they perceived as evil spirits, and heal the sick and afflicted. Though their practices were not recorded in writing, their traditions and magic were passed down through the ages to other earth-based philosophies and religions.

EGYPT

The Egyptian civilization was one of the first great civilizations. They were traders and merchants who traveled long distances, bringing back herbs and spices from faraway lands. They had a complex belief system about gods and goddesses, magic, and the use of herbs and plants in healing.

Egyptians believed the gods were the creators and controllers of life. They believed conception was ruled by the god Thoth, while Bes, another god, decided whether childbirth went smoothly. They believed the human body had forty-six channels that were conduits for the soul's energy. Blockages in any of those channels caused disease and were the result of the evil doings by Wehedu, an evil spirit.

A medical papyrus was discovered by Georg Moritz Ebers, a German novelist and Egyptologist, in Luxor. The papyrus contained more than 700 remedies, magical formulas, and scores of incantations aimed at repelling demons, which they believed caused disease and other bodily afflictions. These incantations allowed the healer to harness the magical aspect of the herbs and use them to alleviate the disease or remove the patients' suffering.

Herbs were used for everything from embalming the dead to creating love spells and just magically improving the quality of life. Their knowledge of herbs embraced all levels of existence, including the physical as well as the spiritual aspects of life.

CELTS/DRUIDS

The Celts were a rural people living very close to nature. The Druids were priests, teachers, and judges of the Celtic people. The earliest records of the Druids come from the third century BCE. The Celtic tribes were a creative and close-knit tribe of people with a love of study, learning, music, and the arts. They viewed themselves as the caretakers of the earth.

Pre-Christian religious faith and beliefs in the Celtic regions of the British Isles included a deep sense of curiosity about the connection between the visible and invisible aspects of the world. Magic, herbs, and ceremony were a part of everyday life. This consciousness allowed them to give greater meaning to life. The eight earth-based ceremonies discussed later in this chapter have their roots in the Celtic tradition.

Listen to your intuition as you begin to explore the use of herbs in your spiritual and magical practices. Indigenous cultures all over the world use herbs for healing. Most of their spirituality, world views, and cosmology is rooted in what we might refer to as magic. Follow your heart and open your mind to the gentle whispers of the mystical. All regions of the world have magic in their history, find the area you most resonate with and deepen your connection and understanding with their practices, plants, and ceremonies.

How to Use This Book

Working with magic is a way of life. It is a sacred endeavor that honors the beauty, wisdom, and mystical qualities that all of life contains. We are all magicians, constantly using the energy of creation to conjure up all sorts of experiences. The study of magic allows us to begin to use that energy consciously.

If you want to know how your mom is doing, you can call her on the phone. Or if she is not available by phone, you can put some Mimosa in a dream pillow along with some Yarrow and Meadowsweet and contact your mother in your dreams. We have been taught to think that the phone is a more accurate means of communication, but I'd like you to challenge that idea. Most of us haven't been trained to engage our other senses, to expand our awareness of the world around us, or to use the plant kingdom to more fully savor life. But when we begin to explore these other realms and fully use all of our senses, we get a glimpse into the magical capabilities we might someday harness.

The world of magical practices is vast and intricate; exploring all of its realms isn't within the scope of this book, or any one book, for that matter. In this chapter, however, I will provide you with some of the basics. Magic is an art that takes practice, discipline, and dedication. Following the instructions in this book, along with your own intuition, will allow you to use herbs, plants, and flowers to enrich your life. Experiment and play with the information in this book. Encourage yourself to build a rich and rewarding relationship with magic, plants, and your own divinity while allowing yourself to enjoy the journey.

How to Reconnect with Herbs, Flowers, and Other Plants

A hundred years ago, an herbal practitioner would know which plants were available in her area. She would have been trained by an elder about how to collect her herbs, where to go, the correct time of day and season to harvest them, and the necessary rituals. There was a sacred connection with the Earth that was honored. That connection was a big part of life and as real as the telephone is to us today.

Sadly, in our high-tech, high-speed modern culture, we've largely forgotten that connection. We are a society out of sync with nature; if we crave a tomato when they're not in season locally, we can still find one at our local grocery store. And it's likely that the seed that created the tomato plant was engineered to give us a bigger, redder, or juicier tomato that ships well but has very little taste. When we begin to explore the world of herbs, we are really gradually teaching ourselves to reconnect with nature. In so doing, we need to remember that wild plants belong to the Earth; they are sacred and must be treated as such. It is their energy we harness, their very essence and spirit. It is a sacred act.

Because many plants are rare in the wild, it is best to grow your own herbs whenever possible. If you do collect wild herbs, do so under the direction of someone who knows the area and has a deep connection to the Earth. Don't just steal plants. Always take a moment to give thanks and say a prayer before you pick any plant, even ones you have grown. The magic begins the moment you decide to use herbs. Approach each step in the process as a sacred act, one that is done mindfully and with full awareness.

Tips for Harvesting, Drying, and Storing Plants

Herbs, plants, and flowers are such wonderful gifts, and every part of working with them should be approached mindfully and with respect. Gathering them, drying them for future use, and even storing them are all part of the magical ritual that connects you with the Earth's healing energy.

Many herbs can be purchased at a farmer's market, supermarket, or specialty store. If you decide to harvest your own herbs and haven't grown them yourself, make sure you ask permission from the landowner. Many plants are rare in the wild. When I was a little girl, I picked the neighbor's daffodils and brought them home to my mother as a gift. She explained to me that I had stolen the flowers and made me give them back. Don't steal your herbs!

If you decide to dry your herbs, wash them and remove any damaged portions. Shake off the excess water, tie the herbs with a piece of ribbon, and then hang them upside down in an airy place, out of direct sunlight. An attic is often a wonderful place for drying herbs. When the leaves easily crumble, they are dry enough to store in bottles. Label them and date them. Herbs lose their strength as they age. I replace mine yearly. I recycle leftover herbs in my compost pile after giving thanks for their presence in my life.

You can store fresh herbs in the refrigerator. First wash them in cool water, remove any damaged portions, and shake off the excess water. Then wrap them in a clean linen towel. Place them in the crisper section of your refrigerator. Check them every day to make sure they aren't wilting or decomposing.

Store your dried herbs, plants, and flowers in glass bottles in a dark place away from heat. I love the color blue, so I store all of my herbs in vivid blue bottles. Both brown and blue bottles keep the light out and help keep your herbs more potent.

Understanding the Magical and Spiritual Meaning of Colors

Each color has a different magical use and spiritual meaning. Depending on your ritual, your desire, and the herb, you can use different color strings to hang your herbs from, bags to put them in, or paper to wrap them in. Choose the color as carefully as you chose the herb.

RED	ORANGE	YELLOW	BLUE	GREEN
power, strength, courage, sexuality	success, legal issues	psychic powers, divination, wisdom, visions	healing, peace, joy	sleep, healing, money, abundance, fertility, employment, youth

PURPLE	PINK	WHITE	BROWN	BLACK
power, divinity, banishing negativity, transformation	love, friendship, loyalty	spirituality, protection, happiness, encouragement	animals, earth, home	cleansing, releasing, freedom

Practicing and Perfecting Your Herbal Magic

Magic is organic. Allow yourself to grow and change with your magical practice. Allow the plant world to fully embrace you, support you, and teach you. Above all else, allow the process to be fun!

Herbal magic is easier to practice than other forms of magic because the herbs have their own power and magical abilities. Once you have a reason for using magic and have decided on which herb to use, the plant will help you. The how and the why of your magical ritual will become self-evident.

For your herbal magic to be successful, there are certain key steps:
1. Define your sincere need.
2. Allow your need to suggest which herb, plant, or flower to use.
3. Once you decide on the herb, plant, or flower, plan the ceremony.
4. Spend some time connecting with the essence of the herb, plant, or flower; preparing for the ritual; and allowing the magical power to build.
5. Perform your ceremony in private or with the support of people who are in alignment with what you are doing.
6. Trust the process, let go of your wishes, and allow the magic to work.

One of the most important principles of magic is to do no harm. So when you decide to use herbs, plants, or flowers, use them for your benefit and the benefit of all involved. Magic is something you feel with your heart and soul rather than a mental exercise.

Creating an Altar for
Your Magical Work

Creating an altar or a workspace for your magical work can be a very enjoyable part of the whole process. Find an area in your home you can set aside to work with your herbs. Add some special objects to your altar, perhaps a few candles, perhaps an icon of your favorite spiritual mentor, or any other objects that will make this space special and sacred to you.

Once you make your altar, where you place things makes a big difference. The diagram shows you which area corresponds to which issue.

Spend some time thinking about where you want your altar to be and how you want it to look. It will be a very important part of your magical practices. Being mindful and fully present whenever you work with magic is extremely important.

PROSPERITY	REPUTATION	LOVE
FAMILY	HEALTH	CREATIVITY
KNOWLEDGE/ WISDOM	CAREER	HELPFUL PEOPLE

Making Herbal Tea and Using Incense

As you work with herbs, you will get an intuitive sense about what is needed for your ritual. This book often recommends using herbs to make a tea or burning them as incense. If you're a beginner, the information below provides you with the basics on these two ways to harness the magical properties of herbs.

The following is a good basic recipe for making herbal tea: In a clean stainless steel pot, bring two cups of water to a vigorous boil. Turn off the heat and add two tablespoons of dried herbs to the pot. Cover the pot and allow the mixture to steep (sit undisturbed) for about ten minutes. In that amount of time, most teas will begin to take on a rich color and develop a full-bodied scent reminiscent of the herb in its pure form. Sometimes, however, this can take up to thirty minutes. Then gently pour off the liquid. You can use a strainer if you'd like, but make sure it is bamboo or stainless steel.

When I add the herbs to the water, I say a short prayer of thanks, expressing my gratitude to the herbs for working with me. Then I mentally picture what I'd like them to do. Practice listening to the herbs each time you work with them. If it "feels right" to simmer them a bit longer, or to boil them more vigorously, do so. There is no right or wrong way; simply allow your intuition to guide you.

You can also buy reusable silk tea bags or stainless steel tea balls. I often place my herbs in a pretty clay teapot and allow them to steep in that. Each time you make tea, you can practice connecting to the spirit of the plants

Another way to harness the magic of herbs is to burn them as incense. You can buy small pieces of charcoal designed specifically for burning incense at health food stores or wherever incense is sold. Place the charcoal in a bowl or shell filled with sand. Light it, and after it has started to glow, sprinkle the dried herb over it. Use your hand or a small fan to move the smoke around the room.

Take some time creating your censer (incense burner). I use a beautiful abalone shell filled with green sand from one of the beaches on the beautiful island of Hawaii where I live. My fan is the wing from a hawk that was given to me years ago. Find things that are meaningful to you. Magic is a sacred act that connects you to the divine nature found in all of creation. Make each part of that act as special as possible without becoming rigid, fearful, or dogmatic about it.

Another way to use incense is in a Native American practice called smudging, which is bathing oneself, the surrounding area, and one's home with smoke from burning herbs. You can use your favorite incense and then fan it over yourself with a small fan. When smudging your home, you walk around the entire structure, fanning the smoke around the rooms while holding the sacred intent of blessing and clearing the area. Traditionally, Sage, Cedar, Juniper, or Sweet Grass was used for smudging. Some tribes also used Tobacco or Copal.

Creating a Magical Herb Garden

Each plant has a spirit and a personality. When we allow ourselves to tune in to that energy we can feel the magic and limitless possibilities when working with the plant kingdom. The mere act of inviting a new life into the world by planting a seed is magical. To cultivate soil and see a new life blossom as the seed unfolds, and then to watch as it continues to grow, mature, and then produce seeds for the next season is to see alchemy before your very eyes. The earth is filled with magic if we take the time to pay attention.

The plant cycle is deeply connected to so many earth-based belief systems. It should come as no surprise that the magic of the garden is one well worth looking into. Your garden can be simple or complex, or it can even be just a few pots of herbs sitting on your window sill.

You can choose to plant your garden according to the phases of the moon, in alignment with an ancient symbol that you resonate with, using Feng Shui principles, or even patterned after a formal English garden. How you organize it is up to you but use an approach that is meaningful to you. Take some time designing your garden. Draw it, cut out pictures of the herbs, play with them until you get a sense that this is your herb garden.

If you decide to plant your herb garden using the moon's cycles, traditionally, the first quarter is when to plant herbs that bloom above ground, such as yarrow or Bergamot. The second quarter, leading up to the full moon, is the time to plant above-ground herbs, such as Job's Tears. During the third quarter, the week following the full moon, you should plant herbs where you primarily use the root, for instance, turmeric, as well as bulbs, such as tulips. According to ancient customs, the last quarter of the moon, or the waning moon, is a time to focus on weeding and nurturing your herb garden rather than planting.

When the moon is full, spend some time under the night sky. Meditate while allowing the moonlight to fill your heart and your mind with its magic. Get acquainted with the earth's magic and say a silent prayer of thanksgiving. The earth lovingly provides us with all our wants and needs. Walk through your garden and invite the herbs to talk to you. If you look closely you may even see a plant diva or fairy. These energies appear differently to everyone. You may see a flash of light or just feel a loving presence. The most important thing is the willingness to acknowledge them, possess an open heart, and know that they are there whether we see them with our physical eyes or with our heart.

Using the Moon's Cycles to Connect with Magical Herbs

The sun and the moon influence the earth energetically, controlling the earth's cycles and the seasons. The earth turns on its axis once a day. The moon orbits the earth once every twenty-nine days and the earth takes a full year to revolve around the sun.

The effect of the moon on the earth and its people has been recognized by the earliest of mankind. The moon was personified as the Triple Moon Goddess. They correspond to the great cycles of life: birth, maturity, death, and rebirth. The maid is the emerging New Moon Goddess; the Mother, the abundant provider, is the Full Moon Goddess, and the Crone, the wise woman, is the inner-realm Dark Goddess.

The moon influences our unconscious, emotional nature. The moon is a reflector and a shadow. As you learn to work with herbs, keep a moon journal. Observe how the moon cycles affect you and the world around you. Connecting with the waxing and waning of the moon can create more balance and harmony to your life.

Magical Herbs, Ceremony, and Connecting with the Earth's Cycles

THE DIRECTIONS AND THE FIVE ELEMENTS

All physical matter is alive with energy. The more you expand your awareness of this energy the more magical and wonderful your life will become. The earth is composed of five elements and each element has a direction associated with it. Whenever you do a ceremony it is a good idea to call upon the four directions for protection and guidance first. The five elements and the directions which I explain in the following section can be used to influence the physical world around you, and help you to consciously create more of what you do want.

If you want to deepen your connection to herbs and the mystical qualities of life, allow yourself to become familiar with the elements, the directions, and spend a year becoming more familiar with the eight ceremonies that celebrate the inherent rhythms of this beautiful planet we live on. Experiment and play with the concepts that follow. There are no hard and fast rules when dealing with elements and the directions. What I present in the following sections are gentle suggestions and some guidelines that have worked for me and may well work for you.

Spirit: Center

Spirit is at the center of all creation. All physical matter is energy and that energy is spirit. Spirit encompasses all of the directions and elements. Whenever you work with herbs connect with your spirit and the spirit of the herbs. Magic is merely a matter of aligning with spirit. Breathe in the sweet smell of spirit and embrace its wonders.

The four directions and elements enfold and encircle spirit while spirit gives birth to the four directions and all the elements. They are interconnected and entwined.

East: Air

East is embodied by air. Air is symbolic of the power of the mind. Air is formless and ever present. It gives life to everything. It represents rebirth, the dawn, and the beginning of new adventures. It is the colors of a magnificent dawn. It has the power of the wind, birds in flight, butterflies, and transformation.

When you think of the east and air imagine clouds skittering across the sky, dragonflies, storms, and a lyrical song sung by a sweet voice. Allow yourself to remember and reconnect with your inner wisdom and release the power of your spirit to create the life of your dreams. Remember your instinctive connection with the plants and allow the herbs to speak to you in your dreams and with your touch.

South: Fire

South is the embodiment of fire. It is aligned with your ability to consciously set energy in motion. At its essence, fire is about the energy of transformation. You can consciously choose to transform all of your limiting beliefs into inspirations that will guide you to new heights of freedom and joy. Imagine the heat of midday as you think of the relationship between fire and the south. Think of passion, power, and creativity.

Call upon the south when you feel you need courage or clarity of purpose. The sun can empower you to creatively bring about change in your life or the lives of those around you. As you begin to boil water to make a cup of tea or infusion, align with the power of fire and use it to activate the magic inherent in the herbs.

West: Water

West conjures up images of beautiful sunsets and the enchantment and mysticism of the conclusion of a wonderful journey. Water is symbolic of our emotional side; it is deep and flowing. Water is often filled with currents and eddies. It is representative of deep cleansing, fertility, and healing.

Imagine yourself standing at the sea watching the sun set and disappear below the horizon. Think about the end of a beautiful fall day. See the magnificence of the fall colors bathed by the twilight. How do you feel as you picture that? Use that energy as you decide which herbs to use.

All of your herbs are filled with the energy of all the directions and the elements. When deciding what herbs you want to use, call upon your psychic perception, which is enhanced by the power of the west. Allow the west to help you sink into the well of sacred energy that lives within you.

North: Earth

The earth supports us bountifully and lovingly. It sustains us and it is the essence of the material world. The earth is solid and a fully manifested physical reality. The cold winter winds come out of the north. The north represents the hidden world that lies within each of us. From that inner world we create the limitless possibilities that life holds. Our inner life precedes our outer manifestations. You manifest your beliefs and thoughts into physical reality.

The earth gives birth to all the plants, seeds, flowers, herbs, trees, and animals. When you allow yourself to connect with Mother Earth and the spirits of nature, knowing how to conjure magic and work with the herbs will become second nature. The north is the direction of our ancestors, so call upon their wisdom and knowledge as you align with the energies of the herbs. Imagine yourself amongst ancient standing stones hearing the voices of the earth and the ancient ones speaking to you and guiding you.

The Eight Ceremonies of the Earth's Yearly Cycle

The winter and summer solstice along with the spring and fall equinoxes make up the four cardinal points for ceremonies that align with the sun's transit in the sky. Solstice comes from Latin and refers to the standing of the sun. At both solstices the sun reaches a point in the sky where it seems to stop, then turn around and begin its journey back across the sky.

A natural extension of working with herbs is connecting with the earth's rhythms and cycles. As the earth revolves around the sun the seasons change. If you allow your awareness to expand, you will begin to feel the changes in the energy of the earth as the moon waxes and wanes. Tuning into those energies, really allowing yourself to feel the elements, the herbs, the changing light of the seasons will deepen your experience of life and allow you to better tune into the magical properties of herbs.

In between the quarter points of the solstices and the equinoxes there were once four other ceremonial times known as the cross quarter points. In the past, these were known as the fire ceremonies and were celebrated by building huge bonfires on the hills and mountains around the villages. These points in the circle of the year are another wonderful opportunity for us to align with our true nature and further deepen our connection with the magical nature of life, the earth, and herbs. You can use these times to feel the sacred qualities of all of life, especially the plant kingdom.

■ **WINTER SOLSTICE DECEMBER 20–23**
Trees: Pine, Oak
Herbs: Yarrow, Thyme, Garlic

The winter solstice is a time to reflect, go within, and then look forward to what you would like to create in the coming year. It is truly the beginning of a new year. The outer ring of Stonehenge is aligned to the Solstice sunset. In Ireland, Newgrange is aligned to the dawn of the winter solstice and a shaft of light travels deep into this burial chamber and fills it with light. These ancient structures are amazing monuments to the power and energy these days held in ancient cultures.

Pine boughs were brought into the homes as a symbol of everlasting life. A Yule log of oak was burned after prayers were offered for the coming year. You can burn a piece of oak after you imbue it with all the thoughts, feelings, and beliefs you wish to let go of. In place of an oak log you can light a candle and place your prayers on a small piece of paper and burn it at dawn.

Allow yourself to connect with the ancient wisdom of this time and create a ceremony that is meaningful to you. You can sprinkle yarrow inside your home or use it to make a tea. Yarrow will strengthen your spirit and protect you from the negative influences of others. For the winter solstice make a dream pillow, fill it with yarrow, and then sprinkle it with a little pine oil. It will help you connect with the sacredness of the season and help you set your intent for the coming year. You can use some of your favorite fabric to create a small dream pillow. You'll find that when you sleep with a dream pillow not only are your night dreams enhanced, but also you will find manifesting your deepest desires easier as well.

As you embrace these earth cycles you can begin to look at life in different way. Instead of thinking linearly you can embrace the cyclical nature of all life. Thyme is a wonderful cleansing tonic for the body. Before you do any ceremony or when you want to invite positive change into your life, drink a cup of your favorite tea and add a pinch of thyme into your cup before you brew it. And garlic makes it easier to connect with the spirit realms when eaten raw. It helps prevent respiratory infections so adding it to your diet will help you remain healthy during the short days of winter.

Fill your home with love and light, allow your dreams to expand and know the coming year will be filled with the gifts of your spirit.

■ **IMBOLIC/CANDELMAS END OF JANUARY/BEGINNING OF FEBRUARY**
Trees: Rowan, Willow
Herbs: Coltsfoot, Ginger

Imbolic is a celebration of the reawakening of the earth. The quarter festivals are an opportunity to connect with the energy of the coming season. During the dark winter months you have had the opportunity to connect with your inner wisdom, with your innate intuitive nature. Spring is a time to plant new seeds. Imbolic is a union of power and magic, the inner and the outer worlds.

In the Celtic traditions the Triple Goddess has been reborn as the virgin known as Bride or Brigit. In other ancient traditions Persephone returns from the underworld as the young spring maiden. These early versions of the Goddess were honored for their fertility and sexuality. The worship of the Goddess was later channeled into worship of the Virgin Mary by the early Christian church. Imbolic is a festival rich in passion and sexuality. The festival later was called Candelmas by the early Christian church and became known as the purification of the Virgin Mary, a time during which her body was purified after childbirth. The days are still cold but they are lengthening. If you look closely there are signs the earth is beginning to awaken. Symbolically the unconscious and conscious are joining to bring about growth, fertility, and manifestation in physical reality.

Imbolic is a time for healing, releasing, and initiation. It is a time for you to reclaim your forgotten talents, your intuitive insights, and to fully embrace your dreams. At the winter solstice you planted seeds and your visions now have the opportunity to begin to emerge.

Make a walking stick out of Rowan wood. It will help you see clearly at night and deepen your connection with the moon. If you haven't already, begin a moon journal. Notice the correlation between the moon's cycles and the events in your life. Meditating near a Rowan tree will help you heal your body, clear your mind and expand your personal power. A wand made of Rowan branch will strengthen your psychic abilities. A Rowan tree planted near your home will protect your family and friends. The berries can be used to make a jelly that is helpful in curing sore throats and will help you speak your truth with a greater sense of purpose.

Meditating near a willow tree will help you remember to be more flexible, will assist you in releasing limiting beliefs, and allow you to release emotions from your unconscious mind. Sleeping with a piece of willow under your pillow will help you remember your dreams and make them more vivid, colorful, and meaningful.

Try burning coltsfoot as an incense to help you open up your connection to your inner wisdom. Ginger root, lemon and honey make an excellent tea that will warm your heart and fill you with a sense of love for everyone and everything.

■ SPRING EQUINOX MARCH 21–22
Trees: Ash, Adler
Herbs: Nettle, Hyssop

Day and night are of equal lengths. The days are starting to get warmer and it is a time of balance. At the equinoxes you can work on finding balance within, a balance of the physical, mental, and spiritual realms. During the spring equinox, the goddess is represented as a young maiden carrying a basket of eggs. The eggs represent the cosmic balance, the rebirth, the male and the female, light and dark, expansion and contraction. The egg is the symbol of creation, the fullness of the potential of all life.

Dragon energy has long been associated with the spring equinox. The Church aligned Easter with this ancient ceremony of rebirth. This is a wonderful time of year to learn to balance your inner male, the conscious mind, with the intuition of your inner female. When you learn to find that inner balance your life becomes magical and miracles occur. Finding balance is a matter of going within, perhaps in a meditation or while listening to relaxing music. The energy of the season will help you find and deepen that balance.

Create a ceremony of balance by tuning into the earth and feeling the balance of day and night at this time of year. Sit and watch the sunrise or sunset while opening up and feeling the unfolding energies in nature. Invite the wisdom of the ages and step fully into this active energy of the season, plant the seeds of your grandest hopes, dreams and aspirations. Clear away the weeds, choose life-affirming thoughts and release any fear-based thoughts of doubt and negativity. Learn to listen to the quiet still voice of your spirit. Tune into your inner wisdom and watch your life become filled with ease.

Ash grows straight and tall so it makes a wonderful walking stick. When found growing with honeysuckle it makes a particularly powerful walking stick. Sleeping with alder leaves under your pillow will help you know when to move forward and when finding the inner stillness is the most important thing to do next on your spiritual journey. Nettle tea is a wonderful tonic to experience before any ceremony. Sprinkle hyssop around an altar or ceremony location for purification.

■ BELTANE/MAY DAY END OF APRIL/BEGINNING OF MAY
Trees: Hawthorn
Herb: Cowslip

Beltane is the celebration of fertility. It is based on having the utmost reverence for all of life. It is a time to celebrate the union of the cosmic male and female. It combines the sacredness and spirituality of love and sexual expression.

Ribbons and pieces of clothing were once tied around trees growing around sacred wells as a gift to the fairies. Beltane means goodly fire, which refers to the bonfires traditionally built along the ridges. People would jump the fires to purify themselves while livestock was driven through the smoke to protect them from diseases. Hot embers from the fires were taken home to rekindle the hearths. The Church renamed Beltane and changed it into Mayday. Once again the focus of the celebration became about virginity, purity, and chastity.

From Beltane until the summer solstice the sun is at its strongest. At dawn and dusk of Beltane and its opposite on the wheel, Samhain, the veil between the two worlds is thin. It is easy to get in touch with your greatest wishes and dreams. You can use this powerful energy of fertility to help you manifest your dreams and desires.

Labyrinths have often been associated with Beltane. Find a local labyrinth and walk it as part of your Beltane celebration. Since a fire is central to a Beltane celebration, it would be ideal to find a labyrinth where you can build a fire in the center. A tall candle can substitute for a bonfire at the center. Placing tea candles in paper bags to light your path around the labyrinth can make for a magic back drop to a powerful ceremony.

Hawthorn trees can be used to heal matters of the heart. If your relationship isn't as intimate as you would like bury the name of your beloved under a Hawthorn tree at Beltane. Use its flowers and leaves to release blocked energy and remove stress from your life. Sprinkled around your home, it will help visitors feel welcomed and loved. Cowslip will help fill your home with a sense of peace and wellbeing.

■ **SUMMER SOLSTICE JUNE 20–23**
Trees: Oak, Rose
Herbs: Lavender, Lemon Balm

During the summer solstice the sun is at its strongest. Trees are fully leafed. Herbs, plants and flowers are flourishing. You are again at a powerful point of transformation in the yearly cycle of life.

This is a wonderful time to celebrate what you have created in your life. Gratitude is an expansive energy that will open up the channels of the universe to help you create more of what you do want. Use this powerful day to focus on healing and infuse your dreams with positive intent. Dance and sing with complete joy and abandon. Allow yourself to celebrate the birth and rebirth of the earth's yearly cycle and the sun's glorious journey across the sky.

This is a time to deepen your connection with your dreams and affirm your ability to manifest them easily and effortless in your life as you align with your spirit and the magic and wonder of the universe. Build a fire from oak leaves, twigs, and logs. Write two letters, one to let go of all your limiting thinking and another containing all your desires, wishes, and dreams. After saying a prayer, throw them into the fire and watch them as they transform into light.

Sit with an oak when you need to find your inner strength and connect with the wisdom of your spirit. Scatter oak leaves around your home to fill it with a sense of deep inner calm and peace. Sleeping under an oak will restore your will and deepen your belief in yourself and life. Combine that with the smell of lavender and you will have a greater sense of clarity and understanding of the true meaning of your life. Sprinkle lemon balm around your home to drive away all of your concerns and dispel any problems.

■ **LAMMAS/FESTIVAL OF THE GRAIN MOTHER END OF JULY/BEGINNING OF AUGUST**
Trees: Hazel
Herbs: Sage, Meadow Sweet

Lammas is held at the height of summer when grains are ripe and ready to harvest. The Grain Mother, the abundance of the Earth Mother was once celebrated. The door to the inner realms is once again opening as the days shorten. A person who was filled with the energy of the Goddess was referred to as an "august."

Traditionally, the first and last sheaf of grain harvested was celebrated. Corn referred to all the grain crops. A Corn Mother or doll would be made from the first or last stalk of grain harvested and hung over the fireplace. Bread would be baked and the cooking fires would be blessed and honored as part of the harvest. Thanks were given to the sun's energy reborn in the hearth as the bread of life.

The sun god is slowly dying, moving once again toward the darkness of winter. The shift from outer energy to the energy of the inner dimensions is the key to fully understanding the energy of Lammas. It is time for each of us to assimilate and gather our own harvest of love, light, and laughter. It is time to give thanks to all the energies of the earth and the beings of light that help the earth.

Hazel will help you find inspiration and insights. Carry a small wand made of hazel to help you overcome emotional blocks and find creative solutions to all of life's concerns. Sage is associated with inner wisdom and used to clear away blockages and purification. Harvest sage in July after the flowers have fully matured. Dry it and create small bundles. You can use it as a tea or burn it using the smoke to purify the area. Never use sage if you are pregnant, however.

■ **AUTUMNAL EQUINOX SEPTEMBER 20–23**
Tree: Apple
Herbs: Fennel, Hops, Marigold

Day and night are once again in prefect balance. The autumnal equinox is the end of summer and the beginning of a long journey into night. Gratitude, thanksgiving, and balance are the cornerstones of the autumnal equinox. It is a wonderful time to gather with your friends and have a feast of earth's bountiful gifts.

This is an ideal time to ask what you can give back to the earth. It is time to prepare the soil for next year's harvest. The double spiral is a symbol often associated with these days. It symbolizes the balance of this time of year and of life. You inhale, you exhale, the seasons change.

The sap in the trees is returning to the earth. Plants are preparing for the long sleep of the coming winter. It is time to begin the inner journey and lovingly harvest and gather the herbs you will use over the coming year. Finish off any garden projects and plant bulbs.

Traditionally, the rafters would be filled with bunches of fragrant herbs drying. It is a time where you can really sense the magic of the season. This is a good time for you to deepen your commitment to your spiritual path, to connect with the magic, and clear anything out of your life that no longer serves you.

Take time to meditate and feel your connection to the earth, the herbs, and the potential held within each moment. Sit with your favorite herb and allow it to teach you the gifts held within. Each cell of every plant holds within it the gift of life and the ability to facilitate change. Align with those gifts. Pay attention to your dreams.

Apple trees have a long history of magic properties. When cut open you find a pentagram long associated with the gift of healing and the magic contained within nature. It is a symbol of abundance. By aligning with that abundance you invite more gifts into your life. Spend time outdoors on the equinox. Go to a farmers market and take in the sights, sounds, and smells.

Place some colorful leaves on your altar and fill a vase with marigolds. Dry the petals for use all winter. They make a wonderful tea and are useful as a cleansing tonic. When the sun is at its weakest, sprinkle the dried flowers around your home to remind yourself of the summer to come. Sit with the flowers in your hands as you meditate to help your dreams come true. Sprinkled around your home, they will dispel any negative energy. Put them in your bath water before an important meeting and all will go well.

This is the perfect time of year to harvest fennel. When you clean, add a few seeds to the water to purify and protect your home. This is the time of year to celebrate abundance so the seeds sprinkled around your home and placed in your wallet are sure to help the abundance in your life flow more freely.

Hang hops around your home as part of the celebration of the equinox. Place some under your pillow to enhance your dreams.

■ SAMHAIN/HALLOWS EVE END OF OCTOBER/ BEGINNING OF NOVEMBER
Trees: Elder, Yew
Herbs: Dandelion, Mugwort, Elderberry

Samhain (pronounced Sow-ein) is a magical time of the year. Like Beltane, the veil between the worlds is at its thinnest. This is a wonderful time to communicate with our ancestors. It is a time to receive messages from the spirits and help lost souls return to the light. The Goddess become the Crone and embraces the wisdom of the ages. This time of year most people are accustomed to celebrating Halloween. The Crone has been turned into an old hag and magic downgraded to a game of trick or treat. Fear of magic over the ages distorted this powerful and wonderful time of the year.

This time of the year is also celebrated as the Feast of the Dead. If you have lost a loved one during the past year, this is a wonderful time to honor their life and lovingly set them free. Thank them for their presence in your life, send them a great deal of love, and see them freely continue on their path bathed in love.

This is the best time of the year for inner exploration. Spend time with yourself, allow your dreams to speak to you, meditate and listen to the wisdom of your ancestors and spiritual guides. This is also an ideal time to deepen and expand your understanding of the herbal kingdom.

Spend time outside when the moon is dark. Listen to the wind, allow the elements to embrace you, and know you are one with everyone and everything. Find an ancient chant that speaks to you and sing it, allowing the wind to carry it into the darkness. Open your heart and your mind to the wisdom of those who have come before you, knowing you are always guided with love.

There are many superstitions about the elder tree. It is thought to be bad luck to cut down the tree. Sprinkle the leaves around your home for protection. Plant it around your home if you want to tap into your inner strength and wisdom.

The yew is often associated with immortality. Some of the yew trees in England are thought to be over 4000 years old. The tree itself is very poisonous. Spending time with a yew is said to remove the fear of death. It is an ancient symbol of renewal. By meditating beneath one you can release your negative thinking and renew your sense of magic and wonder.

Now is the time to harvest dandelion root. A tea made from the root will dispel negative thinking and purify the body. The flowers and the seeds are generally used to carry messages and manifest your dreams. This time of year, as the energy of the earth goes within, the roots are most potent and make a wonderful tonic for the mind and the body. Drink some as you celebrate this extraordinary time of year.

Mugwort has long been used in rituals and magical practices. It enhances clairvoyance, dream work, and encourages astral travel. It tends to grow along the sides of the road and in abandoned lots. As a tea, it is a powerful tonic, cleansing the blood and detoxing the liver. Avoid using it if you are pregnant because it will bring on a late period and ease menstrual cramps. You can use it as an incense to clear your home and prepare a space for ceremony. Used at this time of year it will help you connect with the ancestors and talk to the spirits recently departed.

Elderberry makes a wonderful jelly, deep in flavor and rich in color. You can also use it to dye fabric to make a beautiful altar cloth. The berries when mixed with honey make a wonderful cough syrup and decongestant. The berries will also help you deepen your understanding of core emotional issues, helping you transform them into an expansive understanding of your spiritual nature. The wine is often used in celebrations at this time of year. Take some of the leaves and berries and float them in your bath or make a tea and soak for a while to help heal old emotional wounds. Burning the stems as incense will clear your home of any unwanted energy. Do this just before you do a reading for someone and your intuition will be greatly enhanced.

PART I

Enchanting Herbs

HERBS THAT WILL PROTECT AND HEAL

For information on harvesting, drying, and storing herbs, plants, and flowers, see page 14.
For directions for using them to make tea and incense, see page 18.

Cowslip

Primula veris

Helps you find the hidden treasures in your life

- **COWSLIP WILL:** Discourage visitors, Help you find hidden treasures, Heal your mind, body, and spirit

- **THE PLANT:** Cowslip is a low-growing plant that appears very early in the spring. The leaves are broad and look like an elongated oval. The bright yellow flowers wave gracefully from a tall stalk that comes up from the middle of the plant. The plant is very fresh smelling and the flowers are very fragrant. It is native throughout much of Europe, Asia, and North America.

- **HOW TO HARNESS COWSLIP'S MAGICAL PROPERTIES:** A bouquet of the flowers will fill your home with a sense of peace and well-being.

    To discourage visitors, put the dried herb under your front door.

    Bathing in Cowslip tea is said to restore lost youth. To make the tea, immerse two tablespoons of the dried flowers in a warm cup of water for a half hour. Then add the tea to your bathwater.

    Keeping the herb near you will help you find lost objects and hidden treasure and will remind you of all the gifts in your life.

- **MEDICINAL USES:** The flowers are used in making a fermented liquor called Cowslip Wine. It is made from the yellow flower rings, which are called peeps. To a gallon of peeps you add four pounds of sugar, the rind of three lemons, and a gallon of water. Add a cup of brewer's yeast and stir every day for a week. Then put the mixture into a barrel to ferment. When it has finished fermenting, bottle it. The wine will be pale yellow and perfectly clear and is very useful as a tonic and to quiet coughs.

Oak *Quercus robur*

Shows you how to manifest your magnificence

OAK WILL: Attract money, Bring good luck, Assure you of good health, Enhance fertility, Protect your home

THE PLANT: The Oak is widely distributed over Europe and North America. It is of great symbolic significance in England and is one of the chief trees in most of England's forests. It is a tall, majestic tree, and its fruit, the acorn, was widely used as a food source for both animals and people. The trees are very long lived and will often last for eight hundred years or more. They grow up to 125 feet tall, and it is said their roots go as deep as their top is tall. Oaks were very sacred to the Druids. Symbolically, the Oak tree is often used to represent the tree of life.

■ **HOW TO HARNESS OAK'S MAGICAL PROPERTIES:** Hanging a piece of Oak in your home that you cut from a tree that was hit by lightning is said to be a particularly powerful good luck charm. It will protect your home from lightning, assure abundance, enhance fertility, and repel sickness and disease.

Carrying an acorn in your pocket will protect you from harm. Placing acorns on your altar and around your home will invite the wisdom and protection of the ancestors.

■ **MEDICINAL USES:** The bark is widely used for medical purposes, especially chronic diarrhea and dysentery. A tea made from two tablespoons of bark in a quart of water boiled down to a pint will relieve a chronic sore throat and helps heal bleeding gums when applied regularly.

Myrtle *Myrtus communis*

Makes your life exciting

- **MYRTLE WILL:** Keep love fresh and passionate, Increase fertility, Preserve youth, Attract abundance

- **THE PLANT:** Myrtle is an evergreen shrub native to southern Europe and northern Africa. The leaves are very fragrant. The flowers look like a star and have five petals. They are usually white and turn into very deep, almost black, blue berries. The berries contain several seeds, which are often spread by birds.

- **HOW TO HARNESS MYRTLE'S MAGICAL PROPERTIES:** Myrtle was used in Greek temples and Jewish synagogues as incense. It is good luck for the bride to carry Myrtle on her wedding day; it will ensure fertility, but prevent her from getting pregnant too soon.

Taking a bath with tea made from dried Myrtle will fill you with a sense of peace and well-being. To make the tea, add two tablespoons of dried Myrtle to two cups of boiling water, allow it to steep for about ten minutes, and then strain the tea before adding it to your bathwater.

To keep your home safe and bless it and the occupants, plant some Myrtle in a window box.

Carrying the wood in an amulet will preserve a youthful appearance. It is also a wonderful addition to any love amulet.

- **MEDICINAL USES:** A tea made from the leaves will help treat urinary tract infections, bronchial congestion, and sinus problems. It will also help relieve a dry cough. Used as a douche, it will stop excessive vaginal discharges and relieve itching. Used as a mouthwash, it will clear up gum infections. An herbalist might prescribe washing your face twice a day with the tea to treat acne.

Yucca *Yucca glauca*

Transforms your dreams into reality

YUCCA WILL: Increase spiritual awareness, Purify your thoughts, Transform your life, Provide protection

THE PLANT: Yucca is a perennial that has fibrous, rigid leaves and grows best on arid lands. The leaves have a sharp, pointed tip. The plant will yield ten to fifteen flowers along a spike that is about three feet long. The flowers are greenish white and grow up to two and a half inches long. They produce long black seeds. The roots are often used for making soap and hair rinse. There are about forty different varieties of Yucca. The most famous is the Joshua Tree, which grows up to thirty feet tall and can be found only in the Mojave Desert.

■ **HOW TO HARNESS YUCCA'S MAGICAL PROPERTIES:** Use the yucca fibers to braid a hoop. Place the hoop on your altar to increase your spiritual awareness. You can also wear it while you meditate to purify your thoughts and release negative beliefs.

To fill yourself with a sense of well-being and help transform your life through right action, wash with soap made from the root.

Placing a wreath over your front door will ensure you of success and stop any negativity from entering your home.

■ **MEDICINAL USES:** A soap made from crushed Yucca roots will cure dandruff and soothe skin irritations. A tea made from the root eases the pain of childbirth, speeds labor, and helps expel the placenta. A poultice made from the root will help heal wounds and stop bleeding.

Celery *Apium graveolens*

Helps you sleep soundly

- **CELERY WILL:** Help you sleep, Increase your concentration, Expand your psychic awareness

- **THE PLANT:** The Latin name for celery means strong smelling. It has been cultivated in the Mediterranean region for the last three thousand years. Both the plants and the seeds are used in cooking.

- **HOW TO HARNESS CELERY'S MAGICAL PROPERTIES:** If you've been struggling with insomnia, fill a pillow with celery seeds to induce sleep and improve your mental alertness during the day. Chewing on the seeds will help with concentration.

  To expand your psychic ability, burn the seeds along with incense. To attract your spirit guides, place a celery root on your altar.

  Eating stalks of celery as an appetizer will increase your sexual potency.

- **MEDICINAL USES:** Celery seeds are harvested after the plant's second year. They are used in homeopathic remedies to detoxify and cleanse the body. The seeds are also a digestive stimulant. Seeds soaked in almond oil and massaged into joints will relieve the pain of arthritis and gout. The root is a wonderful diuretic and can be eaten to clear up urinary infections and to treat mild anxiety.

Walnut *Juglans nigra*

Helps you connect with the bounty of Mother Earth

WALNUT WILL: Increase fertility, Deepen your spiritual connection, Help you stay on your path, Enhance mental abilities

THE PLANT: Walnut trees grow forty to sixty feet tall. They have a large spreading canopy and a thick, massive trunk. Some Walnut trees have been measured to be twenty-three feet in diameter, and there are trees in France that are more than three hundred years old that are even wider. Walnut trees will begin to bear fruit when they are ten years old, and the fruits ripen in mid-September. The trees were introduced to Europe from Persia but are now naturalized in much of the Northern Hemisphere.

HOW TO HARNESS WALNUT'S MAGICAL PROPERTIES: If you're looking for help staying on your spiritual path, purchase some Walnut oil and use it in a lamp on your altar. It will illuminate your way, helping you stay on the right path easily and effortlessly.

If you're struggling to make a difficult decision, place a Walnut in each hand and ask for guidance from your spirit. Within a day, you will receive an answer.

For help conceiving a child, place some walnuts under your bed.

When you have to take an exam, carry some walnuts with you to improve your scores.

MEDICINAL USES: The bark and leaves are used in the treatment of skin troubles, particularly herpes and eczema. A tea made from the bark will heal skin ulcers. The fruit, before it is ripe, can be combined with vinegar to make a gargle for sore throats and to heal ulcers in the mouth and throat.

Solomon Seal

Polygonatum multiflorum

Deepens your understanding

- **SOLOMON SEAL WILL:** Invite inner wisdom, Protect you and your home, Repel negativity

- **THE PLANT:** Solomon Seal is a relative of Lily of the Valley. It is native to northern Europe and Siberia. The creeping root is thick, white, and full of twists and knots. Its stems grow from one to two feet tall. They start out standing very straight but eventually bend over very gracefully. The blooms are small dropping clusters of two to seven flowers. The berries are about the size of a pea and vary from black to purple to red.

- **HOW TO HARNESS SOLOMON SEAL'S MAGICAL PROPERTIES:** To help you connect with your innate, inner wisdom, burn some of the dried leaves as incense. The smoke will cleanse the house of any negativity and fill it with a sense of peace, happiness, and joy.
    Placing pieces of the root in the four corners of your home will protect the occupants as well as the house itself.

- **MEDICINAL USES:** Solomon Seal is used to treat congestion and to stop bleeding in the lungs. It helps relieve menstrual discomfort and regulate a woman's flow. The powdered roots make an excellent poultice for bruises, piles, inflammations, and tumors. The bruised roots can be mixed with cream to treat black eyes. When combined with beeswax, the powdered roots make a multipurpose salve for treating bruises, scrapes, and cuts.

Agaric

Amanita muscaria

Enriches your life and your dreams

■ **AGARIC WILL:** Increase fertility, Enhance your dreams, Deepen your connection with the Divine, Attract gnomes and fairies

■ **THE PLANT:** This small mushroom is frequently used as an illustration in books of fairy tales. Classically, Agaric is symbolic of enchanted forests and magical groves where gnomes and fairies live. It is known as a mysterious, magical, and lucky mushroom. It grows in the cooler forests of northern Europe, while close relatives grow throughout much of the world. Although Agaric is considered very poisonous, many mystics and shamans have used it in their sacred rituals.

■ **HOW TO HARNESS AGARIC'S MAGICAL PROP-ERTIES:** Place a dried mushroom or a picture of one on your altar. Take a few deep breaths and go deep within yourself. Then open your heart and your mind to this mushroom's magical spirit. As you connect with the essence of its spirit, you will find yourself having good luck in all of your endeavors. Agaric is specifically associated with increasing fertility, so if you want to have a child, ask for assistance in getting pregnant.

To have more powerful and prophetic dreams, place this mushroom on your nightstand or hang it over your bed.

Putting a small symbol of this mushroom in a dream catcher placed over your baby's crib will ensure the child of a fruitful and happy life. Especially around children, make sure you use only a porcelain or carved version of the mushroom.

■ **MEDICINAL USES:** None, it is poisonous.

Catnip *Nepta cataria*

Reminds you to play

- **CATNIP WILL:** Invite more love into your life, Enhance your good looks, Make you smile more

- **THE PLANT:** Catnip is a member of the Mint family and grows all over southern Europe, the cooler parts of Asia, and North America. It is a perennial that can grow two to three feet tall. Cats love the leaves and seem totally blissed out when they're given some of them. The leaves are grayish and look almost dusty. Catnip flowers from July through September, producing small, whitish pink spiky blossoms.

- **HOW TO HARNESS CATNIP'S MAGICAL PROPERTIES:** When you sprinkle a little bit of dried Catnip around the rooms of your home, your guests will just seem happier, and so will you. Some long-lost friends may even show up at your door.

To become more radiant and allow your inner beauty to shine, make a tea from a quarter cup of dried Catnip leaves simmered in two cups of water for at least ten minutes. Strain the tea and then add it to your bathwater. Use the tea on a daily basis.

- **MEDICINAL USES:** A weak Catnip tea made of two tablespoons of dried leaves gently simmered in a pint of water for about ten minutes and then strained will help reduce a fever. Catnip tea is also relaxing, so it can help people fall asleep. Small quantities of it will relieve colic in young children and help get rid of gas pains. Never boil catnip because boiling causes it to lose its curative properties.

Arnica *Arnica montana*

Brightens up your life

- **ARNICA WILL:** Help you sleep, Increase your confidence, Help you feel safe

- **THE PLANT:** Arnica is a perennial herb that is native to Central Europe. Its bright yellow, daisylike flowers bloom around July. Preparations made from the flowering heads have been used in homeopathic medicine for hundreds of years. It is seldom used internally because it irritates the stomach.

- **HOW TO HARNESS ARNICA'S MAGICAL PROPERTIES:** Sprinkle dried Arnica flowers in a corner of your home to bless and purify the space.

  Use the dried leaves as incense when you meditate to deepen your spiritual connection. If you're hoping to expand your psychic abilities, rub Arnica salve on your temples. You can make your own salve by combining two tablespoons of crushed fresh Arnica leaves with half a cup of fresh beeswax. Or simply buy a tube from a health food store.

- **MEDICINAL USES:** Arnica is a wonderful treatment for bruises, sprains, and stiff muscles. It helps with skin inflammations and rapidly heals bruises. It can also help with any form of blunt trauma or contusions.

Hyssop

Hyssopus officinalis

Purifies your life

- **HYSSOP WILL:** Protect you and your home, Purify your altar or sacred space, Dispel depression

- **THE PLANT:** Hyssop is a hardy evergreen, bushy herb that is native to the Mediterranean and eastern Asia. It has been naturalized throughout most of Europe and North America. It grows two to four feet tall, has a sweet, warm aroma, and blooms between June and August. The leaves can be harvested as needed, but the flowering tops should be harvested only in August.

- **HARNESS HYSSOP'S MAGICAL PROPERTIES:** To remove negativity, tie a bunch of hyssop branches together to symbolicly sweep your home, removing any negative energy or spirits. You can also add about half a cup of Hyssop tea to your mop water to cleanse your house. To make the tea, add two tablespoons of dried Hyssop to two cups of boiling water and allow the mixture to steep for about ten minutes before straining it. Finally, you can use a small bunch of Hyssop leaves to sprinkle water over objects or around a room to bless them.

  Add a pinch of dried Hyssop to your bathwater as part of a ritual of healing and purification, especially if you have been feeling depressed.

  When burned as incense, dried Hyssop will raise the spiritual vibrations of your home and release the energy of protection.

- **MEDICINAL USES:** Hyssop tea will settle an upset stomach and ease the pain of arthritis and rheumatism. A poultice made out of the leaves will heal wounds and help the discoloration from bruises fade more rapidly. Added to soup, Hyssop will help relieve asthma.

Tobacco

Nicotiana tabacum

Teaches you about both the light and the dark side of things

- **TOBACCO WILL:** Purify an area, Release negativity, Induce visions

- **THE PLANT:** Tobacco is native to the mid-Atlantic portion of North America, although it is now cultivated in China, Turkey, and many subtropical regions. It is an annual with long, fibrous roots and long, oval, heavily wrinkled leaves. Native Americans considered it sacred and often left Tobacco and cornmeal as a gift to the spirits. In sacred ceremonies, initiates often had to drink a tea made from its leaves to induce visions as part of their training to become a shaman.

- **HARNESS TOBACCO'S MAGICAL PROPERTIES:** To purify an area and dispel it of spirits, burn some Tobacco leaves as incense. The smoke can also be used to clear your aura and to send sacred prayers off into the heavens.

  For protection and to bless an area, sprinkle a pinch of tobacco and coarsely ground cornmeal in the four corners of your property.

  Before you travel, place a Tobacco leaf on the ground and walk over it to assure your safety. If you are traveling by water, throw some Tobacco into the water before you depart.

  Finally, whenever you work with earth magic, leave some Tobacco and cornmeal behind as an offering of thanks.

- **MEDICINAL USES:** The thousands of people who use it on a regular basis might be surprised to learn that the Tobacco plant is considered extremely toxic and poisonous. It was once used as a relaxant.

Buckeye Nut

Aesculus glabra

Gladdens your heart and fills you with joy

- **BUCKEYE NUT WILL:** Bring you good luck, Help enhance a man's sexual performance, Protect your home

- **THE PLANT:** Buckeye is a tree that grows in the central part of the United States, primarily in the Mississippi and Ohio River valley regions. It grows thirty to fifty feet tall and bears small, inedible nuts in the late fall. It is the first tree to produce leaves in the spring and has greenish yellow blossoms. In the fall, the leaves turn orange and bright red. The Buckeye is related to the Horse Chestnut, but the high tannic acid content of its nuts makes them very bitter. If you rub a bit of oil on the nuts, they will dry nicely with a beautiful, smooth finish.

- **HARNESS BUCKEYE NUT'S MAGICAL PROPERTIES:** For centuries, it was believed that if a man carried Buckeye nuts in his pocket, it would improve his sexual performance and he would have better luck seducing a woman. He would also be sure to win in cards. Even if you're not a card player, you can place Buckeye nuts on your altar to bring you good luck in general.

  Buckeye nuts can be oiled, strung together, and placed over your front door for protection, to attract love, and to assure abundance. They are a beautiful addition to holiday decorations while inviting good fortune in the coming year.

- **MEDICINAL USES:** An herbalist might rub an oil made from the nuts on your joints to prevent rheumatism and arthritis. It can also be rubbed on the forehead to relieve headaches.

▶ Top: Hyssop, Middle: Tobacco, Bottom: Buckeye Nut

Magnolia Leaves *Magnolia acuminata*

Teaches you about loyalty

- **MAGNOLIA LEAVES WILL:** Encourage fidelity, Provide protection, Purify your home

- **THE PLANT:** The Magnolia tree can grow up to eighty feet tall. The leaves are oval and slightly pointed at the tips. The leaves are a deep, rich forest green and are heavily veined. Its flowers are large and very fragrant. The wood of the tree is finely grained and is beautiful when polished. It is used for house interiors and to build large canoes. It is native to North America, although it has been naturalized in much of the world.

- **HOW TO HARNESS MAGNOLIA LEAVES' MAGICAL PROPERTIES:** To ensure your partner's fidelity, place Magnolia leaves under your bed. You can also place some leaves on your altar to purify it and to increase its sanctity.

For protection, scatter a few of the leaves around the inside of your home. And to protect your money, put some leaves in your wallet; this will make sure no one but you touches it. Likewise, if you're worried about someone reading your journal, put a Magnolia leaf on the cover and it will remain untouched.

- **MEDICINAL USES:** A warm tea made from the leaves makes an effective laxative. Drinking Magnolia leaf tea on a regular basis will also prevent malaria.

  Magnolia leaf is also known as an aromatic stimulant and is taken by some people in the spring as a cleansing tonic.

Calamus Root *Acorus calamus*

Reminds you just how sweet life can be

- **CALAMUS ROOT WILL:** Increase your good luck Help you heal, Protect you and your property, Attract abundance

- **THE PLANT:** Calamus grows in all European countries except Spain. It is also found in northern Asia Minor, Japan, the United States, Ceylon, and India. It is a perennial herb that looks very similar to the bearded Iris. The plant grows two to three feet high and has an aromatic odor when bruised. The flowers are sweet-scented and in warmer climates produce berries. Calamus spreads mainly by the rapid growth of its spreading rhizome.

- **HOW TO HARNESS CALAMUS ROOT'S MAGICAL PROPERTIES:** Sprinkling a small amount of the powdered root around the outside of your home will not only protect your home from robbers but will also discourage fleas and other unwanted pests. The dried root can also be used in incense to encourage spiritual, emotional, and physical healing.

  If you find yourself worrying about your finances, cut up the dried roots and place them in the corners of the rooms of your house to assure yourself of always having more than enough money.

  Growing the plants in your garden will attract good luck and help protect the property.

- **MEDICINAL USES:** Some varieties of Calamus are poisonous, so be sure to consult an experienced herbalist before you ingest any. The powdered root mixed into a glass of white wine helps to settle an upset stomach. Drinking a glass before a meal will help with digestion. The candied roots can be chewed to soothe a sore throat or calm a persistent cough.

St. John's Wort *Hypericum perforatum*

Deepens connection to your instinctual nature

- **ST. JOHN'S WORT WILL:** Repel negativity and provide protection, Attract abundance

- **THE PLANT:** St. John's Wort is plentiful throughout most temperate regions of the world. It is thought to be indigenous to Europe and Asia. It is a perennial herb that grows one to three feet tall in uncultivated areas. The leaves are pale green and often have black or red spots. The flowers appear in midsummer and are very bright yellow. The plant produces round, black seeds that have a strong resinous smell. St. John's Wort is believed to chase away negative spirits.

- **HOW TO HARNESS ST. JOHN'S WORT'S MAGICAL PROPERTIES:** It is said you must pick St. John's Wort with your left hand after asking the plant for permission. It is most powerful if picked on Midsummer Night's Eve and dried over a ceremonial bonfire.

For protection and to attract abundance, plant a St. John's Wort bush near your front door. You might also hang a branch of it over your front door to repel negativity.

If you're looking to deepen your spiritual connection, soak the dried leaves in olive oil and then put the mixture in a bottle. Place the bottle outside where the moonlight can shine on it. Leave it there for a month. You can then use the oil to anoint yourself and others to strengthen your spiritual connection.

- **MEDICINAL USES:** Recently St. John's Wort has become a popular treatment for depression. It is also used to treat bladder problems. Given as a tea before bedtime, it will help children who are struggling with wetting the bed at night. It will also help relieve chronic lung congestion and clear up urinary tract infections.

Vanilla

Vanilla planifolia

Teaches you how to simplify your life

- **VANILLA WILL:** Attract love, Clear your mind, Raise the spiritual vibrations

- **THE PLANT:** Vanilla is the seedpod of an Orchid native to Mexico. It is now widely grown throughout the tropics, but there is only one type of bee that will pollinate it. Attempts to export the bees have been unsuccessful, so each flower must be hand pollinated. The blossoms open for only one day, which is why Vanilla beans are so expensive. The Vanilla orchid grows as a vine, climbing on existing trees. In a Vanilla plantation, the vines are grown on poles or shade trees and folded downward by hand each year to make them easier to harvest. Vanilla grows best in partial shade in moist conditions.

- **HOW TO HARNESS VANILLA'S MAGICAL PROPERTIES:** Place a Vanilla bean in a bowl of sugar for several weeks and then use the sugar with your friends and family. It will encourage peaceful and loving communications.

  To bless and purify an area, soak a Vanilla bean in coarse sea salt for several weeks and then scatter the salt around the area. To raise your home's energy, place a bean on your altar.

  If you'd like to attract abundance, carry a Vanilla bean in your wallet.

- **MEDICINAL USES:** In old medicinal texts, Vanilla is described as an aphrodisiac and used as a remedy for fevers.

Pimento

Pimenta dioica

Makes your life run smoothly

- **PIMENTO WILL:** Attract love, Bless your home

- **THE PLANT:** The Pimento tree is indigenous to the Caribbean Islands. It was found in Jamaica by the early Spanish conquerors, who liked its taste. It is an evergreen tree that reaches forty feet in height. It has small white flowers that produce a deep purple berry. It is also found in Mexico and was thought to be carried there by migratory birds.

- **HARNESS PIMENTO'S MAGICAL PROPERTIES:** Pimento has been used for centuries as a love amulet. Place a few berries in a small locket or silk bag and wear it around your neck. Love is sure to find you.

    To fill your home with joy, happiness, and ease, place some of the berries on your altar and in the four corners of your house. When placed on your altar, they will help deepen your loving connection with yourself and your spirit.

- **MEDICINAL USES:** Pimento is a hot and aromatic stimulant. It is seldom used for medical purposes itself but is often added to other mixtures to make them more palatable. It can be made into a poultice and added to flannel to make a plaster for treating neuralgia or rheumatism.

Elecampane

Inula helenium

Nurtures your magical nature

- **ELECAMPANE WILL:** Provide protection, Help you feel loved, Enhance your psychic abilities

- **THE PLANT:** Elecampane can be found growing wild throughout Europe, temperate Asia, Siberia, and parts of India. As a cultivated plant, it is grown in much of North America. Elecampane grows four to five feet tall, is very stout, and produces huge pointed leaves one and a half feet long and four inches wide. It blooms from June through August. The slightly aromatic flowers are large and bright yellow, resembling a double sunflower. Elecampane springs from a fleshy perennial root.

- **HARNESS ELECAMPANE'S MAGICAL PROP-ERTIES:** How to harness Elecampane's magical properties: When the dried leaves are burned as incense, Elecampane will increase your psychic abilities, make it easier to connect with your intuition, and help you hear the voices of friends and family who have passed over.

    If you want to consecrate a relationship, wear white and use the smoke of its incense to surround you as you say your vows to one another.

    Sprinkle a few pinches of the dried herb in a circle around your home to fill it with love, peace, and protection.

- **MEDICINAL USES:** Elecampane is chiefly used to treat coughs, consumption, and other pulmonary complaints. It is also used to treat bronchitis. The powdered root mixed with honey is an effective treatment for hemorrhoids when applied externally. It also helps relieve the pain of neuralgia.

Burning Bush

Dictammus albus

Helps you experience miracles in your life

◀ BURNING BUSH WILL: Help you create success, Remove curses, Enlighten you, Impart courage

THE PLANT: Burning Bush is a small plant indigenous to Southern Europe and Asia Minor. When you brush against the plant, it smells like lemon peel, but when you crush the leaves or flowers, they smell more like balsam. Burning Bush exudes an essential oil that is flammable. When a candle is held near the plant, the air around the plant will ignite but leave the plant unharmed, hence its name.

◀ HARNESS BURNING BUSH'S MAGICAL PROPERTIES: If you're feeling unsure of yourself, carry the dried leaves in your wallet or on your person. They will help you have the courage of your convictions and make decisions that bring you great success. Similarly, whenever you have an important decision to make, rub some of the leaves on your temples.

Add the dried leaves to your favorite incense before you meditate to help you deepen your connection to your spirit and higher self. To remove any curses or negative thoughts, make the sign of the cross three times on your forehead with the leaves.

◀ MEDICINAL USES: Some people consider the plant mildly poisonous, while others claim a tea made from its leaves will reduce fevers and help a person relax. Its tea is also said to settle an upset stomach. When combined with peppermint, it is used to treat epilepsy. The tea is also a wonderfully soothing face wash.

▶ Top: Pimento, Middle: Elecampane
Bottom: Burning Bush

Sage *Salvia officinalis*

Helps you access your innate wisdom

- **SAGE WILL:** Help with divination, Increase abundance, Invite longevity, Protect your home and family

- **THE PLANT:** A member of the Mint family, Sage is native to the Mediterranean and Asia but now grows all over the world. It has been cultivated for many centuries. The plant grows one to three feet tall and all parts of it are used. It blooms from June through September. The flowers range from white to purple to deep red. The leaves are slightly fuzzy and a silvery gray green. The plant is highly aromatic and somewhat bitter in taste.

- **HOW TO HARNESS SAGE'S MAGICAL PROPERTIES:** For magical purposes the leaves are best harvested before the flowers appear. It's believed that if you eat Sage in May, you will live a long life.

  Carrying Sage on your person will encourage wisdom and help you connect with your intuition

  To cleanse your home and property, raise the spiritual vibration, and create a bubble of protection, burn some Sage and walk around your home and property with it. You can also burn it during meditation to help see into the future.

  Finally, to ensure success and attract abundance, plant some Sage in your garden or in a pot on your windowsill.

- **MEDICINAL USES:** Sage tea can be used as a mouthwash to heal bleeding gums and soothe the mouth. When used as a gargle, it will soothe a sore throat and calm inflamed tonsils. When consumed, it has a calming effect and is a wonderful cleansing tonic.

Dittany

Origanum dictamnus

Helps you give birth to your dreams

DITTANY WILL: Deepen love, Help you connect with spirits, Increase your ability to manifest your hopes and dreams

THE PLANT: Dittany was originally a native of the mountains on the island of Crete. It is one of the best-known healing herbs of antiquity. It was also considered a symbol of love, and young men risked climbing the steep mountains to pick bouquets to prove their love.

Today, this perennial herb is grown primarily as a potted plant or as an ornamental plant in a garden. The small green leaves are velvety, and the plant can grow to one and a half feet tall. It has flowers that range from light pink to deep purple during the summer months.

HOW TO HARNESS DITTANY'S MAGICAL PROPERTIES: To contact spirits and facilitate visions, burn the dried leaves and flowers as incense. Spirits will often materialize in the smoke.

A tea made from Dittany will enhance your ability to astral project (separate your consciousness from your physical body). To make the tea, place two tablespoons of the dried leaves in two cups of boiling water and allow the mixture to steep for about ten minutes before straining it.

Placing the leaves on your altar will help you manifest your hopes, dreams, and desires.

To provide an aura of protection, sprinkle a handful of the dried leaves around the outside of your home.

MEDICINAL USES: A tea made from Dittany can be used to heal wounds, soothe pain, cure snake bites, and ease childbirth. Hippocrates recommended for diseases of the digestive system, rheumatism, arthritis, and irregular menses.

Myrrh

Commiphora myrrha

Opens your heart to love

- **MYRRH WILL:** Invoke the divine feminine, Deepen your connection to your spirit, Create a feeling of peace and joy, Facilitate healing

- **THE PLANT:** Myrrh is indigenous to Arabia, East India, and northern Africa. The bushes seldom grow more than nine feet tall. They are compact and sturdy, and the branches are heavily knotted. The bark creates cavities that fill up with secretions that flow freely when the bark is wounded. It flows as a pale yellow liquid that hardens into a reddish brown mass ranging in size from a small teardrop to a large walnut. The surface of the teardrop is powdery and rough, and is semi-transparent. It tastes bitter but is very aromatic. Myrrh has been used for millennia, and its origin is clouded with mystery.

- **HARNESS MYRRH'S MAGICAL PROPERTIES:** Myrrh was used by the Egyptians to honor Isis, the goddess of love. Add it to an amulet to attract love, peace, joy, and happiness.

  To bless and sanctify your home, burn Myrrh with Frankincense as incense. Burn it while you meditate to deepen your meditations.

  To ensure you will always have more than enough of everything, add it to a sachet and hang it in your closet.

- **MEDICINAL USES:** Myrrh is useful for treating congestion and coughs as long as a fever isn't present. It calms an upset stomach, stimulates the appetite, and is often used in toothpowder and as a mouthwash.

Foxglove

Digitalis purpurea

Opens your heart

- **FOXGLOVE WILL:** Provide protection, Call fairies

- **THE PLANT:** Foxglove is a handsome plant that is indigenous to much of Europe; it is common as a wildflower in Great Britain and grows throughout North America. It is a biennial plant, although sometimes the roots will produce flowers for several more years. The first year the plant puts out only leaves, and the second year it puts out flower spikes that are three to four feet tall. The long spikes of bell-shaped flowers often droop and bloom throughout the summer. Foxglove will reseed itself after flowering.

- **HARNESS FOXGLOVE'S MAGICAL PROPERTIES:** Many centuries ago, women in Wales made black dye from the Foxglove plant and painted crossed lines on their floors to prevent evil from entering their homes. You can protect your own home and garden simply by growing Foxglove on your property.

  Fairies can be either friend or foe, depending on your intent. If you have an open heart, you can use Foxglove to make friends with fairies, but if your intent is impure, the fairies will know, and they make formidable enemies. To connect with fairies, simply hold the fresh leaves in your hand and ask them to be present in your life.

- **MEDICINAL USES:** Foxglove provides the main drug, digitalis, used to treat heart problems. An herbalist might prescribe it to improve circulation and to help improve the functioning of the kidneys and liver. It can easily upset the stomach; if it does, talk with your practitioner about cutting back on the dosage. Foxglove is poisonous in large doses, so it should be handled with extreme care.

Senna

Cassia acutifolia

Helps you feel loved

■ **SENNA WILL:** Attract love, Add beauty to your life

■ **THE PLANT:** Senna is a small shrub indigenous to Egypt, northern Africa, and Arabia. It has a smooth, erect, green stem and long spreading branches. Its leaves are about an inch long and have distinct veins on the underside. They have a mildly sweet taste. The flowers are small and vibrant yellow. The pods are about two inches long and contain about six seeds.

■ **HARNESS SENNA'S MAGICAL PROPERTIES:** Senna is a common ingredient in love spells. Putting some of the powdered herb in an amulet and wearing it around your neck will attract love.

　To help you create beauty in your life, sprinkle the powder on your altar or put a very small amount in your bath.

■ **MEDICINAL USES:** When taken internally, Senna will cleanse your entire body. It relieves constipation but can cause cramping. It will color the urine, making it reddish brown within a half hour of taking Senna. If cloves and cinnamon are added to Senna, it is less likely to cause nausea.

▶ Top: Myrrh, Middle: Foxglove, Bottom: Senna

Agrimony *Agrimonia eupatoria*

Shows you how to banish the blues

- **AGRIMONY WILL:** Reverse spells and dispel other people's negativity, Clear negative energies from your home, Accelerate spiritual healing and cleanse the aura

- **THE PLANT:** Agrimony grows throughout Europe, Canada, and the United States. It is a hardy perennial that flourishes in both woods and open fields. It is easily cultivated. It is best to divide the roots in the fall. Agrimony's flowers and leaves give off a lemony scent when crushed. It is best harvested in early summer when the flowers are in full bloom and at their most fragrant.

- **HOW TO HARNESS AGRIMONY'S MAGICAL PROPERTIES:** Agrimony is generally used dried. If you're drying your own herb, make sure it is in full bloom when you pick it.

  If you have trouble sleeping, fill a small pillow with its dried leaves and place it under your head.

  To relieve negative energies that might cause depression and lethargy, put two tablespoons of chopped, dried leaves into a pint of boiling water, stir, and then add the unsteeped tea to your bathwater.

  When you move into a new home, use the tea in your cleaning water to purify and bless the home. You can also add half of cup of the tea to your laundry water to remove any residual negative energy.

  To boost your mood and cleanse your aura, burn some dried leaves and allow the smoke to wash over you. Drinking a weak tea made from the whole plant will fill you with a sense of well-being. To make the tea, add a sprig of the plant to a cup of hot water.

  Sprinkling the leaves around your home will invite good luck and fill your home with love.

- **MEDICINAL USES:** During the Middle Ages, Agrimony was often found in monastery gardens, where the monks used it to treat stomach and eye problems.

Raspberry Leaves

Rubus idaens

Transforms your dreams into reality

◄ **RASPBERRY LEAVES WILL:** Protect your home, Attract love, Ease the pain of childbirth

◄ **THE PLANT:** Raspberries are indigenous to much of Europe and North America. They grow wild in many places. The stems are upright and covered with small thorns. They are a biennial and the roots will easily spread. They flower in May and June, producing a flavorful and sweet red berry.

◄ **HOW TO HARNESS RASPBERRY LEAVES' MAGICAL PROPERTIES:** Raspberry leaves contain very powerful, nurturing magic. They are connected with the Great Earth Mother and will remind you to love and honor your family and community. Meditating with them or simply watching the plants grow will deepen your connection with the Earth.

To protect your home and all who enter, hang some dried Raspberry leaves over your front door. You can also scatter a few handfuls around your property to attract love and good luck.

If you are pregnant, remember to place some of the leaves under the bed where you will be giving birth; they will ease the pain of childbirth.

◄ **MEDICINAL USES:** A tea made by adding two heaping tablespoons of Raspberry leaves to a pint of boiling water and steeping for at least ten minutes, or until the tea is rich in color and smells full-bodied, makes an excellent gargle for sore throats and cankers in the mouth. It can also be used to wash wounds and ulcers of the skin. When combined with Slippery Elm, it can be used to help heal scalds and burns and prevent scarring. The tea will also settle an upset stomach and quiet nausea.

Blue Cohosh *Caulophyllum thalictroides*

Will lift your spirit and fill your life with serendipity

- **BLUE COHOSH WILL:** Bring great joy and happiness, Encourage chastity, Create opportunities for serendipity

- **THE PLANT:** Blue Cohosh is a perennial woodland herb that is becoming endangered due to overharvesting. It grows one to three feet in height. It blooms in early April and is usually found on wooded slopes. It is purple when young. The mature plant is bluish green and has dark blue fruit.

- **HOW TO HARNESS BLUE COHOSH'S MAGICAL PROPERTIES:** Need more spark in your life? Sprinkle a pinch of the dried leaves around the rooms of your home to fill them with a sense of magic and joy. You can also place a branch of Blue Cohosh over the entrance of your home to invite good luck.

When you move into a new home, use Blue Cohosh as incense. Bless the entire house with the smoke from the incense while saying, "Spirits of good fortune, happiness, and ease, bless this home. May all who enter here be blessed with goodwill and abundance. May this home be protected now and always."

To ensure fidelity, hang a branch over your bed. And place a few berries on your altar to ensure the presence of helpful spirits and remove any negative influences from your life.

- **MEDICINAL USES:** A tea made from dried Blue Cohosh root helps regulate difficulties with menstruation. Native Americans often used Blue Cohosh to induce labor.

Note: Blue Cohosh should not be used in pregnancy prior to the ninth month.

Gotu Kola *Hydrocotyle asiatica*

Shows you how to enjoy life's sweet rewards

- **GOTU KOLA WILL:** Help you relax and deepen your meditations, Enhance your dreams, Improve your concentration

- **THE PLANT:** Gotu Kola is a perennial plant that loves partial shade. It is native to Indonesia, India, Malaysia, New Guinea, and other parts of Asia. The more you water the plant, the larger its leaves become. The new leaves taste like a cross between parsley and a carrot and are a wonderful addition to a salad. The flowers are pinkish red. The fruit is smooth and warty looking. The plant is manually harvested about every three months.

- **HOW TO HARNESS GOTU KOLA'S MAGICAL PROPERTIES:** If you have trouble concentrating, eat a few Gotu Kola leaves on a regular basis, which will improve memory.

  To enhance your dream life, drink a tea made from Gotu Kola before you go to sleep. To make the tea, add two tablespoons of the dried leaves and roots to two cups of boiling water and allow the mixture to steep for about ten minutes before straining it. The change in your dream life will be dramatic.

  Burning the root as incense before you meditate will clear the space for a deep and profound meditation.

- **MEDICINAL USES:** The whole Gotu Kola plant has been widely used in India and Fiji to treat skin inflammations, improve blood circulation, and aid in the treatment of bloating, congestion, and depression. When the leaves are eaten on a daily basis, Gotu Kola is said to improve memory, help with learning disabilities, and lessen the effects of Alzheimer's disease and senility. Gotu Kola energizes the thyroid, so it helps overcome fatigue and depression. It was long believed that if you ate two leaves a day, you would keep old age at bay. A poultice of the leaves is also useful in treating open sores.

Gravel Root

Eupatorium purpureum

Teaches you how to bring your dreams into reality

- **GRAVEL ROOT WILL:** Help you find a great job, Attract abundance, Show you how to manifest your dreams

- **THE PLANT:** Gravel Root is a perennial plant that is native to North America and is found in meadows and at the edge of forests from southern Canada to Florida as long as there is sufficient moisture. Gravel Root loves partial shade and normally is five to six feet tall, although it can grow up to twelve feet. Its stems are purple, and in August and September the top of each stem has a cluster of rose pink flowers that is about a foot across. Leaves can be gathered any time, but dig the roots only after frost has killed back the plant.

- **HARNESS GRAVEL ROOT'S MAGICAL PROPERTIES:** When burned as incense, the dried leaves will repel negativity. Scatter dried leaves on your altar when you are in the process of manifesting something. Return them to the ground with a prayer of thanks when your project is completed.

  Carry a piece of the root when you are looking for a job or want to ask for a raise or an increase in benefits.

- **MEDICINAL USES:** The root is the most powerful part of the plant for healing, although the leaves and flowers are used as well. The leaves can be crushed and placed in mesh bags to repel flies. A tea made from the dried root and flowers is a diuretic that will help clear up bladder and kidney problems.

Quinine

Parthenium integrifolium

Protects you from unseen dangers

- **QUININE WILL:** Protect you, Help you connect with your divinity, Ease the pain of loss

- **THE PLANT:** Wild Quinine grows about three feet high. It is native to eastern North America. The leaves are very aromatic and bitter to the taste. From late spring until early summer the plant produces numerous wooly looking white flowers. The blooms are very small and look like buttons. Quinine is found growing in prairies, along roads, and in rock outcroppings as far west as Wisconsin. The plant has large dark brown roots that expand horizontally as well as vertically. The roots and flowers are the parts of the plant that are used.

- **HARNESS QUININE'S MAGICAL PROPERTIES:** To protect your property and all who enter, hang some dried Quinine flowers over your front door. Placing the flowers on your altar will deepen your connection with your spirit and attract helpful spirits.

  To ease the emotional pain of personal loss, wear the flowers as an amulet.

- **MEDICINAL USES:** Wild Quinine strengthens the immune system and is similar in taste to the more familiar quinine that is used in the treatment of malaria. Wild Quinine is used to treat lymphatic congestion, colds, ear infections, sore throats, fevers, and Epstein-Barr virus.

  It will also stop muscle cramps and stimulate the liver. The fresh leaves can be used as a poultice to treat burns and wounds.

Ague Root

Aletris farcinosa

It is as magical as a unicorn, so it will bring you safety, success, and joy

- **AGUE ROOT WILL:** Banish evil, Erase bad luck, Protect you and your property

- **THE PLANT:** Ague Root is also known as Unicorn Root. Native to North America, it is a perennial and a member of the Lily family. It prefers grassy or sandy soil that is consistently damp. Ague Root grows in sunny areas from southern Canada and the northeastern United States to the Gulf of Mexico. The rhizome root is thick and fibrous and grows in a slightly horizontal direction. The root is intensely bitter, although this bitterness fades with drying. The plant is endangered in some areas, so grow it rather than trying to harvest it.

- **HARNESS AGUE ROOT'S MAGICAL PROPERTIES:** Ague Root is primarily used to ward off evil and for protection. To fill your home with a sense of peace and safety, grind up the root into a powder and sprinkle it around the outside of your house or put a pinch in the corner of each room. If you make a cross out of two pieces of the root and place it at the entrance to your home, only friends will be able to enter.

  You can also carry a small piece of the root in your wallet to keep yourself safe and make sure no one steals your money.

  If you have to go to court, wear a sachet filled with the powder or a small piece of the root around your neck to ensure success.

- **MEDICINAL USES:** When dried and made into a tea, Ague Root will relieve gas, settle an upset stomach, and improve digestion. It is also effective in treating the urinary tract.

▶ Top: Gravel Root, Middle: Quinine, Bottom: Ague Root

Black Cohosh

Cimicifuga racemosa

Gives you courage to live the life of your dreams

- **BLACK COHOSH WILL:** Invite love, Give you courage and protect you and your home, Increase fertility

- **THE PLANT:** Black Cohosh is native to North America, where it grows freely in shady woods in Canada and the United States. It flowers in June or early in July. Black Cohosh produces stout blackish rhizomes, or creeping underground stems, which are the most useful part of the plant.

- **HOW TO HARNESS BLACK COHOSH'S MAGI-CAL PROPERTIES:** To attract love, place Black Cohosh powder mixed with Rose and Gardenia petals in a sachet and hang it in your closet.

  To enhance your fertility, add an infusion of one tablespoon of Black Cohosh powder dissolved in a cup of hot water and a few drops of Lavender oil to your bathwater.

  For protection from evil, sprinkle a bit of Black Cohosh powder around the perimeter of your home or at your front door.

  For added courage, wash your hands in a tea made from the powdered root. You can make the tea by adding two tablespoons of the powdered root to two cups of boiling water and allowing the mixture to steep for about ten minutes before straining it. Make sure the tea is sufficiently cool before washing your hands in it.

  Combine a teaspoon of the powdered root with your favorite liquid hand soap and keep it in your bathroom. Use it regularly when you are in the process of changing some old behaviors.

- **MEDICINAL USES:** Black Cohosh can be used to treat menopausal symptoms. It is also said to be an antidote against poison and rattlesnake bites.

Witch Grass

Panicum capillare

Helps you connect with your playful nature

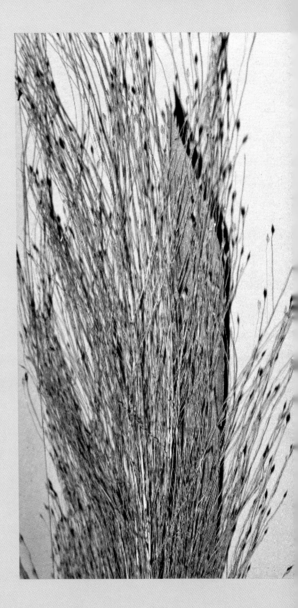

- **WITCH GRASS WILL:** Attract joy and happiness, Chase away negativity, Help you find the love of your life, Increase your sexual enjoyment

- **THE PLANT:** Witch Grass is a native annual grass in much of North America. It grows one to three feet tall. It sends up multiple stalks, called culms. The blades grow up to ten inches long and are rather floppy. The central flower looks much like the tassel of a Corn stalk. The blooming period occurs in late summer and early fall. The entire spiky flower becomes a light tan and can actually fall off the plant, tumbling along the ground much like tumbleweed. The root system is fibrous, and the plants spread by seeding themselves.

- **HOW TO HARNESS WITCH GRASS'S MAGI-CAL PROPERTIES:** The leaves can be harvested anytime and braided for specific purposes. You can gather fresh leaves and, as you braid them, think about what you want to create. Then place the braid on your altar until your dreams have manifested.

   For protection, place a braid over your front door. Use the flower stalk as a broom, hold several together, and sweep your entire house to remove any negative energy.

   For help with your love life, bind a bunch of Witch Grass with a golden cord and place it under your bed. It will increase your sexual pleasure and make sure your mate doesn't stray.

- **MEDICINAL USES:** An infusion of the leaves can be used to induce vomiting. The plant can also be used as a diet aid, although there are healthier and more effective ways to lose weight.

Spikenard

Aralia racemosais

Teaches you the true meaning of loyalty

- **SPIKENARD WILL:** Attract love, Ensure fidelity, Invite ease

- **THE PLANT:** Spikenard is native to North America. It grows up to six feet tall and has large leaves that are thin ovals that are often heart shaped. In July and August the plants are covered with a profusion of small clusters of greenish flowers. The berries are round and deep purple or reddish brown when ripe. The roots are thick and have several layers that contain oil.

- **HOW TO HARNESS SPIKENARD'S MAGICAL PROPERTIES:** Put a few Spikenard berries in an amulet and wear it around your neck to attract love.

  To repel any negativity and ensure loyalty and emotional support, hang a branch of Spikenard with leaves and berries over your front door.

  Make a tea from the root and sprinkle it around your home to make your life easier. For the tea, add two tablespoons of crushed root to two cups of boiling water. Steep the mixture for about ten minutes.

  Place a few berries and a piece of the root on your altar to help you hear the guidance from your inner wisdom.

- **MEDICINAL USES:** Spikenard was popular with Native Americans. They used its roots to relieve backaches and treat gas pains, coughs, and chest pains. Women were given a tea made from the roots to make childbirth less painful and quicker. A poultice made from the root was used to treat wounds and help mend broken bones. Early settlers used the juice from the berries to treat earaches and deafness. The root is also used as a blood purifier.

Turkey Rhubarb

Rheum palmatum

Protects you from your own fears

- **TURKEY RHUBARB WILL:** Protect you from sickness, Attract love and abundance, Remove negative thoughts

- **THE PLANT:** Turkey Rhubarb can be distinguished from familiar garden rhubarb by its huge leaves that are oblong with sharp segments. It has greenish white flowers, and the first buds that appear in the spring are yellow, not red like traditional-grade rhubarb. Turkey Rhubarb is indigenous to India and China.

- **HOW TO HARNESS TURKEY RHUBARB'S MAGICAL PROPERTIES:** Turkey Rhubarb root was used as an amulet during the Black Plague to protect the wearer from getting the plague. Today, you can wear it in an amulet to protect against illness and help release negative thinking.

  To purify your home and raise the spiritual vibrations, sprinkle some of the dried root in the rooms of your home or add it to your cleaning water.

  Put a piece of the root on your altar before you do any ceremonies to manifest abundance, and then bury it afterward to release your fears.

  If you are having a lot of fears about the future, sleep with a root under your bed for a month and then bury it in a sacred location.

- **MEDICINAL USES:** The root makes an excellent laxative. A powder made from the dried root and then made into a tea will cleanse the entire body if taken regularly for a week.

All Heal *Prunella vulgaris*

Helps you connect with the essence of who and what you really are

- **ALL HEAL WILL:** Show you how to open your heart, Help you let go of old fears and phobias, Cleanse your body and your mind, Deepen your connection with your spirit, Aid you in finding a new home or job

- **THE PLANT:** All Heal is a perennial herb found throughout Europe, Asia, Japan, and the United States. It grows in unused lots, in grassland, and along the edge of forests. All Heal thrives in any damp soil in full sun or in light shade. The plants are very hardy, so they are apt to become troublesome weeds. They grow from one to two feet high, with creeping, self-rooting, tough, square, reddish stems that branch. The flowers are two-lipped. The top lip is usually purple and the lower is often white or a light lavender. They bloom from June to August. Its leaves and small flowers are edible.

- **HOW TO HARNESS ALL HEAL'S MAGICAL PROPERTIES:** This herb was once called a gift from God because of all its uses. If you're feeling anxious and stressed, add All Heal tea to your bathwater for relaxation and to release all of your worries. You can make the tea by adding two tablespoons of dried All Heal to two cups of boiling water and allowing the mixture to steep for about ten minutes. Then strain it before adding it to your bathwater. Drinking the tea before you look for a new home or apply for a job will ensure you of success.

  Adding the flowers to a salad served to your beloved will improve your relationship and dispel any misunderstandings.

  To deepen your connection with your inner wisdom, rub fresh or dried All Heal leaves on your forehead before meditating.

- **MEDICINAL USES:** A tea made from one ounce of dried herb boiled in a pint of water for five minutes and sweetened with honey is an overall tonic for the body. As its name implies, it is said to heal anything.

Squaw Vine

Mitchella repens

Opens your heart to true compassion

- **SQUAW VINE WILL:** Open your heart, Repel jealousy, Increase self-confidence

- **THE PLANT:** Squaw Vine is native to the United States and was originally used by Native Americans. It grows in the forests of the Northeast among the Hemlocks and in moist places. It grows close to the ground and has deep green leaves that stay green all winter. It flowers in June and July, producing small red berries. They are edible, although dry and tasteless. The plant is also called Partridge Berry because partridges are said to be very fond of the berries.

- **HOW TO HARNESS SQUAW VINE'S MAGICAL PROPERTIES:** If you're hoping to attract love and increase self-confidence, place the berries in an amulet and wear it around your neck.

    Placing the berries on your altar will deepen your spiritual connection.

    Hanging the plant over your front door will repel jealousy.

    Bathing in the tea during pregnancy will ensure a healthy child and wash away any jealousy. To make the tea, add two tablespoons of dried Squaw Vine to two cups of boiling water. Allow the mixture to steep for about ten minutes before straining it.

MEDICINAL USES: Squaw Vine was used by Native American women to shorten labor and to end unwanted pregnancies. A tea made from the berries can ease menstrual cramps and help clear up urinary tract infections. It was also used to treat fevers. Externally, it can be applied as a poultice for swelling and sore nipples. Adding a tea made from Squaw Vine to hot bathwater can relieve stiff, rheumatic joints.

Orris Root

Iris florentia

Reminds you of the power of love

- **ORRIS ROOT WILL:** Attract love, Assist with divination, Protect your home

- **THE PLANT:** The Orris plant takes two to three years to mature. The flowers are beautiful even when the roots are still immature. In the third year of its growth, the plant is almost as tall as a man. The flowers bloom during May and June, then wither and die in July. The flowers are large and white with tinged purple edges and bright yellow centers. Since the time of ancient Greece, Orris Root was traditionally harvested in Italy.

- **HARNESS ORRIS ROOT'S MAGICAL PROPERTIES:** Orris Root is considered a moon herb, so it is useful in digging deep into the subconscious and uprooting what is hidden there. Place it near your journal or hold it while you are meditating to uncover the causes of unresolved issues.

  To protect yourself and your home and to attract love, sprinkle some of the ground root around the outside of your house. Anything you sprinkle the powder on will always return to its owner, including lovers. It acts like a love magnet, so it is a wonderful addition to any love amulet. The root can also be used like a pendulum to help you find the answers to all your deepest questions.

- **MEDICINAL USES:** The juice of the root is often used as a cosmetic and to remove freckles. The root is mainly used when it is dried, and it is good for complaints of the lungs, coughs, and a hoarse throat. Currently, it is more valued for its violet-like perfume than for any other use.

Cattail

Typha latifolia

Helps you live passionately

- **CATTAIL WILL:** Enhance your sex life, Help you have multiple orgasms, Fill your home with laughter

- **THE PLANT:** Cattails are found throughout most of North America, Europe, Asia, and Africa. They are the most common water-loving plant. The leaves are tall and slender, making an attractive border to most marshlands. The cattails themselves are hotdog-shaped brown flower spikes. Many parts of the plants are edible. The roots are very nutritious and have more starch and protein than rice or potatoes.

- **HARNESS CATTAIL'S MAGICAL PROPERTIES:** Want to liven up your sex life? Place a large bunch of cattails in the bedroom; their presence will also help you have multiple orgasms.

  If you want to attract joy, happiness, and abundance into your life, dry the leaves, weave them into a mat, and use them as a covering for your altar.

  Using the fluffy innards of cattails to make a small dream pillow will make it easier to remember your dreams and use them to find solutions to any issues in your life.

- **MEDICINAL USES:** Cattail roots can be crushed and used as a poultice for cuts, stings, and bruises. The ashes of the burned leaves are a wonderful antiseptic. A tea made from the roots is useful when applied to burns. It can also be used to settle an upset stomach and calm the intestines.

Pennyroyal

Mamentha pulegium

Makes all your burdens fall away

- **PENNYROYAL WILL:** Dispel fatigue while traveling, Protect you and repel negativity, Bring peace

- **THE PLANT:** Pennyroyal is a member of the Mint family. It has a weak stem, which readily takes root wherever it touches the ground. Pennyroyal blooms in July and August.

- **HARNESS PENNYROYAL'S MAGICAL PROPERTIES:** If you're going on a trip, place dried Pennyroyal leaves in your shoes. They will prevent fatigue during your travels, assure your safety, and strengthen your body in general.

  Placing dried Pennyroyal in a green poppet (a magical doll) is said to alleviate all stomach problems.

  To ensure fairness and success during business dealings, wear some Pennyroyal.

  To remove any negativity from your home and your life, sprinkle a bit of the dried herb mixed with sea salt around your house.

  Adding sea salt and tea made from dried Pennyroyal leaves to your bathwater will also help increase your energy, relax your mind, and soothe your spirit. To make the tea, add two tablespoons of dried leaves to two cups of boiling water, allow the mixture to steep for at least ten minutes, and then strain it.

- **MEDICINAL USES:** Pennyroyal was believed to purify water and the blood. When mixed with honey and eaten, it was supposed to cleanse the lungs and all internal organs. When a sprig was worn on the head, it was believed to cure dizziness and relieve headaches. It was also supposed to cure arthritis and rheumatism.

▶ Top: Orris Root, Middle: Cattail, Bottom: Pennyroyal

Little John

Alpinia galangal

Shows you how to overcome any setbacks

- **LITTLE JOHN WILL:** Help you prevail in court, Bring you good luck, Fill your life with ease

- **THE PLANT:** Little John is indigenous to the tropics and has a gingerlike flavor. It's popular as a spice in Caribbean cooking. It grows seven feet tall and has showy but small greenish white flowers. The fruit is an orangey red.

- **HARNESS LITTLE JOHN'S MAGICAL PROPER-TIES:** When you're facing a legal challenge, chew on the root to ensure that you'll be successful in court.

    Cooking with Little John on a regular basis will ensure that you always have good luck. You can add just a tiny pinch of the dried leaves to whatever food you're preparing to harness its magical properties.

    To protect your home and repel any negativity, place the root over your front door.

    Make a tea by boiling a small piece of the root vigorously in a pint of water for about ten minutes and use it to cleanse your altar and your home. Doing so will raise the spiritual vibrations and release any unwanted energies. Drinking the tea will raise your spirits when you find yourself facing a difficult situation.

    If you want to manifest anything, you can write your request on the root and place it on your altar to ensure that it will come to pass.

- **MEDICINAL USES:** The roots are used to treat rheumatism and bronchial congestion, overcome bad breath, quiet whooping cough, clear up throat infections, control incontinence, reduce fever, and calm upset stomachs.

Althea

Althea officinalis

Gives your life a sense of purpose

- **ALTHEA WILL:** Stimulate your psychic abilities, Protect your home and your body, Attract helpful spirits

- **THE PLANT:** Though native to Europe, Althea is cultivated in many areas, including the United States. It is a tenacious perennial that grows more than four feet tall with beautiful white or pink flowers. It is often found in damp places and marshes close to the coast where the water is brackish. It was revered by the Romans for its curative abilities.

- **HARNESS ALTHEA'S MAGICAL PROPERTIES:** Althea is a wonderful herb to use if you want to connect to your divinity. Place the dried herb on your altar to attract spirit helpers. A root placed under your bed will banish nightmares.

    Burn the dried leaves as incense when you are meditating to increase your psychic abilities and deepen your meditations.

    If you feel in need of protection, hang a bunch of dried Althea flowers over your doorway. You can also wear an amulet made from the dried flowers to protect yourself and attract beneficial spirits.

- **MEDICINAL USES:** Althea is a very good remedy for coughs and bronchitis. A tea made from Althea makes a soothing wash for irritated eyes and skin. Althea is effective in treating burns and wounds.

    The roots can be ground up to aid in digestion and alleviate stomach ulcers. Althea will also cleanse the kidneys and ease the pain of colitis.

Wintergreen

Gaultheria procumbens

Brings joy to your life

- **WINTERGREEN WILL:** Protect you from negativity, Remove negative spells, Help heal your mind and body

- **THE PLANT:** Wintergreen is a small shrub indigenous to much of North America. It is low growing, rarely getting higher than six inches from the ground. It often grows under Rhododendrons. It is also found in large patches on sandy and barren plains or mountainous tracts. The stiff branches have drooping white flowers in June and July followed by fleshy red berries that have a sweet taste and peculiar flavor. The odor of the plant is quite strong, and all parts of the plant are used.

- **HARNESS WINTERGREEN'S MAGICAL PROPERTIES:** To ensure your child of a prosperous and happy life, place dried Wintergreen leaves in a dream pillow and put it in a corner of your child's crib.

  For protection, sprinkle the leaves around your home. Use your inner knowing to tell you how many leaves to use and where to sprinkle them.

  When you are tired or in need of healing, bathe in a tea made from the leaves. You can also use the tea to purify and cleanse your altar. To make the tea, add two tablespoons of dried Wintergreen leaves to two cups of boiling water. Allow the tea to steep for about ten minutes before straining it.

- **MEDICINAL USES:** Wintergreen makes a wonderful overall tonic when taken in small doses. It helps relieve the pain of arthritis when applied externally, but because it can irritate the skin, it should be used with caution. The leaves make an excellent flavoring for other herbs that aren't very palatable.

▶ Top: Little John, Middle: Althea, Bottom: Wintergreen

Knotweed *Polyganum aviculare*

Helps you let go of all of your limitations

- **KNOTWEED WILL:** Help you release sadness and grief, Improve your vision, Increase your psychic awareness

- **THE PLANT:** Knotweed is abundant throughout the world and is commonly found along roadsides. The root is an annual. The plant is branched and woody. It is seldom erect and straggles over a broad area. The branches are two to six feet in length. The flowers are tiny and appear in clusters of two or three. They range from pink to red and are occasionally green or dull white.

- **HOW TO HARNESS KNOTWEED'S MAGICAL PROPERTIES:** Write down all your cares and concerns on a piece of paper. Place some Knotweed in an envelope with the letter and put it on your altar. Leave it there for a week and then burn the envelope. Allow the Knotweed to absorb all the emotional pain expressed in your letter and allow the fire to transform it.

  Use a small amount of Knotweed juice in your household cleaning solution to remove any negative energy.

- **MEDICINAL USES:** A poultice made from the leaves makes an excellent treatment for bleeding hemorrhoids. When squirted up the nose, juice from the leaves is said to stop a nosebleed. The tea is useful as a diuretic. A strong tea drunk on a daily basis will kill intestinal worms. When applied externally, it helps wounds heal rapidly.

Chicory *Cichorium intybus*

Attracts influential people into your life

- **CHICORY WILL:** Remove obstacles, Unlock doors

- **THE PLANT:** Chicory is a perennial herb that has a strong taproot much like a Dandelion. It grows two to three feet tall. Chicory blooms from July through September with numerous blue flowers that close up early in the afternoon. The plants often grow at the edge of the road, waving at people as they drive by.

- **HOW TO HARNESS CHICORY'S MAGICAL PROPERTIES:** Chicory is known to open locks and unlock opportunities. If you harvest Chicory leaves at noon on the summer solstice, in silence, with a pure gold knife, they will magically open locks for you and make you appear invisible.

    To remove any obstacles from your life, carry the dried root as an amulet. This will also help you forget about a former lover.

    When the dried root is burned as incense, it will help you with divination.

You can use a tea made from Chicory roots to clean your altar and crystals. To make the tea, add two tablespoons of dried Chicory root to two cups of boiling water. Allow the tea to steep for approximately ten minutes before straining it. You can also use the tea to release any limiting beliefs by washing your third eye (found in the middle of your forehead) with it.

- **MEDICINAL USES:** Chicory has properties similar to those of Dandelion. Though a tea made from its roots is extremely bitter, it can be used as a tonic, laxative, or diuretic. The leaves can be added to a salad to add an interesting flavor and relieve constipation.

Broom Straw *Cytisus scoparius*

Helps you sweep negativity and limitations out of your life

- **BROOM STRAW WILL:** Purify your thoughts and home, Enhance your ability to see into the future, Fortify your home's security

- **THE PLANT:** Broom Straw is a densely growing shrub native to England and found throughout Europe and northern Asia. It easily grows in the sandy pastures and heaths of Europe and grows sparsely in the United States. Broom Straw reaches three to five feet in height and produces long, straight, slender, bright green branches. It has fragrant yellow flowers that bloom from April to July. The seedpods burst open, making a loud cracking noise.

- **HOW TO HARNESS BROOM STRAW'S MAGICAL PROPERTIES:** Make a symbolic broom from several bunches of Broom Straw tied together with a brightly colored ribbon and slowly move from room to room in your home, sweeping away any negativity. If you can't find Broom Straw, you can use a regular house broom. Take a few deep breaths, say a short prayer, and then ask for the guidance and assistance of the universe. Slowly sweep your house with the broom.

You can call up the wind and rejoice in its magic by saying a prayer and then throwing a few sprigs of dried Broom Straw into the air. If you want to quiet the wind, say a prayer and then burn the herb outside, allowing the smoke to curl up toward the heavens.

To dispel negative spirits, boil a small handful of Broom Straw in salt water.

- **MEDICINAL USES:** Broom Straw is a wonderful tonic for the bladder and kidneys. It will help cleanse the urinary system and give you renewed energy.

Wormwood *Artemisia absinthium*

Shows you the folly of resentment, judgment, and rage

- **WORMWOOD WILL:** Attract love, Protect you from negative spirits, Help develop psychic abilities

- **THE PLANT:** Wormwood is a perennial that grows two to four feet tall. It has a woody base, and all parts of the plant are covered with a silvery down. It is native to the Mediterranean and has small yellow flowers that bloom in July and August. Wormwood generally grows by itself because a substance it gives off kills all other plants. Legend has it that this plant sprung up in the path taken by the serpent as it left the Garden of Eden. The leaves and flowers are very bitter, and the root has a warm and aromatic taste.

- **HOW TO HARNESS WORMWOOD'S MAGICAL PROPERTIES:** Collect the leaves only on a dry day, after the sun has dried off the dew.

    Burned as incense, the dried leaves will chase away negative spirits and help you deepen your psychic connections. To protect against negative spells, carry the leaves with you. You can also place Wormwood over your front door as a protective shield.

- **MEDICINAL USES:** Wormwood is considered harmful and is banned by the FDA. It is mind-altering, and Van Gogh was said to be drinking Wormwood tea when he cut off his ear.

Lemon Balm *Melissa officinalis*

Fills your heart with compassion

- **LEMON BALM WILL:** Attract love, Help you release judgments, Deepen your spiritual connection

- **THE PLANT:** Lemon Balm is a member of the Mint family; it is native to Europe but is now grown all over the world. In addition to being grown for its herbal properties, Lemon Balm is also grown for its medicinal properties, for use in cosmetics, and as an ingredient in furniture polish. The plant grows up to two feet high. During the spring and summer, it's covered with clusters of small, light yellow flowers that grow where the leaves meet the stem. The leaves are very wrinkled and range from dark green to yellowish green. If you rub your fingers on the leaves, your fingers will smell like lemons.

- **HOW TO HARNESS LEMON BALM'S MAGICAL PROPERTIES:** Dried Lemon Balm leaves and flowers are a wonderful addition to love amulets.

  To ensure that justice and right action prevail in your life, hang a bunch of Lemon Balm in your home.

  To help make your dreams manifest, wrap the Lemon Balm plant (except the roots) in linen, write down what you want to manifest on a piece of paper, enfold the paper in the linen, tie the bundle with a piece of silk thread, and place it on your altar. Say a prayer and know your dreams have already manifested in your life. Bury the bundle once your prayers have been answered.

- **MEDICINAL USES:** Lemon Balm reduces anxiety, promotes sleep, improves the appetite, and eases the pain and discomfort associated with bloating and gas. An herbalist might prescribe Lemon Balm tea sweetened with a bit of sugar to help a colicky baby sleep.

Basil

Ocimum basilicum

Fill your life with love

- **BASIL WILL:** Calm tempers, Banish evil from your home, Bring luck, prosperity, and harmony, Mend lovers' quarrels

- **THE PLANT:** Basil is a member of the Mint family and grows well almost anywhere. The leaves are extremely fragrant and vary in color from rich green to deep purple. They can be either smooth or crinkled. The flowers are usually white and are popular with bees.

- **HOW TO HARNESS BASIL'S MAGICAL PROP-ERTIES:** Basil is a powerful multipurpose herb. Sprinkle a little bit of dried Basil in the corners of each room to remove negativity, protect your house, and bring you good luck.

    After a tough day, add it to your bath to help you relax and bring balance and harmony into your life.

    If you've been having strained relationships with loved ones lately, Basil can help you improve your communication with them. Its aroma invites understanding between people, so tuck a sprig of it into your pocket to avoid major clashes and protect you while out in public. To mend a lovers' quarrel, place sprigs of it around the bedroom. A Basil plant makes a wonderful housewarming gift because it brings good luck to both parties.

    To find out whether a relationship will last, take two sprigs of Basil and gently place them in a fire. If they pop and jump as they burn, the relationship will be volatile. If they move apart, the relationship won't last. If they stay together, the relationship will be harmonious.

- **MEDICINAL USES:** Basil can help lower blood pressure and ease the symptoms of emphysema and bronchitis. It is also a wonderful insect repellent.

Mistletoe

Viscum album

Reminds you of the love of the Divine

- **MISTLETOE WILL:** Bring peace to difficult situations, Assure you of love and abundance, Heal your mind, body, and spirit, Bless your home

- **THE PLANT:** Mistletoe is an evergreen parasitic plant. It can grow up to five feet tall and is usually found growing on the branches of Apple trees, although it can also be found on Ash, Hawthorn, and occasionally on Oak. It is rarely found on Cedar, Larch, and Pear trees. It is spread by birds. When one of the sticky berries comes into contact with the bark of a tree, it rapidly creates roots that penetrate into the tree, absorbing needed nutrients from the host itself. The leaves are tongue shaped, and the small flowers appear in clusters of three. Mistletoe flowers in May, and the berries ripen in December.

- **HARNESS MISTLETOE'S MAGICAL PROPERTIES:** Because Mistletoe doesn't grow in the earth, it is thought to be a very sacred plant that comes from the place between places. The early Christians adopted the Pagan tradition of using Mistletoe as a symbol of peace and goodwill. When hung in your home, it will provide protection, attract love and peace, bless your home, and heal your mind, body, and spirit. Place it on your altar at the winter solstice to ensure success in the coming year.

- **MEDICINAL USES:** Mistletoe was believed to cure epilepsy and other convulsive disorders. It can also be used to stop internal hemorrhaging. Large doses of the plant or berries can be toxic. People have been known to have convulsions after eating a large number of the berries.

Cinnamon

Cinnamonum zeylanicum

Makes your life easier than you could possibly imagine

- **CINNAMON WILL:** Deepen your spiritual connection, Invite success, Give you the power to change anything

- **THE PLANT:** Cinnamon trees grow twenty to thirty feet tall. They are native to Ceylon and India, but grow well in Jamaica, parts of Mexico, and other tropical climates. Cinnamon bark is made from the dried bark of the branches. The leaves smell spicy and have a very spicy flavor. The tree has small white flowers that produce an oval berry about the size of a small blackberry.

- **HARNESS CINNAMON'S MAGICAL PROPERTIES:** When Cinnamon bark is used in incense, it raises the spiritual vibrations of the home and empowers the magical properties of any herb it is used with. Burning it will help you develop your psychic and spiritual abilities. When combined with Sandalwood, it will deepen your insights.

  Cinnamon oil is one of the oldest aromatic oils and was mentioned in the Old Testament. It is a wonderful love charm. Wear a little when you go out on a date or sprinkle it around the room. Adding a few drops of it to your bath will empower you and invite success into your life.

  For protection, sprinkle a few pinches of the powder around the rooms of your home.

- **MEDICINAL USES:** Cinnamon can stop vomiting, relieve gas, and help treat diarrhea. A tea made from Cinnamon bark will calm your stomach. It is a mild stimulant, so a cup of cinnamon tea in the afternoon is a wonderful pick-me-up. Washing wounds with the tea will prevent infections.

Cancer Bush

Sutherlandia frutescens

Dispels all darkness from your heart and mind

- **CANCER BUSH WILL:** Make you feel beautiful, Energize your love life, Protect your home

- **THE PLANT:** Cancer Bush is known as the plant that dispels darkness. It has very attractive bright ruby red butterfly-like flowers. It grows about two feet tall and is indigenous to Africa. It blooms profusely whenever sufficient rain is present. The leaves are gray green and very bitter to the taste. Cancer Bush has long been valued for both its beauty and its medicinal value. The dried fruit looks like an inflated paper pod and is often used in flower arrangements.

- **HARNESS CANCER BUSH'S MAGICAL PROPER-TIES:** To help you feel and look more beautiful, make a tea from a handful of dried leaves brewed in a quart of water for about ten minutes. Then strain the tea and add it to your bathwater.

  To protect your home from unwelcome guests, crush and scatter a handful of dried Cancer Bush leaves around your property.

  Drinking a cup of the Cancer Bush tea described above every day will help you release limiting thoughts and behaviors.

- **MEDICINAL USES:** Cancer Bush is used to treat internal cancers and stomach problems. Tea made from its leaves can be used to treat chicken pox and fevers.

  A tea made from the roots and leaves is useful in the treatment of eye problems. A weak version of this tea can also treat flu, liver ailments, rheumatism, and diarrhea. Finally, a little bit of Cancer Bush tea will improve the appetite.

▶ Top: Mistletoe, Middle: Cinnamon, Bottom: Cancer Bush

Dill *Peucedanum graveolens*

Sweeps limitations right out of your life and invites miracles instead

- **DILL WILL:** Attract abundance, Protect your home, Prevent envy, Make you sexually alluring

- **THE PLANT:** Dill is a hardy annual that is a native of the Mediterranean region and southern Russia. It grows wild in the cornfields of Spain and Portugal. It has a wonderful smell and lacy, feathery-looking leaves. It grows several feet tall and has a large, umbrella-like yellow flower.

- **HOW TO HARNESS DILL'S MAGICAL PROPERTIES:** Float a handful of Dill seeds in your bathwater before a romantic date to make yourself irresistible.

  To protect your home from evil influences, place Dill seeds on your windowsills. Hanging a bunch of Dill over your front door will prevent people from envying you.

  You can hang stalks of Dill over your baby's cradle to keep away bad dreams and calm your child.

Place the flowers (fresh or dried) on your altar to attract love. To attract abundance, put some Dill seeds in your wallet. Planting some in your garden will ensure that you always have all the resources you need.

Put some seeds in your shoes on your wedding day or when you go for a job interview to ensure success.

- **MEDICINAL USES:** The leaves, seeds, and oil of Dill can be used to calm the digestive tract, stimulate the appetite, and relieve bloating and gas. Oil of Dill can be used to make Dill water, which is a time-tested treatment for gas and colic in infants. When a few drops of the oil are added to a glass of water with a little bit of sugar, the Dill water is easily tolerated and effective in calming hiccups or soothing an upset stomach.

Blue Flag *Iris versicolor*

Reminds you of the limitless possibilities life holds

- **BLUE FLAG WILL:** Vastly increase your financial resources, Help you feel safe, Attract money

- **THE PLANT:** Native to North America, Blue Flag also grows throughout the British Isles. It is often cultivated as a garden plant but also grows in the wild in damp and marshy areas. A perennial, it grows to about three feet tall, with erect stems, sword-shaped leaves, and two or three blue or violet irislike flowers per stem. The flower petals are long with a pleasant aroma. The fruit is a large pod with a number of sections filled with brown seeds that are lined up like a roll of coins. The rhizome is thick and short and best harvested in autumn.

- **HOW TO HARNESS BLUE FLAG'S MAGICAL PROPERTIES:** Placing a bouquet of the flowers on your altar is sure to bring abundance into your life. Carrying a piece of the root in your wallet will ensure you of always having enough money for all your wants and needs.

  To help you feel safe, hang a rhizome over your front door.

- **MEDICINAL USES:** Blue Flag was a popular medicinal plant with Native Americans, who used it to treat wounds and sores and to relieve colds, earaches, and cholera. The plant was also used for treating liver problems.

Wolfberry

Lycium barbatum

Helps you live with passion

- **WOLFBERRY WILL:** Invite loyalty and friendships, Enhance your social life, Help you manifest your deepest dreams

- **THE PLANT:** Wolfberry grows throughout much of China and Tibet and is extensively cultivated in the northern regions. The shrub was popular in Europe as a hedging plant. The root is harvested in spring. They flower in June and July, and the bright orange-red berries are harvested in the fall.

- **HOW TO HARNESS WOLFBERRY'S MAGICAL PROPERTIES:** Wolfberry was so named because peasants saw wolves eating the berries. Placing a bowl of the berries on your altar will invite new friendships and greatly enhance your social life.

  Wolfberry can also improve your social life if it's being disrupted by people quarreling around you. Simply offer some of the berries to the people who are quarreling. As soon as they eat them, the fighting will stop and an amicable solution to the issue will easily be found.

  To deepen your connection to spirit, eat a few of the berries before meditating.

  To keep yourself and your home safe, put some of the berries in the four corners of your property.

- **MEDICINAL USES:** For at least two thousand years, Wolfberry bushes have grown wild in China and been used in common recipes and traditional Chinese medicine. The Chinese revere Wolfberry as a national treasure, and it is one of the most nutrient-dense medicinal herbs. They owe much of their popularity to the herbalist Li Ch'ing Yuen, who was a proponent of eating and using the berries and is said to have lived for 252 years.

Cedar Wood

Cedrus libani

Reminds you just how sweet life can be

CEDAR WOOD WILL: Banish nightmares, Attract money, Purify your home, Mark rites of passage

THE PLANT: Cedar is native to North America, Europe, northern Africa, and much of Asia. Cedars are graceful and conical in shape and make wonderful wind breaks or hedgerows. The flowers appear in the fall. They are very small and fragrant. The wood has been used for centuries to make incense and was probably the first essence extracted from plants.

HOW TO HARNESS CEDAR WOOD'S MAGICAL PROPERTIES: When used as incense, the dried leaves will purify your home. Use the incense on a regular basis to cleanse your altar. You can also place cedar boughs around your home to protect it from negativity.

To increase your psychic abilities, burn a few Cedar twigs in your fireplace, allowing yourself to inhale the sweet aroma of the smoke before you meditate.

Placing Cedar leaves in your wallet will attract abundance. Putting them in a sachet and hanging it in your closet will invite love into your life as well as repel moths from your clothes.

MEDICINAL USES: Native Americans burned Cedar branches in sweat lodges to relieve head colds and purify the body. When combined with fat, the leaves are a great remedy for rheumatism as well as muscular aches and pains. Boiling the leaves and pinecones in milk makes a wonderful poultice to dispel fevers and relieve pain. The smoke helps stop coughs and clear up stuffy noses.

Fern

Pteris aquilina

Teaches you about the power of patience

- **FERN WILL:** Help you contact the dead, Attract love, Return lost youth, Make you appear invisible, Protect you and your family

- **THE PLANT:** There are many species of Ferns. They are perennial with a creeping rootstock or rhizome. Most Ferns thrive with a northern exposure and prefer shaded areas. They flourish in a soil rich in composted leaves. A Fern's leaves are called fronds.

- **HOW TO HARNESS FERN'S MAGICAL PROPERTIES:** Fern's magic is most strongly associated with thresholds. It is most powerful at the change of season, or at midnight when one day becomes the next. At these moments, Fern will assist you in having access into other worlds. You can use it to contact the dead or call upon assistance from the spiritual realms by burning Fern as incense.

  Fern is a sacred plant of midsummer, so burning it as incense or throwing it into a bonfire on Midsummer Night's Eve will invite prophetic dreams. As you watch the smoke rise, speak forth your dreams for the coming summer and they will manifest.

  Include Ferns in a vase of flowers for protection and to attract love. A Fern plant in or around your home will protect your home and the inhabitants.

  If you could collect enough sap from the female Fern, it is said to impart eternal youth.

  Finally, carrying Fern seeds is said to make you appear invisible.

- **MEDICINAL USES:** For centuries, an oil distilled from the rhizomes of the plant has been used to rid people and animals of worms.

Borage

Borago officinalis

Brings you the courage to be yourself

- **BORAGE WILL:** Enhance your psychic abilities, Bestow courage, Help you feel safe

- **THE PLANT:** Borage is a hardy annual plant that originated in the Middle East but is now grown throughout Europe and the United States. For centuries, it was grown in kitchen gardens. The flowers used to be preserved and candied. The flowers are bright blue and star shaped. The plant has white prickly hairs and grows about one and a half feet tall.

- **HOW TO HARNESS BORAGE'S MAGICAL PROPERTIES:** If you drink a cup of tea made from a handful of dried Borage leaves boiled in a pint of water for about five minutes and then sweetened with honey, you will rapidly develop or enhance your psychic abilities.

  Fresh Borage flowers placed on the table before you read Tarot cards will improve the accuracy of the reading. If you place the flowers on your altar, it will deepen your connection with your spirit.

  For protection, sprinkle a scant handful of the dried herb around the outside of your home.

  If you're feeling nervous before an important meeting, carry the dried herb on your person to bring you added courage and insights.

- **MEDICINAL USES:** The candied flowers can be used to give a person renewed strength after a long illness. Leaves boiled in distilled water and then cooled are useful as an eyewash to soothe inflammation and soreness. Green leaves boiled in mead or honeyed water and then used as a gargle are excellent at relieving inflammation and ulcers in the mouth or throat.

Yerba Mate

Ilex paraguariensis

Shows you the true meaning of friendship

- **YERBA MATE WILL:** Attract friendship and love, Keep your mate faithful, Deepen your capacity to care for others

- **THE PLANT:** Yerba Mate is a species of Holly that is indigenous to South America. It was introduced to the world by the Guarani Indians. It is an evergreen shrub that grows up to forty feet tall. The flowers are small with four petals and yield bright red berries. More than just an herb used for tea, it has become a cultural phenomenon in South America.

- **HOW TO HARNESS YERBA MATE'S MAGICAL PROPERTIES:** To attract a life partner, wear Yerba Mate around your neck. This plant is about friendship, support, and loyalty, so don't use it if you are just looking for a fling.

  If you drink Yerba Mate tea from the same cup with someone, you will be friends for life. If you drink it on a regular basis, it will expand your capacity to be compassionate and care for others. To make the tea, add two tablespoons of dried Yerba Mate to two cups of boiling water. Allow the mixture to steep for about ten minutes before straining it.

  If you want to end a relationship, brew a cup of tea with the person in mind and then spill the drink on the ground.

- **MEDICINAL USES:** Yerba Mate is used to boost the immune system, cleanse and detoxify the blood, tone and soothe the nervous system, clear the mind, combat fatigue, control the appetite, reduce stress, and eliminate insomnia. In Brazil, people carry Yerba Mate with them.

Garlic

Allium sativum

Reminds you of your roots

- **GARLIC WILL:** Bring good luck, Guard against jealousy, Repel vampires, Protect sleeping children

- **THE PLANT:** Garlic's origins are hard to trace because it goes so far back into antiquity. It's a member of the Lily family and a cousin to Onions. Its leaves are long, narrow, and flat. The part that's usually eaten is actually the bulb, which has many divisions, or little bulblets, known as cloves. Garlic is harvested after the leaves have withered and turned brown. It is best stored in a cool, dry place and can last for several months. It also dries very well and retains its flavor.

- **HOW TO HARNESS GARLIC'S MAGICAL PROPERTIES:** If you've ever watched a vampire movie, you've undoubtedly seen Garlic used as protection against the evil creatures. If your concern is more with repelling negative energy in general, hang Garlic over your front door. In addition to keeping you safe from negative energy, it will stop people from feeling jealous of you and bring you good luck. You can also hang it over your children's beds to keep them safe and ensure pleasant dreams. And if you do want to keep vampires away from your home, the Garlic must be harvested in May.

  If you are about to face a difficult situation, eat some Garlic to give you the necessary strength. Garlic can be carried as an amulet to ensure that your magical spells will be effective.

- **MEDICINAL USES:** When rubbed into a wound, Garlic is an excellent treatment to avoid infection. It can be applied externally to reduce swelling. When pounded and applied as a poultice, it can heal even the most stubborn wounds.

Angelica *Angelica archangelica*

Surrounds you with a sense of peace, love, and protection

- **ANGELICA WILL:** Surround you with protection, Release negative thinking, Attract abundance, Help with divination

- **THE PLANT:** Angelica is thought to be native to Syria. It has spread to the cooler parts of Europe, where it has become naturalized. It's highly prized for both its healing properties and its magical abilities. Angelica has a large root and stems that are hollow. It grows as tall as six feet. It has a profusion of small flowers in July that produce an oblong pale, yellow fruit. The odor and taste of the fruits are pleasantly aromatic.

- **HOW TO HARNESS ANGELICA'S MAGICAL PROPERTIES:** Because Angelica is the master herb of protection, it was once called the root of the Holy Ghost. It is effective against negative thoughts, misfortune, and even lustful peeping Toms! Wear a pinch of dried Angelica in an amulet or grow it around your property to repel negativity and invite angels and fairies into your life.

To attract good fortune, sprinkle a few pinches of dried Angelica around the outside of your home or scatter it in the corners of your rooms. You can also bless your home by burning the dried Angelica plant as incense; the incense will also aid in your own divination and purification.

To soothe grief, pour Angelica tea into your bathwater. Make the tea by adding one-quarter cup of dried herb to a pint of boiling water and steeping it for a few minutes before adding it to the bath. Meditating in the bath will deepen your connection to your spirit.

- **MEDICINAL USES:** A tea made from Angelica is a wonderful remedy for colds, coughs, pleurisy, colic, rheumatism, and diseases of the urinary tract. Note: Angelica shouldn't be used by people who have diabetes.

Sandalwood

Santalum album

Makes your entire life a sacred act

◼ **SANDALWOOD WILL:** Help you focus your attention, Attract love, Increase clairvoyance, Call spirit helpers

◼ **THE PLANT:** Sandalwood is a semiparasitic evergreen tree native to India, Malaysia, and parts of Australia. It grows twenty to thirty feet high by burying its roots in other trees. The leaves are lance shaped, and the slender branches droop. The bark is smooth and grayish brown. It has numerous small flowers that are pale yellow to purple. They produce spherical pea-size fruit. The wood has a strong aroma and is used for carving and to make boxes.

◼ **HOW TO HARNESS SANDALWOOD'S MAGICAL PROPERTIES:** To make your deepest hopes, dreams, and desires come true, burn Sandalwood as incense once a day while clearly visualizing your desired outcomes.

Place Sandalwood on your altar to open a doorway for spiritual helpers to come to your aid. Hold it to your forehead to enhance your clairvoyant abilities.

◼ **MEDICINAL USES:** Sandalwood is used to treat chronic bronchitis. It will also help relieve the symptoms of gonorrhea and chronic cystitis. It eases joint pain and, when combined with Epsom salts, makes a healing bath that will cleanse the body of toxins.

Cumin *Cuminum cyminum*

Expands your awareness of love

- **CUMIN WILL:** Prevent theft and protect your home, Invite peace of mind, Encourage loyalty

- **THE PLANT:** Cumin grows to about one to two feet tall and is harvested by hand. It is a member of the Parsley family and native to Iran, India, Syria, Pakistan, and Turkey. Cumin tends to droop under its own weight. The leaves are bluish green and the flowers range from white to pink. The flowers bloom in June and July. The plants have a wonderful aroma when brushed against.

- **HOW TO HARNESS CUMIN'S MAGICAL PROPERTIES:** In the past, Cumin was baked into bread in Germany and Italy to prevent mischievous spirits from stealing the loaves. Today, sprinkling a bit of powdered Cumin on an object will prevent it from being stolen.

  When worn at your wedding, Cumin will ensure a long and loving relationship. It will also ensure that the wedding proceeds smoothly.

When the powder is placed under the marriage bed, Cumin will prevent the partners from being unfaithful.

Scatter a handful or two of Cumin and sea salt around the outside of your home to banish fear and negativity. Worn in an amulet, Cumin will encourage peace of mind as well as help you attract love.

Feeling nervous about your future? To ensure abundance and success, burn dried Cumin leaves as incense.

- **MEDICINAL USES:** Cumin is used to stimulate the appetite and relieve gas. A tea made from the seeds will help with nausea due to morning sickness. It is also good for colic. A poultice of crushed seeds will help reduce swelling.

Sweetgrass *Hierochloe odorata*

Reminds you of the importance of spirit

- **SWEETGRASS WILL:** Attract spirit helpers, Cleanse and purify a space, Lift your spirits

- **THE PLANT:** Sweetgrass is a grass common to the plains of the United States. It has short leaves and stems that shoot up four to twelve inches tall.

  The stems are hollow and erect. It has rhizomes that are slender and creeping, forming a dense mat just beneath the surface of the soil. Its Latin name, Hierochloe, literally means sacred grass. It has a very sweet odor and is used ceremonially by many Native American tribes.

- **HOW TO HARNESS SWEETGRASS'S MAGICAL PROPERTIES:** To protect your home and its occupants, braid some Sweetgrass and hang it near the entrance to your house.

  You can purify your home by burning Sweetgrass as incense; it will also call your spirit guides and helpers.

  Crushing the fresh leaves and inhaling the smell is a wonderful way to enhance your divination and to connect with the ancestors. The smell of the grass is emotionally uplifting.

- **MEDICINAL USES:** A tea can be made from Sweetgrass to thin the blood. An herbalist might use the smoke to treat colds. It is a traditional herb used by Native American tribes and was considered an all-around panacea.

Caraway Seed

Carum carvi

Makes sure no one breaks your heart

- **CARAWAY SEED WILL:** Protect your child from getting sick, Ensure fidelity, Repel negativity

- **THE PLANT:** The Caraway plant is a biennial that grows one and a half feet tall. It has large umbrella-like white flowers that bloom profusely in June. The fruits are incorrectly called seeds. They have a pleasant, aromatic odor when crushed and are rather tasty. The leaves have a similar taste and smell. The Caraway plant grows throughout central Europe and Asia.

- **HOW TO HARNESS CARAWAY SEED'S MAGICAL PROPERTIES:** To keep away sickness and disease, place a small, tightly sealed bag of Caraway seeds under your child's crib.

  Wearing an amulet of the seeds will improve your memory, protect you from evil spirits, encourage fidelity, and attract love. Chewing Caraway seeds before an important date will help assure you of creating a loving relationship.

  To protect against unwanted visitors, sprinkle the seeds around the outside of your home. As an added bonus, they will also repel bugs.

- **MEDICINAL USES:** Caraway seeds improve digestion and help relieve gas. A tea made from the seeds helps relieve colic in babies and is well tolerated. Ground seeds made into a poultice will help fade bruises and is an old-fashioned cure for earaches.

Kava Kava

Piper methysticum

Helps you relax and deepen your connection to your spirit

- **KAVA KAVA WILL:** Protect you and your home, Invite good luck, Deepen your spiritual connection

- **THE PLANT:** Kava Kava is indigenous to much of Polynesia, including Hawai'i. It is a shrub that grows several feet high. It has spikes of flowers and a fibrous rhizome. A fermented liquor is prepared from the upper portion of the rhizome and the base of the stems. It is mildly narcotic and is a stimulant. The liquor was often consumed before important religious rites in the Polynesian culture.

  When chewed and mixed with saliva in the mouth, the root of the plant creates a spicy and intoxicating juice. Kava Kava rhizomes are whitish or grayish brown.

- **HOW TO HARNESS KAVA KAVA'S MAGICAL PROPERTIES:** Sprinkle a small handful of the chopped root around the outside of your home to protect it and keep unwelcome visitors from entering.

  To invite good luck, hang a small piece of the root over your front door or put a small piece in an amulet worn around your neck.

  To induce visions, soak a quarter of a cup of leaves and roots in half a gallon of water in the refrigerator overnight. Strain out the Kava Kava and drink a cup before you meditate.

- **MEDICINAL USES:** Kava Kava acts as a stimulant but then depresses the nervous system and slows the respiratory center. It is a useful treatment for the symptoms of gonorrhea and nighttime incontinence. A tea made from the leaves and the roots will calm the nerves.

Sesame

Sesamum indicum

Opens your mind and your heart

- **SESAME WILL:** Attract money, Help you find hidden treasure, Increase sexual desire

- **THE PLANT:** The Sesame plant is an annual plant that grows from two to four feet tall. Its origin is unknown, but it grows in Africa and Asia. It has deeply veined oval leaves. The flowers are white or pink and mature into a pod containing the Sesame seeds. The pods burst open and pop when the seeds are ripe. If you walk through a field of them late in the summer when the seeds are ripe, you will cause massive explosions. Sesame seeds are usually harvested before they ripen to avoid the losses due to the explosions.

   Its origin is in dispute, but usage of the seeds goes back to at least 3000 b.c. Five thousand years ago the Chinese burned oil made from the seeds for a light source and used the soot for ink. Sesame seeds have a nutty, sweet flavor and aroma.

- **HARNESS SESAME'S MAGICAL PROPERTIES:** Eating Sesame seeds will increase your sexual desire.

   Place some seeds on your altar to help you find the hidden aspects of yourself and attract abundance.

   Carrying Sesame seeds in a purple velvet bag while you are hunting for treasure will ensure you of success.

- **MEDICINAL USES:** Sesame seeds will detoxify the kidneys and liver and relax the bowel. They will relieve constipation and are also useful in the treatment of tinnitus, anemia, dizziness, and poor vision. The seeds and fresh leaves may be used as a poultice for bruises and sore muscles.

Acacia

Acacia Nilotica

Brings peace and harmony, thus assuring you of a wonderful future

- **ACACIA WILL:** Enhance psychic abilities, Protect you and your property, Attract abundance, Deepen your friendships

- **THE PLANT:** Acacia is a small, spiny bush or small tree. It likes dry, warm climates and lives in the Holy Land, northern Africa, throughout Asia, and in parts of Australia. It is considered a sacred tree by Jews, Christians, and Muslims. It is said Moses was instructed to build the Ark of the Covenant from it, and Muslims hung their weapons and garments on it as they went to Mecca. It was used to make Christ's crown of thorns.

   The resin from the Acacia tree is collected after the rainy season and can be harvested anytime by stripping off pieces of the bark. The gum hardens into tear-shaped drops when it touches the air.

- **HARNESS ACACIA'S MAGICAL PROPERTIES:** Acacia is generally bought as a resin, although you can also buy it in powdered form as Gum Arabic. If you can find a box made of its wood, write all of your hopes, dreams, and prayers on small slips of paper and then place them inside. Take a moment to give thanks for the magic that is about to occur and know your request will be granted. To ensure financial abundance, sprinkle the powder on your money.

   If you combine Acacia resin with equal parts of Sandalwood, you can wear them in an amulet or burn them as incense to facilitate your psychic abilities and deepen your meditations. The scent will also bring harmony to your home, clear your mind, and stimulate your mental process.

- **MEDICINAL USES:** Drinking a tea made from Acacia leaves will prevent premature ejaculation.

Gorse

Ulex europaeus

Shows you what actions to take

- **GORSE WILL:** Protect your home, Bring hope, Increase your personal power, Purify your mind, heart, and spirit

- **THE PLANT:** Gorse is a perennial, evergreen shrub that grows from three feet to more than ten feet tall. Gorse is native to western and central Europe but can be found all over the world. In many places it has become an invasive species. It can take nitrogen from the atmosphere and fix it in the soil. Fire plays a role in its ecology. The seeds open after a fire and easily sprout when the rains come.

HARNESS GORSE'S MAGICAL PROPERTIES: The flowers are a powerful love amulet, and when given to someone, they bring that person good luck, abundance, and love. Scatter the flowers in your bathwater to increase your personal power and purify your mind, body, and spirit.

If you're feeling "stuck" or overwhelmed, burn some dried Gorse leaves as incense. It will infuse you with hope and encourage you to take actions to create whatever you want.

Drinking it as tea on a regular basis will help you connect with your soul. To make the tea, add two tablespoons of dried Gorse to two cups of boiling water. Allow the mixture to steep for approximately ten minutes before straining it.

- **MEDICINAL USES:** The flowers of the plant help purify the liver and relieve jaundice. Gargling with tea made from the flowers will sweeten the breath and heal any sores in your mouth. The powdered herb can be used to repel mosquitoes and fleas. A poultice made from its root can be used to treat snake bites.

▶ Top: Sesame, Middle: Acacia, Bottom: Gorse

Bladderwrack

Focus visiculos

Brings you luck and keeps you safe

- **BLADDERWRACK WILL:** Ensure safety at sea, Boost your magical spells, Help you control the wind, Attract abundance

- **THE PLANT:** Bladderwrack is a seaweed commonly found on the sheltered shores of the North Sea, Baltic Sea, and Atlantic and Pacific oceans. It is a brown algae that has numerous air sacks scattered along its many branches.

- **HOW TO HARNESS BLADDERWRACK'S MAGICAL PROPERTIES:** To ensure your safety when you travel, carry a small sprig of the plant with you, especially when you are traveling over the water.

  Stand at the edge of the sea while holding Bladderwrack in your hand and call upon the sea spirits to aid you on your journey of life. Ask for their help, state your concerns, and then throw the seaweed into the ocean. To call up the wind, hold Bladderwrack over your head and twirl it until you feel the winds begin to stir.

  If you've been having financial problems, put dried, ground Bladderwrack in your cleaning water and wash your floors and all the doorknobs in your home to attract abundance and bring in supportive energy.

  Finally, Bladderwrack is a great herb to add to the soil in your garden as an amendment for protection and fertility.

- **MEDICINAL USES:** Bladderwrack has been used for centuries to augment low thyroid hormone. It has also been used to treat arteriosclerosis, menstrual problems, and heart disease. It relieves constipation, settles upset stomachs, and helps lower high cholesterol.

Rue *Ruta graveolens*

Reminds you of your magical nature

- **RUE WILL:** Invoke divine grace, Repel negativity and demons, Remove envy, Dispel worry

- **THE PLANT:** Rue is a hardy evergreen shrubby plant that is native to southern Europe. The stem is woody and erect. It grows up to six feet tall. The greenish yellow flowers first appear in June, but the plant continues to bloom throughout the summer. Its Latin name means strong smelling. It is an old garden plant cultivated for its medical purposes. The first flower that opens has ten stamens while the rest of the flowers have only eight.

- **HOW TO HARNESS RUE'S MAGICAL PROPERTIES:** In the Middle Ages, anyone found with Rue was considered a witch.

  Bringing Rue into a building will immediately invite divine grace and create a sacred space. You can also burn dried Rue as incense; it is excellent for purification, protection, and consecration, and to restore rational, levelheaded thinking.

If you're feeling anxious about a problem, hang a bunch of Rue tied with a red ribbon by your front door. It will help you see solutions for your concerns rather than worrying about them. You can also do this to prevent envy.

- **MEDICINAL USES:** Rue is used to treat coughs, colic, excessive gas, and upset stomachs. When the leaves are applied to a bruise, the pain is immediately relieved and the bruise will fade very rapidly. Juice made from the leaves will stop nightmares. When the juice is applied to the chest, it is beneficial for treating chronic bronchitis and asthma. Tea made from Rue will alleviate a nervous headache.

Chickweed

Stellaria media

Purifies your life

- **CHICKWEED WILL:** Attract love, Increase fertility, Enhance the effect of magic

- **THE PLANT:** Chickweed is a hardy annual plant with small starlike white flowers. Folklore says that if the flowers are fully open, the sun will shine the rest of the day, but if the flowers close up, expect rain within a few hours.

    It is said that there is no part of the world where Chickweed is not found. It has naturalized itself wherever white people have settled, thus becoming one of the most common weeds.

- **HARNESS CHICKWEED'S MAGICAL PROPERTIES:** You can increase the effect of any magic performed in your house by planting Chickweed on the south side of your home.

    Adding some Chickweed tea, a quarter of a cup of vinegar, and a tablespoon of salt to your bathwater will help you release any negative energy, attract love, and deepen your connection with your spirit. To make the tea, add two tablespoons of dried Chickweed to two cups of boiling water and allow the mixture to steep for about ten minutes before straining it.

    Drinking Chickweed tea on a daily basis will help you conceive a child. (Note: Chickweed tea is not recommended for use once you become pregnant.)

- **MEDICINAL USES:** A poultice made from Chickweed and enclosed in muslin is a wonderful remedy for external abscesses. Or Chickweed can be soaked in water and the water can be used to bathe the affected area. A tea made with the fresh plant is good for constipation, while tea made from the dried herb will help treat coughs, sore throats, and hoarseness.

Masterwort

Imperatorial ostruthium

Gives you the courage to stand up for what matters to you

- **MASTERWORT WILL:** Infuse you with courage, Strengthen your willpower, Protect you, your family, and your home

- **THE PLANT:** It is rare to find Masterwort in the wild anymore. It was native to central Europe but is now widely cultivated. Occasionally it escapes from the garden, and it grows well in most meadows in the cooler sections of the world. It is a perennial with stout stems growing two to three feet tall. The leaves are a very dark green and the flowers are large white corollas.

- **HARNESS MASTERWORT'S MAGICAL PROPERTIES:** If you wear a small piece of the plant about your body, you will have the strength to finish any project. If you want to be rid of an unwanted habit, carry a piece of the plant with you. It will enhance your willpower.

    To protect yourself, your family, and your home, simply grow Masterwort in your yard or garden. Having it around will also calm your emotions and help you remain balanced.

    Place a bit of Masterwort on your altar to ensure success.

- **MEDICINAL USES:** The root is the strongest part of the plant and is very useful for relieving diseases of the stomach. It is a wonderful stimulant and is often used to treat menstrual complaints.

Licorice Root

Glycyrrhiza glabra

Helps you connect with your magical essence

- **LICORICE ROOT WILL:** Attract love, Bring you good luck, Help you stop smoking

- **THE PLANT:** Licorice plants are shrubs that are natives of southeastern Europe and southwestern Asia. The leaves hang down at night and perk up again after daybreak. Licorice has small pale blue, violet, yellow, or purple flowers. The fruit looks like small pods that resemble peas.

- **HARNESS LICORICE ROOT'S MAGICAL PROPERTIES:** Energetically, Licorice plants make wonderful wands.

    If you're trying to stop smoking, chew on the fresh or dried root. As an added bonus, doing so will also bring you good luck.

    Drinking Licorice root tea will increase your libido and enhance your sexual pleasure. To make the tea, add two tablespoons of the dried root to two cups of boiling water, allow the mixture to steep for about ten minutes, and then strain it.

    To attract love, add Licorice root to an amulet.

    Putting Licorice root in a sachet and hanging it in your closet will banish negative energy and make you feel more attractive.

- **MEDICINAL USES:** Licorice root is a popular treatment for coughs, congestion, bronchitis, and other chest complaints. It is an ingredient in almost all popular cough medicines because of its soothing properties.

▶ Top: Chickweed, Middle: Masterwort, Bottom: Licorice Root

Valerian Root *Glycyrrhiza glabra*

Helps you connect with your magical essence

- **VALERIAN ROOT WILL:** Attract love, Ensure a good night's sleep, Create a protective shield, Purify your home

- **THE PLANT:** Valerian is a perennial plant native to Europe and northern Asia. It grows in marshy thickets and on the borders of ditches and rivers. It prefers cool roots and warm leaves. It grows two to five feet tall. Valerian has a short, fibrous root, which produces offshoots after the second year. The stem is grooved and hollow. Numerous clusters of pale pink flowers appear between June and August. The rich dark green leaves and towering flowers make the plant quite noticeable. When bruised, the roots have a somewhat unpleasant smell.

- **HOW TO HARNESS VALERIAN ROOT'S MAGICAL PROPERTIES:** To surround your home in a protective bubble, hang the root over your door.

  To attract love, place a small piece of the root in an amulet and wear it around your neck.

  When two people are fighting, place some of the root near them, and the fighting will stop immediately.

- **MEDICINAL USES:** Valerian roots are powerful painkillers and induce sleep. During World War II the English used the roots to help people overcome the stress of the constant bombings. It is an effective treatment for many nervous ailments because it doesn't have the aftereffects of narcotics.

Lobelia *Lobelia inflata*

Helps you live in the present moment

■ **LOBELIA WILL:** Increase spiritual awareness, Purify your thoughts, Transform your life, Provide protection

THE PLANT: Lobelia is native to North America and is commonly called Indian Tobacco. It grows one to two feet tall and has violet flowers that are yellow in the center. It starts blooming in midsummer and continues into early fall. The seeds are the most potent part of the plant. It is an annual and self-seeding.

■ **HOW TO HARNESS LOBELIA'S MAGICAL PROPERTIES:** Grinding up the leaves and throwing them into the wind will quiet approaching storms.

Use a tea made from Lobelia to cleanse your altar. Drinking it prior to meditating will help deepen your connection to your inner wisdom. To make the tea, add two tablespoons of dried Lobelia leaves to two cups of boiling water. Allow the mixture to steep for at least ten minutes before straining it.

Placing the dried flowers in an amulet will remind you to stay present in the moment.

■ **MEDICINAL USES:** Lobelia helps relieve the congestion from bronchitis and asthma. As a poultice, it eases the pain and swelling from sprains and bruises. An herbalist might prescribe a tea made from the dried leaves for relaxation or, when taken regularly, to prevent anemia.

Centaury *Erythraea Centaurium*

Chases away the blues

- **CENTAURY WILL:** Open your connection to the plant kingdom, Enhance beauty, Repel snakes

- **THE PLANT:** Centaury is an annual plant that is native to most of Europe, Asia, and northern Africa. It grows up to two feet tall and is commonly found in dry pastures, stable sand dunes, and at the edge of forests. It is not easily grown in the garden, so it is often collected in the wild. The flowers are rose colored and open up during the day during clear weather and close up early in the afternoon or if the sun stops shining.

- **HOW TO HARNESS CENTAURY'S MAGICAL PROPERTIES:** Drinking a cup of tea made from a teaspoon of dried Centaury brewed in a cup of boiling water for about ten minutes and then strained will help you communicate with the plant kingdom. Before you work with any other herbs, drink a cup of the tea as an opening or dedication of your desire to work with the spiritual energy embodied in the herbs.

You can burn the dried plant as incense to bless your home and chase away any snakes.

Adding some tea to your bathwater will enhance your looks and make you glow.

- **MEDICINAL USES:** Centaury acts on the liver and kidneys. It purifies the blood and is an excellent overall tonic. A tea made out of two tablespoons of dried leaves simmered for ten minutes in a pint of boiling water and then strained is great for indigestion or when you are feeling rundown. Drinking the tea three times a day helps relieve the pain of arthritis.

Peppermint *Mentha piperita*

Refreshes your hopes, dreams, and desires

■ **PEPPERMINT WILL:** Purify your thoughts, Cure insomnia, Enhance your psychic abilities, Attract love

■ **THE PLANT:** Peppermint plants tend to be short and huddle close to the ground. Occasionally, the stems will stand erect, growing two to four feet high. The plants will easily spread and overtake any area of ground available to them. The leaves are short and slightly hairy underneath, and their edges are finely toothed. When tasted, they are very hot at first and then produce a cool sensation because of the menthol. Peppermint produces small reddish violet flowers.

■ **HOW TO HARNESS PEPPERMINT'S MAGICAL PROPERTIES:** To cleanse your house of any negative energies and raise the spiritual vibration, add a small handful of fresh Peppermint leaves to your cleaning solutions.

If you've been tossing and turning at night, place some dried Peppermint leaves under your pillow; they will ensure you of a quiet night's rest.

Rubbing the dried leaves on your money and putting a few in your purse will ensure you of always having more than enough money.

When you have to make a decision, ponder it while holding a bunch of leaves against your forehead. The leaves will help you make the right choice. You can use the leaves in the same way to get rid of a headache.

■ **MEDICINAL USES:** Peppermint is used to disguise the flavor of other medicines. Peppermint tea will settle the stomach and relieve nausea. It will settle the nerves, stop stomach cramps, and relieve the discomfort of menstrual cramps. A weak tea can be given to children suffering from colic and is very good at dissipating gas.

Tansy

Tanacetum vulgare

Teaches you to enjoy every moment of your life

- **TANSY WILL:** Improve health, Help you live longer

- **THE PLANT:** Tansy is a hardy perennial with an erect, almost hairless stem. It grows two to three feet tall and has bright yellow flowers and dark green leaves. It blooms from July through September. Tansy is native to Asia and Europe and has been naturalized in the United States. It can be invasive, so it is best to plant it in a contained area. In ancient times, Tansy was used to preserve bodies, so the herb became associated with immortality and long life.

- **HARNESS TANSY'S MAGICAL PROPERTIES:** Tansy will protect all gentle spirits. If you've been suffering from a bout of ill health, hang some in your home; it will improve your health.

  You can also use the plant in healing rituals. During the ritual, cleanse the ill person's aura by fanning him or her with the plant. After the healing session is complete, burn it or bury it in a sacred location.

  If you're about to set off on a trip, place some dried Tansy in your shoes to ensure safe travel.

- **MEDICINAL USES:** In the past, Tansy was used to treat kidney and urinary problems. It helps relieve fevers and calms the nerves. It also helps the digestive system work more effectively and relieves gas. It will stop stomach cramping, and some women find it effective in stopping the pain of menstrual cramps. It is best not used internally.

  Tansy discourages ants and will stop flies from coming in if hung on the screen door.

Aztec Sweet Herb

Lippia dulcis

Lightens your mood and clears your mind

- **AZTEC SWEET HERB WILL:** Bring joy into your life, Purify your thoughts and bless your life, Quiet your mind, Fill your heart with gratitude

- **THE PLANT:** Aztec Sweet Herb is a vine that does well in hanging baskets and as a ground cover. Its leaves are very sweet and can be added to salads or eaten like candy. In large quantities the leaves can be toxic.

- **HARNESS AZTEC SWEET HERB'S MAGICAL PROPERTIES:** If you're feeling gloomy or depressed, sprinkle the dried leaves around the inside of your home to lighten your mood and enhance the quality of your life.

  To clear your mind, add a tea made from Aztec Sweet Herb to your bathwater. You can make the tea by placing two tablespoons of dried leaves in a cup of boiling water. Allow the mixture to steep for about ten minutes before straining it and adding it to your bathwater.

  Make an infusion by packing a jar with the dried leaves and then filling it with cold-pressed sunflower oil. Set it outside during the full moon and leave it there for a month. Strain the oil and store it in a cool place. Rubbing the oil on your temples when you are feeling worried or stressed will fill you with a sense of peace and ease. You can also rub a few drops of it on your heart each night to remind yourself to feel grateful.

- **MEDICINAL USES:** Tea made from the leaves can be used as a mouthwash to fight tooth decay and gum disease. Also, use the tea to wash wounds, prevent infection, and treat coughs, colds, asthma, and colic.

Meadowsweet

Spiraea ulmaris

Empowers you to express your gentle, loving nature

- **MEADOWSWEET WILL:** Attract love, Ensure the success of a marriage, Imbue an aura of peace and happiness

- **THE PLANT:** Meadowsweet is a wonderfully fragrant wildflower that is native to Europe, parts of Asia, and North America. It is a hardy perennial with fernlike foliage and tufts of delicate, graceful, creamy white flowers, which have a very sweet, strong aroma. It blossoms from June until early September. The leaves are dark green on the top and downy white underneath. Meadowsweet grows two to four feet high and sometimes the entire plant looks purple. The whole plant tastes sweet and smells something like an almond. Traditionally, it was used in bed chambers to make them smell good.

  Meadowsweet leaves should be gathered before the plant blossoms, and the flowers should be picked right after they open.

- **HARNESS MEADOWSWEET'S MAGICAL PROPERTIES:** Meadowsweet was one of the most sacred herbs to Druids. To ensure a happy marriage, include some in the bridal bouquet and strew the flowers in front of the couple after the ceremony.

  To create a sense of peace, joy, and sacredness in your home, place the fresh flowers on your altar.

  Hang some of the leaves over your front door to discourage thieves and protect your home.

- **MEDICINAL USES:** Meadowsweet is used to treat diarrhea and settle the stomach. When sweetened with honey, it has a very pleasant taste and can be used as a tonic by people who are feeling weak.

▶ Top: Tansy, Middle: Aztec Sweet Herb, Bottom: Meadowsweet

Henbane

Hyosycamus niger

Helps you release all judgment so you can fully love

- **HENBANE WILL:** Attract love, Increase psychic awareness, Dispel negativity

- **THE PLANT:** Henbane is a hairy, slightly sticky annual or biennial plant. It is found throughout central and southern Europe. It also grows in western Asia, India, and Siberia. It grows one to two feet tall. The annual flowers in July and August while the biennial blooms in May and June. Henbane's flowers are bell shaped and are dirty yellow with numerous violet-colored veins. The fruit have up to five hundred grayish brown seeds.

- **HOW TO HARNESS HENBANE'S MAGICAL PROPERTIES:** Hang the root over an infant's crib to relieve the pain of teething.

  To attract new love, place some of the root in an amulet. Burning it as incense will dispel negative energy and increase psychic insights. If burned on Samhain (Halloween), it will call up the spirits of the dead. Make sure you are clear about your intent for doing this. You can ask for guidance and also help spirits cross over into the light.

- **MEDICINAL USES:** Henbane can be poisonous, so it is primarily used externally. An oil made from pressing the leaves is effective in treating earaches, neuralgia, sciatica, and rheumatism.

Birch

Betula alba

Refreshes your life and fills it with excitement

- **BIRCH WILL:** Protect your home, Invite abundance, Secure love

- **THE PLANT:** The bark on Birch trees is generally white and the leaves flutter most gracefully in the wind, making gentle noises that are very soothing. Birch trees grow throughout northern Europe and North America.

- **HOW TO HARNESS BIRCH'S MAGICAL PROPERTIES:** Birch leaves are a sign of spring and vibrate with the energy of new beginnings. You can use a broom made of Birch to sweep your life free from all limitations. To make a broom, gather a handful of Birch branches and tie them together with a piece of your favorite-colored ribbon. Slowly walk through each room of your house, mentally sweeping it clean. As you do, also sweep out any negativity residing with the people, places, and things in your life. Doing this will not only clear out negativity but will also invite abundance and fill your life with newness, purity, and limitless possibilities.

  You can also use Birch sticks to create a circle of protection by putting a circle of them on the ground around anything you'd like to protect.

  Burning the dried leaves as incense will release trapped spirits and help you attract love. Traditionally, a couple was considered married if they jumped over a broom made from Birch.

- **MEDICINAL USES:** Birch tea made out of two tablespoons of dried leaves simmered in a pint of boiling water and steeped for five minutes can be used to treat gout and rheumatism and to dissolve kidney stones. An oil made from the bark of the Birch tree is used to treat skin problems, including eczema and acne.

Echinacea *Echinacea angustifolia*

Gives you inner strength

- **ECHINACEA WILL:** Keep love fresh and passionate, Increase fertility, Preserve youth, Attract abundance

- **THE PLANT:** Echinacea is commonly called Purple Coneflower and is indigenous to the eastern and central part of North America. An easily grown perennial, Echinacea has showy purple flowers that blossom from early summer until the first frost. It has a conical taproot that has a thin bark and is fibrous. The root has a faintly aromatic smell and is sweet tasting. When chewed, it leaves a tingling sensation in the mouth.

- **HOW TO HARNESS ECHINACEA'S MAGICAL PROPERTIES:** Just as Echinacea strengthens the immune system, it will increase the power of other herbs, prayers, potions, and spells. Place a bouquet of the dried flowers on your altar to ensure the success of all your magical requests.

To attract abundance, sprinkle some dried flowers into your wallet. Add some to an amulet to enhance the strength of any other herb. Plant it in your yard to protect your home and bring magic and miracles into your life.

- **MEDICINAL USES:** Echinacea increases the body's resistance to infection and strengthens the immune system. It is a wonderful antiseptic and cleanses the blood from impurities. It has been used to treat cancer and syphilis. It is also believed to be an aphrodisiac. A tea made from the fresh root has been useful in the treatment of diphtheria and fevers.

Sumac Berries

Rhus glabra

Spreads peace of mind and harmony

- **SUMAC BERRIES WILL:** Bring harmony, Resolve conflicts

- **THE PLANT:** Native to North America, Sumac grows up to fifteen feet tall. It often grows in clumps and is frequently found on abandoned land. It has straggling branches with pale gray bark. The flowers are reddish green.

  There are several varieties of Sumac, so make sure you pick the nonpoisonous variety! The fruit of the nonlethal variety is covered with crimson hairs, while the poisonous variety has smooth fruit. Be sure to gather the fruit before rain washes off the downy covering or the berries become very bitter.

- **HOW TO HARNESS SUMAC BERRIES MAGICAL PROPERTIES:** Sumac berries are known to bring peace and harmony. Scatter a few of them around your home to avoid conflicts and arguments.

  To avoid legal problems and make sure only people of goodwill enter your home, place a small pile of the berries at the four corners of your property. If you have already lost a legal case, or been found guilty, carry nine berries in your left pocket when you go back to court so you receive a lighter sentence or smaller fine.

- **MEDICINAL USES:** The bark makes a wonderful tonic and has been used to treat sexually transmitted diseases such as gonorrhea and syphilis. When combined with slippery elm, it makes an effective mouthwash, and when used as a gargle, it will soothe a sore throat. You can also use the mixture to wash wounds and treat lesions and skin infections.

Dulse *Palmaria palmate*

Teaches you about tenacity

- **DULSE WILL:** Encourage harmony, Increase sexual pleasure, Protect your home

- **THE PLANT:** Dulse is a red seaweed that grows attached to rocks in the cooler waters of the North Atlantic and North Pacific oceans and the cold waters of the North Sea. It grows in the intertidal region, the area between high and low tides. Dulse that grows in areas shaded by cliffs so that it receives very little sun is said to be more flavorful and potent.

  Between June and September, it is hand picked during low tide and spread out in what are called drying fields. It is then shaken to remove the shells and debris before it's rolled into large bales and shipped to market. Dulse grows rapidly, so it's usually picked every two weeks during the season. It has a variety of uses, including as a brown dye for cloth.

- **HOW TO HARNESS DULSE'S MAGICAL PROPERTIES:** Before an evening with your beloved, add a sprinkle of dried Dulse to the beverage of your choice to enhance your sexual pleasure and increase your desire.

  Sprinkle a pinch of the dried seaweed around the rooms of your home to encourage a sense of harmony, peace, and love. To protect your house, hang some over your front door.

- **MEDICINAL USES:** Dulse makes an excellent cold compress to dress wounds and reduce the swelling of sprains. When eaten after a fast of several days, it will expel intestinal worms, and when eaten on a regular basis, it will treat constipation and cure various stomach discomforts. Raw Dulse can be chewed while working to stop hunger. The high mineral content is also useful in balancing levels of hormones, particularly the thyroid hormones.

Willow *Salix alba*

Helps you release sadness and grief

■ **WILLOW WILL:** Attract love, Help you find the perfect mate, Protect your home, Heal your mind and body

■ **THE PLANT:** Willow is a large tree that can live for more than 120 years and grows upwards of 75 feet tall. It has rough gray bark and its limbs are very flexible. Its flowers and leaves appear at the same time in April and May. The bark is very easily separated throughout the summer. The tree has long been associated with magic. Wands and staffs are often made from its wood. It is a water-loving plant and will often be found along lakes and streams.

■ **HOW TO HARNESS WILLOW'S MAGICAL PROPERTIES:** Collect nine willow branches and braid them together while they are fresh. Symbolically sweep the area with the branches to clear spirits from your home. You can also do this whenever you are performing a healing ritual.

You can form the braid into a circle and place it on your altar. Write your dreams and desires on a piece of paper and place them in the center of the circle until they manifest. Alternately, try writing your desires on a piece of Willow bark and place the bark on your altar.

To attract the perfect mate, sleep with a Willow branch under your bed.

■ **MEDICINAL USES:** Willow bark is useful for relieving pain. A tea made from the bark will lower fevers, ease sore throats, and stop headaches. It is also useful as a treatment for rheumatism. A poultice made from the bark can be applied to open wounds to help them heal and avoid infection.

Mojo Beans

Vicia faba

Assures that you always have an abundance of energy

- **MOJO BEANS WILL:** Assure you of an abundant harvest, Deepen your connection with spirit, Help you overcome difficulties

- **THE PLANT:** Mojo beans are an erect plant that stand about three feet tall. They don't have the ability to climb like other beans. The flowers are small with five petals with a blue or purple spot. The fruit is a leathery pod that, when matured, is blackish brown with a fuzzy surface.

- **HOW TO HARNESS MOJO BEANS'S MAGICAL PROPERTIES:** Mojo beans are seen as a profound blessing from God. In Catholicism, they are associated with St. Joseph's Day and are placed on the altar. During one of Sicily's severe famines, the people prayed to St. Joseph to be delivered from the crisis. As a result of their prayers, the Mojo beans thrived while other crops failed. They became a symbol of abundance and prosperity. If you carry a few of these beans, you will always have money. If you place them on your altar, they will ensure you of a deep and abiding connection with your spirit and the Divine.

    Mojo beans are considered a good luck charm. You can write your desire on a bean and then plant it. If the plant thrives and yields beans, you know your wish will come true.

- **MEDICINAL USES:** Mojo beans are believed to be effective in treating Parkinson's disease and are rumored to be a natural alternative to Viagra.

Hops

Humulus lupulus

Fills your heart with love

HOPS WILL: Ensure pleasant dreams, Cure insomnia, Heal your mind, body, and spirit

THE PLANT: Hops are native to the Northern Hemisphere. The roots are very stout and perennial. The stems come up every year and twine around one another. The stems are very fibrous, and the fibers are used to make a coarse white cloth and paper. Hops are dioecious, which means that the male and female flowers grow on separate plants.

HOW TO HARNESS HOPS' MAGICAL PROPERTIES: In Celtic mythology, Hops are associated with wolf medicine and with the power of the winter months.

Sleeping on a pillow stuffed with Hops will invite powerful and peaceful dreams. It will also help you sleep soundly and overcome insomnia.

Carrying Hops as an amulet will promote healing.

MEDICINAL USES: Hops have been used as a tonic for overall health and to settle upset stomachs. They improve appetite and encourage a restful night's sleep.

Bittersweet

Celastrus scandens

Helps you forget the past and live happily in the present moment

- **BITTERSWEET WILL:** Bring you peace, Help you overcome a broken heart, Protect your home, Manifest your dreams

- **THE PLANT:** American Bittersweet is native to the central and eastern portions of the United States. It is a rambling, woody vine that blooms in the spring. In the fall, its yellow berries burst open, creating a beautiful show of orange centers surrounded by bright yellow jackets. American Bittersweet is not to be confused with the invasive Asian Bittersweet.

- **HARNESS BITTERSWEET'S MAGICAL PROPERTIES:** In the fall, place Bittersweet branches on your altar to begin to release the old year and get ready for the new one. After the Winter Solstice, write whatever you want to create on a piece of paper and burn it along with the Bittersweet.

  To help you forget about an unhappy love affair, place a sprig of Bittersweet under your bed.

  Traditionally, Bittersweet was used to remove spells and hexes. Wearing some around your neck will alleviate dizziness and help you stay focused.

  Bittersweet can also be used to keep your entire family—even your pets—safe. Put a small piece of it on your pets' collars to help keep them free from harm. And place some bouquets of it around the rooms of your home to protect your family and to help heal old emotional wounds.

- **MEDICINAL USES:** Bittersweet is mildly poisonous, so it should never be ingested. A weak tea made from the berries can be used to treat eczema topically.

Oregano

Origanum vulgare

Brings passion to your life

- **OREGANO WILL:** Encourage freedom of expression, Protect you and your home, Make traveling easy and enjoyable

- **THE PLANT:** Oregano is a perennial herb in the Mint family. It is widely used in Spanish, Italian, and Mexican cooking. It may grow up to two feet tall and spread almost two feet. It has white or pinkish purple flowers that appear in the late summer as numerous spikes all over the plant. It is native to the Mediterranean and will live in colder climates if protected during the winter months.

- **HARNESS OREGANO'S MAGICAL PROPERTIES:** To fill your house with a sense of joy and lightheartedness, sprinkle a handful of Oregano around the perimeter of your home. If you plant Oregano in your garden, it will bless your home and protect it.

  To make travel easy, safe, and enjoyable, put a few Oregano leaves in your shoes. Using it in your cooking when you are having guests will encourage lively and uplifting communications at the dinner table.

- **MEDICINAL USES:** Oregano is a powerful germ killer. A poultice made from its crushed leaves will remove inflammation and relieve pain. Cooking with it or making a tea from the dried leaves aids in digestion and helps cleanse the liver.

Comfrey

Symphytum officinale

Makes you feel comfortable in the most challenging situations

- **COMFREY WILL:** Ensure safe and easy travel, Protect your suitcases, Attract abundance

- **THE PLANT:** Comfrey is native to North America, Europe, and temperate Asia. The plant is erect and stands two to three feet tall. The leaves are covered with fuzzy hair. The lower leaves are large and decrease in size as they get closer to the top of the plant. The top of the plant is branched and covered with creamy yellow flowers. Comfrey starts blooming in April or May and continues until fall.

- **HARNESS COMFREY'S MAGICAL PROPERTIES:** If you're about to travel, place a piece of Comfrey root in the bottom of your suitcase to ensure that it arrives safely. Carry a small piece of the root in your pocket to make sure you arrive on time, too.

  Sprinkle small pieces of the root around your property as a blessing. When burned as incense, it creates an atmosphere of peace and well-being.

- **MEDICINAL USES:** Comfrey root is very effective in treating lung problems and whooping cough. A strong tea made from the roots is said to stop internal hemorrhaging from the lungs, stomach, and bowels. The fresh leaves can be rubbed on joints to relieve pain. The roots can be mashed and used as a plaster to set broken bones.

  Comfrey leaves are useful as a poultice for sprains, cuts, boils, abscesses, and any kind of inflammation or swelling.

▶ Top: Bittersweet, Middle: Oregano, Bottom: Comfrey

Bishop's Weed *Carum copticum*

Surrounds you with friendships

- **BISHOP'S WEED WILL:** Invite friendship, Remind you how beautiful and unique you are, Encourage romance

- **THE PLANT:** Bishop's Weed is a small, erect shrub that has soft, fine, feathery leaves that look very similar to wild parsley. The seeds are gray and irregular in size and shape. They have a hot, spicy taste. Bishop's Weed grows almost anywhere but is native to India. The seeds are used as a spice. Raw Bishop's Weed smells almost exactly like thyme.

- **HOW TO HARNESS BISHOP'S WEED'S MAGICAL PROPERTIES:** Bishop's Weed is perfect to use when you're feeling lonely or that you lack connections in your life. To invite love, friendships, partnerships, romance, and attraction, plant some Bishop's Weed in your yard.

Washing your face in a weak infusion made from two tablespoons of dried leaves and seeds soaked in two cups of hot water overnight and then strained will not only help clear up your skin, but it will also give you the confidence to go out to meet a partner. It will help you remember how beautiful and special you are.

Sprinkling the dried leaves in room corners will encourage romance and deepen relationships.

- **MEDICINAL USES:** Bishop's Weed is an excellent antispasmodic. A tea made from the seeds helps expel gas from the stomach and intestines, relieving abdominal pain and distension. Bishop's Weed is also helpful for stimulating the appetite and enhancing digestion. Incense made from burning the dried leaves and seeds is an effective treatment for most forms of respiratory distress.

To relieve a stuffy nose, put one-quarter cup of seeds into a few cups of boiling water and carefully inhale the steam.

Mandrake *Mandragora officinale*

Helps you manifest your deepest dreams

- **MANDRAKE WILL:** Help you conceive a child, Attract love, Bring good luck

- **THE PLANT:** A native of southern Europe, Mandrake will grow in warmer gardens but will seldom survive severe winters. It has a large root that looks somewhat like a parsnip but will grow up to four feet in the ground. From the top of the root arise several dark green leaves that can grow to a foot or more in length. They are pointed and have a foul odor. The flowers are white with a bit of purple. The fruit is about the size of a small apple and is a deep yellow when fully ripe.

- **HOW TO HARNESS MANDRAKE'S MAGICAL PROPERTIES:** Mandrake root chases away demons. To attract good luck and protect your house, hang a Mandrake root in your home.

  Hang a Mandrake root over your bed if you are concerned about conceiving a child, chasing away bad dreams, or simply getting a good night's rest.

  If you wear a piece of Mandrake root around your neck, it will keep you healthy.

- **MEDICINAL USES:** The leaves can be used as an ointment for cuts and burns. When the leaves are boiled in milk, they make a soothing poultice for ulcers. The fresh roots are used to cleanse and purge the body. The Romans used Mandrake as an aphrodisiac. If used in large quantities, it causes delirium and madness.

Betony

Betonica officinalis

Will bless your life three times over

- **BETONY WILL:** Help you think clearly, Protect you from negativity, Purify your mind, body, and soul, Protect you from drunkenness

- **THE PLANT:** Betony is a perennial herb that grows across much of Europe, Siberia, and North America. It was revered by the Greeks and Celts as a sacred plant of healing. It has hairy, aromatic leaves and grows one to two feet tall. Betony is believed to lose all of its magical and medicinal properties if touched by iron. It has small, fragrant pink or purple flowers that bloom throughout June and July.

- **HARNESS BETONY'S MAGICAL PROPERTIES:** Betony is such a powerful herb that planting it in your yard will create security in all areas of your life. It will create such a strong aura of protection that no evil can pass through it.

  In the past, Betony was considered an important addition to the gardens of healers and monasteries. Putting a few dried leaves under your pillow will prevent nightmares.

  To alleviate depression and ease the pain caused by the loss of a loved one, add a sprinkling of dried flowers to your bath. The vapors from the bathwater will also release fears.

  Wear Betony when you go out on a date with that special someone to ensure that the relationship will deepen and grow.

  If you're hoping to avoid quarrels and smooth over disagreements, sprinkle a few pinches of the dried leaves around the rooms of your home.

- **MEDICINAL USES:** Betony is used to relieve headaches and cold symptoms. Tea made from it will strengthen the immune system.

Dragon's Blood

Daemomorops draco

Brings joy and laughter into your life

- **DRAGON'S BLOOD WILL:** Fill your life with lo Increase your vitality, Remind you to laugh

- **THE PLANT:** Dragon's Blood is a slender rattan palm tree with a tendency to climb and is indigenous to Sumatra, Malaysia, and Indonesia. The leaves are prickly and often have long tails. The berries are the size of a cherry and somewhat pointy. When ripe, they are covered with a dark red, resinous substance, which is used to make beads, rolled into small sticks around eighteen inches long and packed in leaves, or sold in irreg lar lumps or powder. The resin is separated from the berries in several ways, producing a variety o qualities.

- **HARNESS DRAGON'S BLOOD'S MAGICAL PROPERTIES:** Dragon's Blood is considered an herb of empowerment. It will enhance the effectiveness of other spells and herbs.

  If you want to enhance your love life or cure impotence, place a stick of Dragon's Blood unde your pillow.

  When the resin or powder is burned as incens it will protect your home, invite love, and bring a sense of happiness and joy into your home. A pinch added to other incenses will increase their potency.

  Worn in an amulet, Dragon's Blood will increase your energy and help you attract love. Add other herbs, and their effects will be increased exponentially.

- **MEDICINAL USES:** In former times, Dragon's Blood was used to treat syphilis.

Patchouli Leaf

Pogostemon patchouli

Helps ground you and sets you free

- **PATCHOULI LEAF WILL:** Attract money, Ensure fertility, Deepen your connection to Mother Earth

- **THE PLANT:** Patchouli Leaf is indigenous to the East and West Indies and Paraguay. Its leaves are egg shaped, and the plant grows two to three feet tall. It has white flowers tinged with purple that grow in small conical spikes. It is a very fragrant plant that can be harvested three or four times a year. The plants are dried and packaged into bales that are used to make oil for perfumes. Patchouli leaves are widely used in India and Asia. The smell improves with age.

- **HARNESS PATCHOULI LEAF'S MAGICAL PROPERTIES:** If you've been feeling out of sorts, burn some Patchouli Leaf as incense. It will deepen your connection to the Earth and bring a sense of peace and calm into your home.

  When placed in an amulet and worn, Patchouli Leaf will act as an aphrodisiac, arouse sexual interest, and attract love. Placed under your bed, it will help you become pregnant. When rubbed on your money and placed in your wallet, it will attract money.

- **MEDICINAL USES:** Patchouli Leaf is said to cause loss of appetite, disturb sleep, and create nervous attacks, so it is not highly recommended for medical uses. It can be used to soothe the itching from insect bites. When put on wounds, it helps them heal more rapidly.

▶ Top: Betony, Middle: Dragon's Blood, Bottom: Patchouli Leaf

Winter's Bark _Drimys winteri_

Shines the light of love on all your endeavors

- **WINTER'S BARK WILL:** Ensure success in all of your efforts, Attract money, Bless your home with love

- **THE PLANT:** This large evergreen tree took its name from Captain Winter, who discovered its medicinal properties while taking care of Sir Francis Drake on his voyage around the world. It grows up to fifty feet tall. It is native to the Antarctic and southern parts of South America. Its bark is green and wrinkled. The branches are smooth and erect in nature. It has small flowers. The fruit has a warm but pungent taste. The bark is increasingly rare.

- **HOW TO HARNESS WINTER'S BARK'S MAGICAL PROPERTIES:** To attract abundance and help you attain success in all of your endeavors, burn the bark as incense.

  To bless your home and fill it with a feeling of peace and well-being, sprinkle a small amount of the bark around the outside of your house.

- **MEDICINAL USES:** The bark is very scarce, so it is seldom used medicinally anymore. It is an excellent remedy for nausea and any disharmony of the digestive tract. It will stop diarrhea and soothe the intestines.

Skullcap *Scutellaria galerirulata*

Enfolds you in peace and love

- **SKULLCAP WILL:** Increase sexual potency, Deepen meditative states, Create an aura of peace

- **THE PLANT:** Skullcap is native to North America and is found from New York to West Virginia and southward to South Carolina, Alabama, and Missouri. It is a perennial herb that grows in sunny locations along forests, thickets, bluffs, and roadsides. It has a short rhizome that sends up stems that grow about a foot and a half in height. Its hooded flowers bloom from May until August.

- **HOW TO HARNESS SKULLCAP'S MAGICAL PROPERTIES:** If your home life has been chaotic lately, burn some Skullcap as incense. It will fill your home with a sense of relaxation and peace, as well as deepen your meditations.

To encourage your ability to contact the ancestors while meditating, drink a tea made of one ounce of the dried herb boiled in a quart of water for a half hour. This tea can also be used to increase sexual potency.

Before a wedding ceremony, sprinkle the dried plant around the area where the vows will be spoken to ensure a long and happy marriage.

- **MEDICINAL USES:** Skullcap is a powerful medicinal herb frequently used as an anti-inflammatory and to help stop muscle cramps and spasms. It can be used as a sedative and is a wonderful overall tonic. It can be used to treat epilepsy, insomnia, and anxiety, and to ease the withdrawal symptoms from barbiturates and other drugs.

Note: Skullcap can cause a miscarriage, so it should never be used by pregnant women. As with all herbs, always consult a qualified herbalist before using it.

Allspice *Pimento officinalis*

Brings you luck and spices up your love life

- **ALLSPICE WILL:** Bring you good luck and attract abundance, Help overcome rifts in relationships, Chase away negative energies

- **THE PLANT:** Pimento or Jamaica Pepper is called Allspice because it tastes like a combination of Cloves, Juniper berries, Cinnamon, and Pepper. It is indigenous to the Caribbean Islands and South America. It grows extensively in Jamaica, where it flourishes on the limestone hills near the sea. The tree grows to more than thirty feet tall and begins fruiting when it's three years old. The flowers appear in June, July, and August and are quickly succeeded by the berries.

  The spice is harvested from the rinds of the berries. It loses its aroma when the berries are ripe, so they are harvested before they have attained their full size.

- **HOW TO HARNESS ALLSPICE'S MAGICAL PROPERTIES:** When placed in your closet, powdered Allspice will not only freshen your clothes, but it will also remove any negative energies you might have picked up.

  If you have had a disagreement with someone, sprinkle some of the powder on the threshold before you enter your house so you won't bring the anger home.

  To spice up your love life, sprinkle a small pinch of Allspice in the corner of your bedroom. Burning the powder as incense will ensure you of abundance.

- **MEDICINAL USES:** Allspice will settle your stomach, relieve gas, stop diarrhea, and get rid of indigestion.

  It is also an effective antiseptic.

Motherwort

Leonurus cardiaca

Brings out your ability to nurture yourself

MOTHERWORT WILL: Remind you of the importance of love, Help you accept yourself unconditionally, Help you release judgment

■ **THE PLANT:** Motherwort is a native of many parts of Europe and can be found along riverbanks and under hedges. It is frequently found in old gardens, where it was previously grown for medicinal purposes. Except when it flowers, it resembles Mugwort. The flowers are whitish on the outside and purple on the inside. They have short, flat lips with long wooly hairs. The plant blooms in August and has a very bitter taste and pungent odor.

■ **HOW TO HARNESS MOTHERWORT'S MAGICAL PROPERTIES:** Place some of the herb on your altar and scatter it around your home to increase the spiritual vibrations.

Adding some tea made from Motherwort to your bathwater will improve your mood, relax you, and deepen your connection to your spirit. To make the tea, add two tablespoons of dried Motherwort to two cups of boiling water, steep for about ten minutes, and strain.

Keep a sprig of Motherwort near your bathroom mirror and take a few moments each day to look at yourself. The herb will help you recognize your perfection.

Finally, to release the past and help forgive anyone who has hurt you, put some Motherwort under your pillow. Doing so will also help heal anyone you may have hurt in the past.

■ **MEDICINAL USES:** Motherwort acts as a tonic to quiet the entire nervous system. It helps balance the hormonal system and eases any problems with the menstrual cycle. It will strengthen the heart and relieve depression.

Datura *Datura stramonium*

Helps you see the divinity in all of life

- **DATURA WILL:** Cure insomnia, Remove curses, Encourage visions

- **THE PLANT:** Datura is commonly called Jimson Weed or Thornapple and grows almost everywhere except the Arctic. It grows one to five feet tall and has purple stems. The flowers are trumpet shaped and open at irregular times during the evening, earning it the nickname of Moonflower. The fruits are oval shaped and covered with spikes. Any part of the plant that is bruised will produce a foul odor.

- **HOW TO HARNESS DATURA'S MAGICAL PROPERTIES:** Centuries ago, Datura was considered useful in strengthening incantations, but during the witch trials in Europe and Salem, Massachusetts, it was unlucky for people to have it growing in their gardens. It was considered sacred by the Aztec.

  You can scatter the leaves around the outside of your home for protection against evil spirits, to remove negative spells, and to banish fear.

  If you put the dried leaves under your pillow, they will cure insomnia. Burning the leaves as incense will encourage visions.

- **MEDICINAL USES:** Datura is extremely toxic when ingested and can cause severe hallucinations. A poultice made from the crushed seeds and roots and applied to the joints will relieve the pain of arthritis and rheumatism.

Anise *Pimpinella anisum*

Sweetens your experience of life

- **ANISE WILL:** Protect you, Restore your youthful appearance, Purify your mind, body, and spirit, Help you see into the future

- **THE PLANT:** Anise is an annual plant native to Egypt and the Eastern Mediterranean. It grows about three feet tall and has fragrant white flowers that smell like licorice.

  It is easy to grow but needs at least four warm months. It has been placed in wedding cakes for good luck since ancient Roman times.

- **HOW TO HARNESS ANISE'S MAGICAL PROPERTIES:** Put some dried Anise under your pillow to prevent nightmares and to be assured of a good night's sleep. Sleeping with a bunch of the fresh leaves and flowers hanging on your bedpost will make you look young again.

  In ancient Rome, brides and grooms bathed in Anise tea to ensure a loving and long-lasting relationship. For help with your love life, place some of the seeds in your wallet; they'll act as a love charm as well as attract abundance.

  To dispel negativity and increase your sense of well-being and self-esteem, sprinkle a few fresh Anise leaves around the inside of your home. Burn Anise as incense when you want guidance from the gods.

  Two tablespoons of dried Anise added to a cup of boiling water and steeped for about ten minutes before straining will improve your insights and deepen your connection to spirit.

  Carrying a sprig of Anise will help you find happiness.

- **MEDICINAL USES:** Anise makes a good antiseptic. Wounds can be cleaned with Anise tea to avoid infection. Placing a few crushed seeds in a warm glass of milk will alleviate insomnia. Burning Anise as incense is said to cure headaches.

Ginseng *Panax quinquefolium*

Lights up your life

- **GINSENG WILL:** Protect you against illness, Attract love, Enhance fertility, Ensure abundance

- **THE PLANT:** American Ginseng is an attractive plant with shiny, deep green leaves. The fleshy roots are slow growing. It is a perennial and grows in the rich woodlands of North America. Although American Ginseng is related to Asian Ginseng, it is said to be more powerful and better suited to the metabolism of Westerners. There is an old adage in herbal medicine and that is to use herbs indigenous to the area in which you live. They carry a similar vibration and will be more effective.

- **HOW TO HARNESS GINSENG'S MAGICAL PROPERTIES:** Carry the root to attract love, promote good health, attract money, and ensure sexual potency. When burned as incense, it creates an aura of peace and well-being. It will purify the area, repel evil spirits, and release any negative spells or hexes.

Worn as an amulet, Ginseng will ensure you of success.

To make your dreams come true, find an attractive root and write your deepest wish on the surface. Place it on your altar for a month and then throw it into a body of water on the night of a full moon.

- **MEDICINAL USES:** Ginseng has a long history of use as a healing herb. It is reputed to stop aging, improve overall well-being, balance the internal organs, calm the emotions, and increase sexual potency. It settles the stomach and improves digestion. Make sure the roots aren't touched by metal objects or they will lose their potency.

Tonka Beans *Coumarouna odorata*

Teaches you about courage

■ **TONKA BEANS WILL:** Invite good luck, Attract abundance, Enhance the power of the will

■ **THE PLANT:** Tonka beans come from a tree that grows in the forest of Brazil. The seed is black, wrinkled on the outside, and smooth on the inside. It is most commonly known for its smell, which is similar to a mixture of Vanilla, Almonds, Cloves, and Cinnamon. It is often used to flavor Tobacco.

■ **HOW TO HARNESS TONKA BEANS'S MAGICAL PROPERTIES:** To remove any residual negative energy, put the ground beans in a sachet and hang it in your closet. To invite good fortune, place a few beans in the four corners of your house. Then simply wait—the good fortune may show up in the form of money or good luck.

Whenever you are in need of courage, carry a few Tonka beans in your pocket.

Tonka beans can also be used in a ritual to manifest something you've been hoping for in your life. First place the beans on your altar for a month while each day spending some time visualizing manifesting whatever it is you specifically want to attract into your life. At the end of the month, throw the beans into a body of running water. Finally, wash your hands in the water and know your desires are on their way to you.

■ **MEDICINAL USES:** Tonka beans should be used with extreme care because they can be poisonous. A trained herbalist might use a juice made from the beans to treat whooping cough, but because it paralyzes the heart in large doses, it should always be used with extreme caution.

Mace

Myristica fragrans

Reminds you about the gift of giving

- **MACE WILL:** Enhance fertility, Bring good luck, Increase abundance

- **THE PLANT:** Native to New Guinea and the West Indies, Mace comes from an evergreen tree that grows up to forty feet tall. The leaves are dark green and smooth. The flowers are small and produce a smooth yellow fruit that looks like a pear. The nuts are about an inch long. The nut itself is nutmeg; the covering of the nut is red and brittle. Mace is the covering of the nut. The name comes from a medieval word for nut that means "suitable for ointment."

- **HARNESS MACE'S MAGICAL PROPERTIES:** If you'd like to conceive a child, add dried Mace to your bathwater.

  When you clean your home, add a sprinkle of dried Mace to your cleaning water to ensure good luck and to invite abundance.

  Place some dried Mace in a small, open container on your altar before you begin any new projects. Done mindfully, this act will bless your endeavors, ensuring success.

  To ensure a baby of a happy, carefree, and abundant life, add a small pinch of dried Mace to the water used at his or her baptism.

- **MEDICINAL USES:** Mace should always be used in moderation. It helps aid digestion and increases circulation. A tea made with Mace, Ginger, Lemon juice, and honey will soothe a sore throat and reduce a fever.

Fenugreek Seed

Foenum-graecum

Lightens up your mood

- **FENUGREEK SEED WILL:** Purify your home, Bring abundance, Bring your dreams to life

- **THE PLANT:** Fenugreek is indigenous to the countries on the eastern shores of the Mediterranean and is cultivated in India, Africa, Egypt, Morocco, and occasionally England. It is an erect annual herb growing about two feet tall. Centuries ago, it was used to scent inferior hay so it could be sold for a better price. The seeds are brownish and are contained in narrow pods that hold ten to twenty seeds.

- **HARNESS FENUGREEK SEED'S MAGICAL PROPERTIES:** Fenugreek seeds attract money, so add them to your cleaning solution when you mop the floors in your home. (They're small, so no need to be concerned about the seeds scratching your floors.)

  Keep an open jar of the seeds in your kitchen and add a few every day to make sure you always have more than enough money. When the jar is full, empty them into your backyard and start over.

  To bless your home, burn Fenugreek seeds as incense. Placing the seeds under your bed will stop nightmares.

- **MEDICINAL USES:** Fenugreek seeds can be soaked in water until they swell into a thick paste. When rubbed on the forehead, the paste will reduce a fever. Adding the seeds to a glass of water and drinking it will calm the stomach and relieve gas. Sprouting the seeds until the baby plants are two to three inches tall and then eating the seeds and all is a wonderful tonic for the liver and also strengthens the immune system.

Lemon Verbena

Aloysia triphylla

Protects you from nightmares

LEMON VERBENA WILL: Stop bad dreams, Purify your home, Encourage love, Lighten your mood

THE PLANT: Lemon Verbena has small lavender flower clusters along the woody stems. The flowers aren't very showy, but the plant is worth growing just for its foliage. Its leaves give off a wonderful citrus scent when crushed. Lemon Verbena grows into a bushy shrub that stands five feet tall and five feet wide, although it can be kept smaller when grown in a container. It can grow larger in warmer climates.

HARNESS LEMON VERBENA'S MAGICAL PROPERTIES: If you want to avoid dreaming, place a leaf under your pillow at night.

Adding the dried crushed leaves to a candle and burning the candle on your altar will purify your home and invoke spiritual blessings. When the dried leaves are burned as incense, they will dispel negative energies and encourage love.

Hang the leaves in your closet to lighten your mood and help you feel more special when you get dressed in the morning.

MEDICINAL USES: A tea made from Lemon Verbena can be used to relieve indigestion, nausea, stomach cramps, menstrual pain, and gas. The oil is also effective in treating migraine headaches, asthma, neuralgia, vertigo, and depression.

▶ Top: Mace, Middle: Fenugreek Seed, Bottom: Lemon Verbena

Country Mallow *Malva syvestris*

Brings beauty into your life

- **COUNTRY MALLOW WILL:** Get rid of negative entities, Protect you and your home, Attract love

- **THE PLANT:** Country Mallow grows three to four feet tall in hedgerows, fields, and empty lots. The flowers are very showy and are a beautiful shade of purplish mauve with prominent dark veins. Country Mallow is a deep, lush green when it first appears in June, but as the season advances, it becomes ragged looking.

- **HOW TO HARNESS COUNTRY MALLOW'S MAGICAL PROPERTIES:** Heat a cup of olive oil until warm and then stir in a cup of dried Country Mallow leaves. Put the mixture in a clean, clear jar and place it outside where the sun, stars, and moon can shine on it. Leave it there for at least one moon cycle and then strain it. You can use this oil to remove negativity and protect yourself from the effects of black magic. Simply rub the oil on your body, add a few drops to your bathwater, or sprinkle it around the room.

If you regret how a past relationship with a lover ended, place a bouquet of the flowers near an open window or by your front door. This will cause a lost love to think more favorably of you and perhaps even return to you. Or you can place the dried herb in an amulet to attract love.

- **MEDICINAL USES:** The flowers and the leaves make a useful poultice to ease the pain of a bruise or strained muscles. A tea made from the leaves will relieve a nagging cough.

Alkanet Root

Alkana tinctoria

Purifies your heart and clears your mind

ALKANET ROOT WILL: Clear negativity out of an area, Attract prosperity, Add color to your life

THE PLANT: Alkanet Root is a biennial or perennial herb that grows to twelve inches high. It has rough leaves and a thick taproot. For centuries the root has been used as a dye for clothing, cosmetics, and wine. Depending on the root, you can create rich reds or beautiful purples.

HOW TO HARNESS ALKANET ROOT'S MAGICAL PROPERTIES: Harvest the leaves when the moon is full. If you want to use the flowers, pick them during the day when the sun is high. Use care when you handle the root so your hands don't turn red. You can wear gloves, but doing so diminishes your connection with the plant.

To attract abundance, sprinkle small pieces of the dried roots around your property.

To purify an area and remove negativity, burn the dried leaves as incense.

If you find your mind racing, the incense will help quiet it. After burning the leaves as incense, go outside and imagine yourself deeply rooted in the earth, drawing all of your sustenance from the Earth Mother.

When you have a heavy heart, rub the dried leaves between your hands, hold them in front of your nose, and allow yourself to be filled with their earthy scent. Breathe in, quiet your mind, and connect with the magic of the moment.

MEDICINAL USES: Alkanet Root is primarily used as a dye, but when mixed with beeswax, it can be applied topically to relieve the pain of arthritis. It is also said to cure poisonous snake bites.

Juniper *Juniperus communis*

Surrounds you with love

- **JUNIPER WILL:** Protect you, Attract love, Keep you safe from accidents

- **THE PLANT:** Juniper is native to Europe, northern Africa, northern Asia, and North America. It is a small shrub that grows four to six feet tall. It loves limestone hills and flourishes there. Instead of pinecones, Juniper bears small blue berries. The berries have very little flavor until crushed, and their taste diminishes shortly after they are picked or if dried. New berries appear on the tree in the spring, but it takes several years for the berries to ripen to dark blue.

- **HOW TO HARNESS JUNIPER'S MAGICAL PROPERTIES:** Hang a branch of Juniper over your front door to protect your home and keep negative energies from entering.

  To prevent accidents and attract love, place some berries in an amulet and wear it around your neck.

  To purify an area, burn the dried leaves as incense.

- **MEDICINAL USES:** Juniper berries are used to treat urinary tract and bladder infections. They help with kidney problems and ease the pain of arthritis and rheumatism. When they're boiled in water, the steam helps break up congestion from colds and the flu or asthma.

  Mixing the berries with beeswax relieves the irritation from insect bites and prevents infection when rubbed on open wounds.

Uva Ursi *Arctostaphylos uva-ursi*

Enhances your creativity

UVA URSI WILL: Increase psychic awareness, Deepen your connection to your spirit

THE PLANT: Uva Ursi is a small shrub that is native to the northern latitudes. Its evergreen leaves are leathery and about an inch long. The waxy-looking flowers appear in May and June before the new leaves appear. The flowers are white with a red lip and are urn shaped. The berries ripen in autumn and are about the size of a small currant. The berries are very red, smooth, and glossy. They have a tough skin and have multiple stones.

■ **HOW TO HARNESS UVA URSI'S MAGICAL PROPERTIES:** When used as incense, the dried leaves will purify the area and create a sacred space.

To enhance your psychic awareness and deepen your connection to your spirit, drink a tea made from Uva Ursi. To make the tea, add two tablespoons of dried Uva Ursi to two cups of boiling water. Allow the mixture to steep for about ten minutes before straining it.

Crumbling the dried leaves and placing them in the corner of a room invokes protective spirits. Place a few under your altar to consecrate it for sacred purposes.

■ **MEDICINAL USES:** Uva Ursi leaves were first written about by a thirteenth-century Welsh physician. They are used to treat kidney and bladder troubles. An infusion made of half an ounce of leaves in a pint of boiling water strengthens and tones the urinary tract. The leaves can also be used for tanning leather hides.

Chamomile *Anthemis nobilis*

Brings calmness, ease, and abundance to your life

- **CHAMOMILE WILL:** Relieve stress and increase confidence, Invite abundance, Attract love

- **THE PLANT:** Chamomile is a member of the Daisy family and is indigenous to much of North America and Europe. It is a perennial with feathery, parsleylike leaves and a fibrous root. Chamomile grows up to ten inches high and produces small, daisylike white flowers with yellow centers. A tea made from it tastes like apple or pineapple.

- **HOW TO HARNESS CHAMOMILE'S MAGICAL PROPERTIES:** Washing your hands in Chamomile tea attracts abundance. To make the tea, add two tablespoons of dried leaves to two cups of boiling water, steep for about ten minutes, and then strain the tea.

  You can add some Chamomile tea to your bath-water to purify your body, relax, and attract love.

A handful of dried Chamomile sprinkled lightly around the outside of your home will create a circle of protection and remove curses. Sprinkle powdered Chamomile inside your shoes to release any unnecessary energy you may have collected during the day.

When you need to be assertive, gargling for thirty seconds with a cup of Chamomile tea will help you speak up. It will also help you feel confident and comfortable speaking in front of groups of people.

- **MEDICINAL USES:** Chamomile is often used as a sedative and tonic. It can be used to ease depression and help you relax when you're under stress. It is said to calm the digestive system, settle nervous indigestion and gastritis, and relieve headaches, menstrual pain, and disorders of the kidney, liver, and bladder. It may also be used to treat hay fever, insomnia, stomach cramps, vomiting, spastic pain, arthritis, and appetite loss, as well as to relieve teething pain and colic in babies.

Huckleberry Leaves *Vaccinium myrtillus*

Brings you good luck

HUCKLEBERRY LEAVES WILL: Bring you good luck, Help you manifest your dreams, Repel negativity

■ **THE PLANT:** Huckleberry is a small bush that grows about a foot tall and is covered with plump, deep blue berries. It is native to northern Europe, Asia, and North America. It thrives in damp, acidic soil. The fruit ripens in late July through September. It is related to the Blueberry bush.

■ **HOW TO HARNESS HUCKLEBERRY LEAVES' MAGICAL PROPERTIES:** When you place Huckleberry leaves in an amulet, it brings good luck and repels negativity.

To help you manifest your dreams, place the leaves in your pillow. You can also make a tea out of one-quarter cup of dried leaves boiled in a quart of water for at least ten minutes and then strained. Add the tea to your bathwater every night for a month while you visualize yourself manifesting your deepest desires.

■ **MEDICINAL USES:** Huckleberry leaves can be used to treat eye irritations and, when eaten, improve eyesight. A poultice made from the leaves and berries is useful to treat hemorrhoids. The berries soothe stomach ulcers and stop diarrhea. Drinking Huckleberry tea on a daily basis will help relieve arthritis. It also helps improve circulation.

Pine Needles

Pinus sylvestris

Refreshes your life

- **PINE NEEDLES WILL:** Attract good luck and abundance, Bless and protect your home, Heal a broken heart, Increase fertility

- **THE PLANT:** The Scotch Pine lives to be 150 to 300 years old. They thrive in sandy soils at low to moderate altitudes. They were indigenous to Scotland and Ireland but have been naturalized over much of Europe and North America. There are literally hundreds of types of Pine trees; each one has its own unique smell and has slightly different properties. Scotch Pine needles are longer and more fragrant than some of the other shorter-needled pines.

- **HARNESS PINE NEEDLES' MAGICAL PROPERTIES:** Pine is the symbol of everlasting life. Even in the middle of the winter when everything else has died, the trees are bright green, reminding us that new life is only a few months away. Placing Pine needles in your home will attract abundance and invite new life.

  Pine trees were symbolically decorated at the winter solstice to honor the energy of divinity and to remind people of their hopes and dreams. Keep a small bowl of Pine needles on your altar all year round. They enhance the ability to heal and transform any situation and remind you of the limitless possibilities of life.

- **MEDICINAL USES:** The scent from the needles will help break up congestion and ease a cough. If Pine oil isn't available, boil a handful of the needles in water and inhale the steam, taking care not to burn yourself with the steam.

Sarsaparilla Root

Sarsaparilla papyracea

Shows you how to use your money wisely

- **SARSAPARILLA ROOT WILL:** Help you balance your checkbook, Attract love, Ignite passion

- **THE PLANT:** Sarsaparilla is native to the southern United States and grows mainly in swampy woods and thickets. It has a thick but flexible stem covered with a few small hooked thorns. The leaves are elliptical with strong veins. The flowers appear from May to August and are yellowish white. They ripen into red and black berries. The roots are fleshy, creep a short distance under the ground, and are very sweet and spicy with a pleasant aroma.

- **HARNESS SARSAPARILLA ROOT'S MAGICAL PROPERTIES:** To attract money, burn the root as incense.

  Before you make any major purchases, meditate with a piece of the root in your right hand. It will help you make good choices.

  If you're hoping to attract love or ignite passion in a relationship, place a small piece of the root in an amulet and wear it around your neck.

  To help protect the environment, sprinkle powder from the ground root around your property.

  Sarsaparilla root is often used in conjunction with Cinnamon and Sandalwood to attract love and abundance.

- **MEDICINAL USES:** An herbalist might use a tea made by combining a quarter of a cup of the ground root with a quart of water to topically treat shingles and recent wounds. Sarsaparilla tea will also calm the nerves and strengthen the heart muscle.

Burdock

Arctium lappa

Helps you let go of life's little annoyances

■ **BURDOCK WILL:** Protect you and your home, Purify your altar

■ **THE PLANT:** Burdock is a sturdy and handsome biennial plant that grows throughout much of Europe and North America. It has large leaves and round heads of purple flowers. The plant is pale green and grows about three to four feet tall. The flowers are seen during the latter part of the summer and well into the autumn. They produce small hooked prickers that attach themselves to anything that brushes against them. The plant owes its large distribution to these burrs.

■ **HARNESS BURDOCK'S MAGICAL PROPERTIES:** Wear a necklace of dried Burdock leaves to protect yourself from negative magical influences.

To protect your home and yourself, sprinkle a small handful of dried Burdock around the outside of your house or wear it in an amulet.

You can also use a tea made from the root to purify your home. Add two tablespoons of dried Burdock root to a pint of boiling water and allow it to steep for about ten minutes before straining it. Then add a few tablespoons of the tea to your cleaning water. Use the tea at least once a year to clean your altar.

■ **MEDICINAL USES:** Three Burdock seeds placed in a small bag worn around the neck is an old gypsy cure for arthritis. A poultice made from the leaves and the ground-up root will speed the healing of wounds and ulcers on the skin.

▶ Top: Pine Needles, Middle: Sarsaparilla Root, Bottom: Burdock

Wahoo Root *Euonymus atropurpureus*

Shows you your life's purpose

- **WAHOO ROOT WILL:** Remove negativity, Give you courage, Attract abundance and success

- **THE PLANT:** Wahoo Root, or Spindle Tree, is a smooth-leaved shrub. The leaves have very short stalks. It bears small clusters of greenish white flowers during May and June. The bushes produce an abundance of fruits. The fruit is a beautiful rose-red color. It bursts open when ripe, exposing deep-orange-colored seeds. The berries tend to attract children, but are harmful.

- **HOW TO HARNESS WAHOO ROOT'S MAGICAL PROPERTIES:** Carrying Wahoo Root will bring you success in all of your endeavors. Sprinkled around your home, it will infuse you with the courage of your convictions and give you the strength of will to overcome any obstacles.

  To remove negativity, make a tea from the bark and rub it on your forehead. To make the tea, add two tablespoons of the bark to two cups of boiling water, steep for about ten minutes, and then strain the tea.

- **MEDICINAL USES:** Wahoo Root is toxic in large doses. In smaller amounts, it makes a good laxative, although it can cause severe cramping. It stimulates the appetite and the flow of gastric juices. As a tonic, it cleanses the liver and reduces fevers.

Elderberry *Sambucuus nigra*

Sweetens up your life

- **ELDERBERRY WILL:** Heal your emotional and spiritual wounds, Protect your home, Attract abundance

- **THE PLANT:** The massive canopy of white, flat-topped Elderberry flowers is a familiar sight in the English and North American countryside. It is said summer hasn't arrived until the Elderberry bush blooms and summer has ended when the berries ripen. The leaves are elongated and pointed. The young stems are hollow and were often used as pipes. People also often carried the hollow stems to assist them in starting a fire; they would blow through the stem to help ignite the tinder. The berries are a deep purple when ripe and make delicious jelly.

- **HOW TO HARNESS ELDERBERRY'S MAGICAL PROPERTIES:** Sharing a glass of beer with Elderberry flowers floating on it with a partner will ensure that you are married within a year.

  Drinking juice from the berries will increase your intuition.

  To help heal spiritual and emotional wounds, add Elderberry tea to your bath. To make the tea, add a handful of the dried leaves to two cups of boiling water and allow the mixture to steep for about ten minutes, strain it, and then add it to your bathwater.

  Burning the stems as incense will cleanse your home and fill it with protection.

- **MEDICINAL USES:** A salve made from dried Elderberry leaves mixed with beeswax can be used to treat bruises, sprains, or shin splints. It also makes a good ointment for cuts and burns and can be used to help fade blemishes and freckles.

Mimosa *Mimosa pudica*

Keeps your life free of problems

- **MIMOSA WILL:** Protect you, Purify your home, Attract love, Enhance your dreams

- **THE PLANT:** Also called Sleeping Grass, the Mimosa plant is very peculiar because of the way the leaves fold up when touched. At night or when Mimosa is exposed to extreme heat or touched, the leaves all fold up. The harder the plant is touched, the quicker the leaves fold up. It is native to southern Mexico and Central America. Where the plant has been introduced, such as in Hawaii, it has become an invasive weed.

- **HOW TO HARNESS MIMOSA'S MAGICAL PROPERTIES:** If your home life has been chaotic lately, scatter a few Mimosa leaves around your house. They will encourage love and create a feeling of peace and an aura of healing.

To encourage dreaming and help you connect with the wisdom of the ancestors, place some leaves beneath your pillow. Make sure you remove the thorns before using the leaves, however, because the thorns will embed themselves under the skin and are difficult to remove.

Adding a tea made from the leaves and flowers to your bathwater will remove negativity and protect you from curses and other people's negative energy. To make the tea, add two tablespoons of dried leaves and flowers to two cups of boiling water. Allow the mixture to steep for at least ten minutes before straining it.

- **MEDICINAL USES:** Mimosa can be used as an antibiotic. A tea made from its leaves relieves muscle spasms, acts as a diuretic, and is very relaxing.

Pepper, Black *Piper nigrum*

Helps you connect with your inner strength

- **BLACK PEPPER WILL:** Stop jealousy, Repel negativity, Protect your home

- **THE PLANT:** Black Pepper grows wild in southern India and in parts of China. It is cultivated in the East and West Indies. Black Pepper is mentioned by Roman writers as early as the fifth century. In its wild state, the tree will grow twenty feet tall, but when cultivated, it is generally kept under twelve feet. It is a perennial. The flowers are small and white and produce small red berries that are wrinkled when ripe. The berries are picked before they are fully ripe and then dried in the sun. They turn black when dried. The plants are propagated by making cuttings. They begin to yield in the third or fourth year and are no longer commercially useful after fifteen years.

- **HOW TO HARNESS BLACK PEPPER'S MAGICAL PROPERTIES:** To protect yourself against negativity, add Black Pepper to an amulet worn around your neck. It will also help you release jealousy and free your mind from negative thoughts.

  You can also mix the peppercorns with coarse sea salt and scatter it around your property for protection and to dispel negative energy. Let your intuition guide you in this process—it will show you how much to use and where to scatter it.

- **MEDICINAL USES:** Black Pepper acts as a stimulant, so it is good for the relief of constipation and to treat urinary tract infections. When used as a gargle, it paralyzes the tongue and stops the pain of a sore throat. It relieves gas and is said to help vertigo. When rubbed on the skin, it stops the pain of arthritis. However, it can irritate the skin, so it should be used with care.

Celandine

Chelidonium majus

Teaches you how to escape your limitations

- **CELANDINE WILL:** Help you break away from an abusive relationship, Ensure that you prevail in court, Cure depression

- **THE PLANT:** Celandine is often found by old walls or in abandoned lots. It likes moist places and can become an aggressive weed if left unchecked. It is indigenous to much of Europe and North America. It has bright yellow flowers during most of the summer. The plant gives off an unpleasant odor when the leaves are brushed against or bruised.

- **HOW TO HARNESS CELANDINE'S MAGICAL PROPERTIES:** Celandine can help you escape from anything that you find limiting. If you want to break away from an abusive relationship, wear a few dried leaves next to your heart in a small silk bag. Replace them every three days until you feel a sense of freedom and release that allows you to end the relationship.

  Place dried Celandine leaves in a blue bottle on your altar to relieve depression and create a sense of ease in your life.

- **MEDICINAL USES:** Celandine is used to treat jaundice, eczema, and diseases of the lymph nodes. A bath with an infusion of two tablespoons of the dried herb to a pint of boiling water makes an excellent treatment for eczema. Adding a few Anise seeds to Celandine tea and drinking a cup three times a day will cleanse the liver and gallbladder.

  Rubbing the sap from the leaves on warts or skin patches affected by ringworm is said to cure them, although it can irritate the skin.

Job's Tears

Coix lacryma-jobi

Makes your wishes come true

◼ **JOB'S TEARS WILL:** Ease teething pain, Heal your mind and body, Manifest your dreams

◼ **THE PLANT:** Job's Tears is a tall grain-bearing tropical plant. It is native to eastern Asia and is grown in the southern United States. It is also called Chinese Barley, although it tastes very different from traditional Barley and has different nutritional qualities. Its individual grains are tear shaped.

◼ **HOW TO HARNESS JOB'S TEARS' MAGICAL PROPERTIES:** String Job's Tears on a red silk thread and place it over your child's crib to relieve the pain of teething.

The seeds have the ability to absorb physical, emotional, and spiritual pain. When strung and put around a person's neck, they will immediately absorb his or her illness. You can also carry the seeds in your pocket for good luck.

To manifest your dreams, place an empty jar on your altar. Then every day for a week, count out seven seeds and place them in the jar while focusing your attention on your deepest dreams. At the end of the week, bury the seeds in a sacred place. Your dreams will come true.

◼ **MEDICINAL USES:** Job's Tears are a diuretic; they reduce edema and other swelling and ease joint pain. They are also used to stop diarrhea. A poultice will clear infections and clean out abscesses.

Buckwheat

Fagopyrum esculentum

Helps you experience the magic each moment contains

- **BUCKWHEAT WILL:** Improve your dreaming, Help you sleep better, Assure you of always having abundance, Keep your home safe and secure

- **THE PLANT:** Buckwheat is native to Central Asia and other Eastern countries. It was first brought to Europe by the Crusaders and was originally called Saracen Corn or French Wheat. The plant grows a foot or two high. The seed, the so-called nut, is triangular and dark brown and has a tough rind. The hulls are often used in pillows. The flowers are very attractive to bees and produce a very flavorful honey.

- **HARNESS BUCKWHEAT'S MAGICAL PROPERTIES:** Sleeping on a pillow made of Buckwheat hulls will not only produce a more restful night's sleep but will also give you more visual and prophetic dreams.

    To attract abundance into your life, burn some of the crushed hulls with your favorite incense.

    For protection, sprinkle a small handful of the ground seeds around the outside of your home.

    Add Buckwheat flour to your holiday baking to bring good luck, love, and prosperity to your family and friends.

- **MEDICINAL USES:** Buckwheat contains a chemical that helps strengthen blood vessels and reduces bleeding in people with high blood pressure. A tea made from the dried leaves helps people with diabetes to better process sugar and is said to reduce cholesterol.

    A poultice made from Buckwheat flour and milk smoothes the skin. When it's applied to the breast, it restores milk production in nursing women.

Frankincense

Boswellia thurifera

Helps deepen your spiritual connection

- **FRANKINCENSE WILL:** Purify and raise the spiritual vibration of your home, Create peace of mind, Improve concentration

- **THE PLANT:** Frankincense is a resin obtained from the leafy Boswellia thurifera tree, which is native to the Middle East and Somalia. It is a deciduous tree with white and pale pink flowers that often grows on rock outcroppings without the benefit of soil. The resin is collected from May until the rains come in September. To obtain the resin, the harvester makes a long cut on the trunk of the tree. The young trees yield the best-quality incense. It will take several months for the gum to become the right consistency, and then large, clear tears are scraped off and collected. The name Frankincense comes from a tenth-century French word that means "luxuriant incenses."

- **HARNESS FRANKINCENSE'S MAGICAL PROPERTIES:** When the dried herb is burned as incense, Frankincense gives off very powerful spiritual vibrations. Frankincense cleanses, purifies, consecrates, and blesses the area by clearing it of negative energies and releasing any trapped spirits. It will quiet the mind and improve the ability to concentrate. The smoke releases vibrations that deepen your connection to the spirit.

    You can put a piece of Frankincense in an amulet for good luck and to attract love and abundance. If you burn it while meditating, it will enhance your meditation and induce visions.

- **MEDICINAL USES:** Frankincense is a stimulant but is seldom used internally anymore. In China, it was used to treat leprosy. The incense relieves bronchitis and helps soothe laryngitis.

Alfalfa

Medicavo sativa

Helps you feel safe by giving you the knowledge that you have more than enough of everything

ALFALFA WILL: Bring prosperity into your life, Increase fertility, Create harmony

THE PLANT: Alfalfa is a perennial member of the Pea family. Its tenacious roots grow more than twenty feet deep, allowing the plant to find rich sources of nutrients not always found in topsoil. Alfalfa grows two to three feet tall and blooms between June and October.

HARNESS ALFALFA'S MAGICAL PROPERTIES: To attract abundance into your life and home, grow Alfalfa seeds in a pot on your windowsill.

To protect your family from harm, sprinkle a few pinches of the dried leaves around the foundation of your house. And if you're looking to add a family member, burn the leaves outside on a calm day and then scatter the ashes around your property; this will attract abundance to your life in general.

If you're nervous about an important meeting, drink a tea before the meeting made by placing two heaping tablespoons of dried Alfalfa leaves in a pint of boiling water, allowing the mixture to steep for approximately ten minutes, and then straining it. You'll be assured of a successful outcome. Drinking this tea at other times will help you let go of all your fears.

MEDICINAL USES: Your herbalist might suggest Alfalfa as a remedy for water retention and urinary and bowel upsets. It is also used to help people who are recovering from narcotic and alcohol addiction. Alfalfa tea is useful in strengthening the body after serious or prolonged illness or weakness.

▶ Top: Buckwheat, Middle: Frankincense, Bottom: Alfalfa

Hazel *Corylus avellana*

Helps you connect with your inner wisdom

- **HAZEL WILL:** Protect your home, Make wishes come true, Increase fertility, Attract abundance

- **THE PLANT:** Hazel is a deciduous tree native to the temperate areas of the Northern Hemisphere. It blossoms very early in the spring, and the flowers come out before the leaves. The male flowers are yellow and the female flowers are very small and reddish. Hazel can grow up to twenty feet tall and will easily rebound even when cut back severely. The nuts are ripe in September.

  The Hazel tree was very sacred to the Celts, and cutting one down was punishable by death. The nuts were a symbol of concentrated wisdom; the sweet gift of wisdom required the patience and strength to break through the hard shell of ignorance.

- **HOW TO HARNESS HAZEL'S MAGICAL PROPERTIES:** Hazel wood is used to make powerful magic wands. If you put three pieces of Hazel wood in the walls of your home, it will be protected from fire.

  Keep a bowl of unopened Hazel nuts on your altar to ensure prosperity and impart wisdom.

  Use a wand made of Hazel to draw a circle around your home for protection. If you wish to conceive a child, place the wand under your bed.

  Hazel nuts given to a bride will ensure a happy union.

- **MEDICINAL USES:** Oil made from the nuts makes an excellent lotion for treating bruises and insect bites.

Lovage

Levisticum officinale

Shows the real meaning of love

LOVAGE WILL: Attract love, Expand your social circle, Help you travel safely

■ THE PLANT: Lovage is indigenous to the Mediterranean, Greece, and the Balkans. It is a stout perennial plant with a thick, fleshy root that is five to six inches long. Lovage grows three to four feet tall and has dark green leaves that look like a coarse form of celery. In June or July the plants blossom with umbel yellow flowers similar to those of Fennel. The whole plant has a strong aromatic odor. Lovage produces an abundance of yellow, gummy resinous juice.

■ HOW TO HARNESS LOVAGE'S MAGICAL PROPERTIES: Put a Lovage leaf in each of your shoes to ensure safe travel and to remove fatigue.

Adding the dried leaves to your bathwater will help you feel more attractive and open your heart to love. Once you know you are special, you will project that energy and people will respond. Bathing in this water before you meditate will also deepen your spiritual connection.

■ MEDICINAL USES: Both the roots and the fruit of Lovage are used as a diuretic, to treat stomach disorders, and to relieve colic and gas. Adding the leaves to a salad improves circulation and lessens constipation. A tea made from boiling the leaves in distilled water soothes the eyes and removes redness. The tea can also be used as a mouthwash.

Thyme *Thymus serpyllum*

Strengthens your will

- **THYME WILL:** Help you sleep, Purify your home, Give you courage, Attract love

- **THE PLANT:** Thyme is a member of the Mint family with small leaves and tiny flowers that are most often purple, lavender, or mauve. The plant grows only about six inches tall and is very fragrant. Thyme flowers from early June through the entire summer.

- **HOW TO HARNESS THYME'S MAGICAL PROPERTIES:** When used as incense, dried Thyme will make everyone in your house healthy. It will also purify the space and fill your home with love and peace.

  Adding a tea made from Thyme to your bathwater will help you release the past and fill you with a sense of peace and love. It will also increase your willpower and give you the courage to do anything. To make the tea, add two tablespoons of dried Thyme to two cups of boiling water. Allow the mixture to steep for about ten minutes before straining it and adding it to your bathwater.

  Wear Thyme around your neck to attract love.

  Place some Thyme under your pillow to ensure you of a peaceful night's sleep and help you access information in your dreams.

- **MEDICINAL USES:** Thyme can be used as an infusion to treat any kind of chest malady. The infusion is made with an ounce of the dried herb placed in a pint of boiling water and then sweetened with sugar or honey. When used as a tea, it relieves gas and calms the stomach. The tea will also calm the nerves and is an excellent remedy for headaches. Carrying a bunch of Thyme is said to prevent drunkenness, although avoiding drinking to excess is probably more effective!

Coltsfoot

Tussilago farfara

Enfolds your life in peace

- **COLTSFOOT WILL:** Bring a sense of peace, Induce visions, Promote tranquility

- **THE PLANT:** Coltsfoot grows abundantly throughout Europe, Asia, and much of North America. It is a perennial with leaves shaped like a horse's hoof. Early in the spring, the tall, star-shaped yellow flowers appear long before the leaves do. When young, the leaves are covered with white fuzz that easily rubs off. Before matches were readily available, the fuzz was used as tinder for lighting fires.

- **HOW TO HARNESS COLTSFOOT'S MAGICAL PROPERTIES:** The dried herb was known as English Tobacco and was often added to shamanic smoking mixtures to facilitate visions.

  When burned as incense, dried Coltsfoot promotes a feeling of tranquility, peace, and calm.

  If you're looking for romance, sprinkle a small handful of the dried leaves around the outside of your home. They will help you attract love. You can also wear some in an amulet around your neck to attract a relationship.

- **MEDICINAL USES:** Coltsfoot has been used for centuries to treat coughs, colds, and asthma. Smoking the dried leaves will suppress coughing and relieve the symptoms of asthma and bronchitis. A tea made from boiling two tablespoons of dried leaves in a quart of water until it's reduced to a pint and then sweetened with honey is a wonderful treatment for all of the symptoms of a cold or the flu.

Endive

Cichorum endiva

Sets you free from all bitterness about the past

- **ENDIVE WILL:** Attract love, Increase libido, Help you let go of the past

- **THE PLANT:** Endive has two varieties, the narrow leaf Endive called Curly Endive and the broad leaf Endive called Escarole. The outside leaves of both types are green and bitter. The inner leaves are a light green to creamy white and are milder in flavor. Both types are used in salads. Endive is more popular in Europe than it is in the Unites States. Its roots are often used as a substitute for coffee.

- **HARNESS ENDIVE'S MAGICAL PROPERTIES:** There are many superstitions about how Endive must be harvested in order to be of any use magically, but however it is picked, when eaten it will help you let go of the past.

  Eating Endive on a daily basis will increase your sexual drive. Adding dried Endive to an amulet will help you attract love.

- **MEDICINAL USES:** The seeds can be brewed into tea by adding two tablespoons of seeds to a quart of water and boiling vigorously for fifteen minutes. When cooled, it is a wonderful treatment for fevers, headaches, and jaundice.

  The leaves are a wonderful tonic for the digestive system and will help cleanse the liver.

Meadow Rue

Ruta graveolens

Helps you see the future

- **MEADOW RUE WILL:** Help with divination, Attract love, Help you maintain inner peace

- **THE PLANT:** Meadow Rue is a beautiful plant with clusters of tiny lavender or pink flowers and ferny foliage. It grows three to four feet tall and prefers a partly shady location, especially in warmer climates. The flowers appear in spring.

- **HARNESS MEADOW RUE'S MAGICAL PROPERTIES:** Native Americans would frequently wear Meadow Rue around their necks as a protective amulet; you can do the same. You can also add Meadow Rue to an amulet to increase its ability to attract love.

  Drinking a tea made from Meadow Rue before you meditate will help deepen your meditation and assist you in having visions of the future. To make the tea, add two tablespoons of the dried leaves to two cups of boiling water. Allow the mixture to steep for about ten minutes before straining it.

  To bless your home and fill it with a sense of peace and ease, place a bouquet of the dried or fresh flowers on your altar. Sprinkle the dried flowers around the inside of your home to raise the spiritual energy and help you feel nurtured and loved whenever you enter.

- **MEDICINAL USES:** The crushed stems and leaves are used to treat headaches. A poultice of the pounded leaves will reduce the swelling when applied to a sprain. It will also relieve the pain of bruises and help them fade more rapidly. Meadow Rue also makes a beautiful yellow dye.

Cascara Sagrada Bark

Rhammus purshiana

Reminds you of the sacred nature of all of life

- **CASCARA SAGRADA BARK WILL:** Help you prevail in legal matters, Attract abundance into your life, Protect your home

- **THE PLANT:** Cascara Sagrada bark is produced from a tree in the Buckthorn family native to the Pacific Northwest. The bark is aged for at least a year so that the active components become milder. Otherwise, freshly dried bark would produce too strong a laxative effect to use safely; it also induces vomiting.

- **HARNESS CASCARA SAGRADA BARK'S MAGICAL PROPERTIES:** If you have any legal matters pending in your life, sprinkle a few handfuls of the ground bark around the outside of your home to ensure success. Make sure you walk through the bark and get some on the soles of your shoes.

    Sprinkling the powder in your wallet and rubbing it on all of your money will ensure you of financial security.

- **MEDICINAL USES:** The aged bark is used as a mild laxative. A weak tea made from a teaspoon of ground aged Cascara Sagrada bark boiled in a quart of water for about ten minutes and then strained is useful in the treatment of constipation, colon disorders, liver problems, poor digestion, colitis, hemorrhoids, and skin problems.

Note: Large doses can cause nausea and vomiting. Cascara Sagrada bark should never be used if there is a fever present.

▶ Top: Endive, Middle: Meadow Rue,
Bottom: Cascara Sagrada Bark

Ginger *Zingiber officinale*

Brings you great success

- **GINGER WILL:** Make your magic more effective, Protect you and your home, Attract love

- **THE PLANT:** Ginger is said to be a native of Asia and is cultivated in the West Indies, Jamaica, and Africa. There are a variety of species, but the best roots are believed to come from the West Indies and are light brown in color. Ginger is a perennial root that creeps and spreads underground. It sends up two-foot-tall leaves that are narrow and bright green. The flowers rise directly from the root and are either white or yellow. Commercial Ginger is called black or white depending on whether it is peeled or unpeeled. The roots are harvested after the plant has died back.

- **HOW TO HARNESS GINGER'S MAGICAL PROPERTIES:** Placing Ginger on your altar will enhance any of your endeavors and bring great success to all of your activities.

  Chewing on Ginger before you work with any other herbs will increase their power and effectiveness.

  To attract passion and love, wear some dried Ginger in an amulet. To cleanse an area and dispel any negativity, burn some dried Ginger as incense.

- **MEDICINAL USES:** Ginger is an excellent treatment for diarrhea and upset stomach. It also helps stop seasickness and relieves gas pains and colic. Ginger tea is very calming and when mixed with Lemon and honey will soothe a sore throat and help break up a stuffy nose.

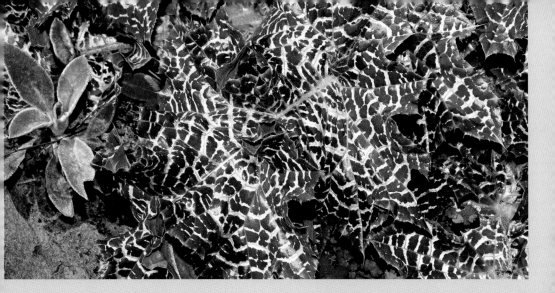

Blessed Thistle *Cnicus benedictus*

Is your connection to the Great Earth Mother

- **BLESSED THISTLE WILL:** Protect you from bad luck and harm, Bring you joy, Energize your life

- **THE PLANT:** Blessed Thistle grows about two feet high and is a reddish, slender plant that is barely able to keep upright under the weight of its leaves and flower heads. The flowers are pale yellow with a long, brown bristle. The entire plant, including the flowers, is covered with a thin, downy fuzz. Blessed Thistle is native to southern Europe, Asia, and the Mediterranean. It blooms from May through July.

- **HOW TO HARNESS BLESSED THISTLE'S MAGICAL PROPERTIES:** Blessed Thistle has long been associated with the tender, nurturing aspects of the goddess. Connecting with Blessed Thistle will allow you to connect with the wisdom and strength of the goddess. If you carry a sprig of it with you, it will bring you a profound sense of happiness, joy, and ease.

  Sprinkling the dried herb around the outside of your home will help you feel safe and repel envy and jealousy.

  Use Blessed Thistle in your wedding flowers to consecrate your marriage.

- **MEDICINAL USES:** Blessed Thistle can be used to purify the blood and improve circulation. Drinking a tea made from Blessed Thistle will improve memory. Drinking the tea will also help a woman stimulate milk production while nursing her baby.

Lemon

Citrus limonum

Refreshes you and purifies your home

- **LEMON WILL:** Purify your home, Attract love, Deepen friendships, Renew youth

- **THE PLANT:** The Lemon tree is indigenous to northern India and widely cultivated in the Mediterranean and other tropical countries. It is a small tree that seldom grows more than ten feet tall. The leaves range from dark green to almost purple. The flowers are very fragrant, and the plant usually has fruits and blossoms at the same time. The tree is evergreen and the leaves are oval shaped, ending with a spiny point. The branches frequently have large thorns.

- **HOW TO HARNESS LEMON'S MAGICAL PROPERTIES:** To remove any stale or negative energy left on your clothes, place some dried Lemon leaves in sachets and hang them in your closets.

  To ensure a restful night's sleep, put the dried leaves in your linen closet.

  To purify your home, crush the fresh leaves and allow the smell of the oil to fill your home. Or you can add the leaves to your mop water the next time you wash the floors.

  A few drops of Lemon oil added to your laundry is sure to attract friends and lovers. Putting some of the dried flowers in an amulet worn around your neck will strengthen its ability to call love.

- **MEDICINAL USES:** In the past, Lemon juice was used to cure scurvy. English law required ships to carry enough Lemons or Limes for each sailor to have an ounce of its juice daily. The juice is high in vitamins and is effective in bringing down a fever or soothing a sore throat.

Rowan

Pyrus aucuparia

Empowers you to do anything

- **ROWAN WILL:** Protect your home, your family, and you, Attract success, Expand your intuition, Invite love

- **THE PLANT:** Rowan is a small deciduous tree that grows up to thirty feet tall. It is native to North America and much of Europe. Rowan can also grow as a bush. It has slender, pointy leaves. Its bark is shiny and it has clusters of five-petalled white flowers, which bloom in May and June. The berries are bright red or orange and very bitter. Birds love the berries and widely distribute the seeds in their droppings.

- **HOW TO HARNESS ROWAN'S MAGICAL PROPERTIES:** Rowan's branches and leaves are very powerful when brought into the home, especially when they are shaped like a cross. They will ward off evil, attract success, invite love, and deepen your spiritual connection.

  When you are troubled by an issue, hold some leaves against your forehead and ask for guidance. When you go to harvest Rowan twigs, make sure you take a different route coming and going.

- **MEDICINAL USES:** Juice made from fresh Rowan berries is an excellent laxative. It can also be used as a gargle for sore throats and to soothe inflamed tonsils and alleviate hoarseness. Rowan berries are a good source of vitamins A and C. Jelly made from the berries will stop diarrhea. The bark can be brewed into a tea and used to treat vaginal and eye irritations.

Cayenne

Capsicum mimimum

Spices up your life

- **CAYENNE WILL:** Help you take action, Enliven your spiritual connection, Repel negativity

- **THE PLANT:** Cayenne is a shrublike perennial that grows from two to six feet tall. It is indigenous to warmer climates such as that in India. It produces a hot red chile pepper that is related to the bell pepper and is used to flavor spicy dishes and for a variety of medicinal purposes. The pepper is very pungent and loses its color if it isn't kept in a dark-colored receptacle.

- **HOW TO HARNESS CAYENNE'S MAGICAL PROPERTIES:** Using a few sprinkles of dried Cayenne in your cleaning water will help purify your home and repel negativity.
  Sprinkling it on your altar will deepen your spiritual connection.
  Adding Cayenne to other herbs will strengthen their impact.

- **MEDICINAL USES:** Cayenne is a powerful stimulant that will help relieve chronic constipation when taken in small doses. It will strengthen a weak digestive system and regulate your appetite. When rubbed on joints, a very weak tea made out of half a teaspoon of Cayenne boiled in a pint of Rose water for about ten minutes will help alleviate joint pain, but make sure you don't get it in your eyes or nose.
  Gargling with a weak tea helps relieve sore throats. Sprinkling Cayenne pepper in orange juice and drinking it several times a day will rapidly break up a cold.

Mugwort

Artemisa vulgaris

*Helps you connect with the spiritual nature
of all of life*

■ **MUGWORT WILL:** Enhance your dreams, Provide protection, Heal your mind, body, and spirit, Increase abundance

■ **THE PLANT:** Mugwort grows about three feet tall and has angular stems that are often a purplish hue. The plant is gathered when in flower and is then dried. In the past it was used to flavor table beer brewed by cottagers.

■ **HOW TO HARNESS MUGWORT'S MAGICAL PROPERTIES:** To increase the frequency of your dreams, help you remember them, and allow you to see into the future, make a dream pillow out of Mugwort. To make a dream pillow, simply stuff a small pillow with the dried herb and keep it near your head when you sleep.

Hang a dried Mugwort plant over your front door to keep out evil spirits and keep away elves and fairies.

Use a tea made from Mugwort to clean your crystals and magical instruments. To make the tea, add two tablespoons of dried Mugwort to two cups of boiling water and allow it to steep for about ten minutes before straining it. You can either simply wash your crystals and magical instruments in the tea or soak them overnight. I like to put my crystals in a bowl of the tea and place them outside on the night of the full moon, making sure the moonlight will shine on them.

To attract love and increase fertility, place a bit of the dried plant in an amulet.

■ **MEDICINAL USES:** Mugwort is a stimulant and is a wonderful tonic. It is frequently used to help women with menstrual complaints, including mood swings and cramps.

Bergamot *Mentha citrate*

Fills your life with abundance

- **BERGAMOT WILL:** Attract abundance, Deepen your meditations, Open you up to clairvoyant visions

- **THE PLANT:** Bergamot is a hardy perennial plant indigenous to North America. It grows two to three feet tall and has scruffy-looking scarlet blossoms. The leaves are best harvested during the spring and early summer. The flowers can be harvested whenever they are available. Bergamot bears a small acidic orange. The peel of this orange provides an essential oil that gives Earl Grey tea its distinctive flavor.

- **HOW TO HARNESS BERGAMOT'S MAGICAL PROPERTIES:** Feeling lonely? Rubbing the dried leaves or oil in your palms will attract friendship and love.

   To ensure a good night's sleep, fill a small pillow with the dried leaves and tuck it under your head.

   Putting a few dried leaves in your wallet or rubbing your money with the oil will ensure you always have enough money.

   To attract success and surround yourself with protection, justice, and compassion, sprinkle a few pinches of the dried leaves around your home and workplace.

   Using Bergamot oil in an aromatherapy lamp will fill your home with a sense of peace and well-being. It will also make your house smell wonderful.

- **MEDICINAL USES:** A tea made out of two tablespoons of dried Bergamot leaves simmered in a pint of boiling water for about ten minutes and then strained relieves nausea, menstrual pain, headaches, and insomnia. Inhaling the steam from the tea helps ease sore throats and loosen chest congestion. It is said that using the tea as a hair rinse will prevent hair from thinning. The tea is also used to help regulate appetite. A hot compress made of Bergamot leaves will draw out infection.

Flax Seed *Linum usitatissimum*

Helps you weave wonderful stories

FLAX SEED WILL: Keep you safe, Attract abundance, Assist you when you're performing healing rituals

THE PLANT: The Flax is a graceful plant with stunning turquoise blue blossoms that appear between May and August. The plant grows four feet tall and is native to most temperate and tropical regions of the world. It is an annual that will easily reseed itself. The plants produce a copious amount of shiny brown seeds. Flax was said to be a gift from the gods. Linen woven from flax has been found in ancient Egyptian tombs.

■ **HOW TO HARNESS FLAX SEED'S MAGICAL PROPERTIES:** Putting Flax seeds and Cayenne pepper in a box under your front porch will prevent evil from entering, while ensuring abundance and good fortune to all who enter. Flax is sacred to the goddess who weaves the web of life, so place an offering of Flax seeds on your altar. The presence of Flax seeds will assist with healing rituals.

To ensure success and abundance, place Flax seeds in your wallet. You can also place them under your bed to protect you while you sleep.

■ **MEDICINAL USES:** Flax seed oil is said to help lower blood cholesterol and blood pressure, increase vitality, reduce the threat of blood clots, protect against cancer, regulate blood sugar levels, ease the pain of arthritis, and treat eczema and psoriasis.

The crushed seeds make a useful poultice, either alone or with ground Mustard. Flax seeds are used to treat abscesses and other local infections.

Lotus Root *Nelumbo nucifera*

Reminds you of your godlike nature

- **LOTUS ROOT WILL:** Invite the blessings of the gods, Bring you good luck, Deepen your connection with your spirit

- **THE PLANT:** Lotus are members of the Water Lily family. They live in warm climates and don't like to be cold. The plants have round leaves that float elegantly on the water's surface. Some of the leaves stand a foot or two above the water. The flowers have long been considered sacred and stand several feet above the water. The plants offer edible leaves, roots, seeds, and flowers. When cut perpendicularly, the rhizomes make a beautiful geometric pattern. The roots can be up to four feet in length. The leaves often have beaded droplets of water that reflect rainbows.

- **HOW TO HARNESS LOTUS ROOT'S MAGICAL PROPERTIES:** The Lotus has long been a symbol of spirituality and enlightenment. If you are fortunate enough to be present when a Lotus is in blossom, the smell will impart protection and deepen your spiritual connection.

  Putting a Lotus root in your home will invite the blessings of the gods. A Lotus flower on your altar will deepen your connection with the Divine

  Burning a floating candle made to look like a Lotus flower in a bowl of water will bring you good luck and help you manifest your dreams.

- **MEDICINAL USES:** Lotus root strengthens the liver, heart, spleen, and stomach. It is said to prevent anemia in women, settle upset stomachs, and increase stamina when eaten regularly.

Quassia Root *Picrarena excelsa*

Reminds you of the power of love

QUASSIA ROOT WILL: Attract love, Deepen relationships, Heal a broken heart

THE PLANT: Quassia is indigenous to Jamaica. The tree grows fifty to a hundred feet tall and more than three feet in diameter. It flowers in October and November with a profusion of pale yellowish green blossoms. The fruit are the size of a pea and mature in January. They are black and very shiny. The wood is split into quarters. It is tough, has a very fine grain, and is white. The bark is thin, grayish brown, odorless, and very bitter. Quassia root is really the chips of the wood and bark of the tree.

■ HOW TO HARNESS QUASSIA ROOT'S MAGICAL PROPERTIES: To attract love or maintain an ongoing relationship, put some Quassia root in an amulet and wear it around your neck. If your goal is to stop your mate from straying and help improve communication in the relationship, place some Quassia root under your bed.

Adding tea made from the bark to your bathwater will help ease the pain of loss and heal a wounded heart. To make the tea, add two tablespoons of the bark to two cups of boiling water, allow the mixture to steep for about ten minutes, and then strain it before pouring it into your bathwater.

■ MEDICINAL USES: Quassia is found in shops in the form of chips or raspings. It has no smell but does have an intense bitter taste, which will always distinguish the real thing from cheap imitations. A tea made from the pure form can be used to kill flies. In small doses, it helps people when they are convalescing from serious illnesses. The tea will increase the appetite and improve digestion. It will also help break a fever.

Aloe

Aloe vera

Helps keep you young at heart

■ **ALOE WILL:** Prevent accidents, Ease the pain of loss, Protect you, Bring you good luck

■ **THE PLANT:** There are more than 350 species of Aloe. It is a perennial indigenous to islands in the Indian Ocean, the Caribbean, and Africa. Its fleshy leaves have spikes along the edges and grow approximately a foot high. Aloe prefers warm, sunny, and slightly dry locations and is a popular houseplant. It blooms only once in its lifetime.

■ **HOW TO HARNESS ALOE'S MAGICAL PROPERTIES:** Keep an Aloe plant in your home to bring you good fortune and to prevent accidents. You can protect your home from negativity and ward off evil by hanging a leaf over your front door. The essence of the plant will remind you to be patient and help you remember that you were meant to blossom and grow.

   To invoke the wisdom, love, and protection of the Moon Goddess, burn the dried leaves as incense. You can rub the juice of the leaves on your third eye (found in the middle of your forehead) to deepen your meditations and expand your awareness.

   When a loved one dies, place the plant on his or her grave to bring peace to everyone touched by the person's life.

■ **MEDICINAL USES:** The gel from the leaves can be used to heal burns, cuts, and scratches. Aloe is also useful in the treatment of eczema, acne, and dermatitis. It is believed Cleopatra used aloe on her skin to preserve her beauty and youth. The juice is also a wonderful tonic and can relieve stomach problems.

Sagebrush *Artemisia tridentata*

Helps you release anything that no longer serves you

■ **SAGEBRUSH WILL:** Purify your home and body, Chase away negativity, Help heal the land and your body

■ **THE PLANT:** Sagebrush is indigenous to the western part of the United States. The leaves are silver gray and fuzzy. The young stems are smooth, but as the plant ages, the bark begins to grow in long strips. The leaves are small, seldom growing more than two inches in length. Sagebrush has dense clusters of tiny yellow or cream-colored flowers. The seeds are tiny and black.

Navajo weavers boiled the leaves and flowers to create a yellow-gold dye. The Ute Indians wove the shredded bark into wicks for candles and made sacks from the bark and lined them with grass for storing food.

■ **HOW TO HARNESS SAGEBRUSH'S MAGICAL PROPERTIES:** Hanging Sagebrush near your front door will prevent negativity from entering your home.

To prevent hardships and repel negative people, place a piece of Sagebrush in an amulet and wear it around your neck or carry it in your medicine bag.

To ensure success and reduce stress before a meeting or ceremony, add tea made with Sagebrush to your bathwater. To make the tea, add two tablespoons of Sagebrush to two cups of boiling water, allow the mixture to steep for about ten minutes, and then strain.

When burned as incense, Sagebrush will raise the spiritual vibrations in your home.

Before you travel, place a few leaves in your suitcase. This will ensure you arrive safely and with your luggage.

■ **MEDICINAL USES:** When applied to bruises, poultices made from wet Sagebrush leaves reduce swelling and alleviate the pain.

Chinese Snake Gourd

Trichosanthes anguina

Helps you nurture your dreams

- **CHINESE SNAKE GOURD WILL:** Help you manifest your deepest dreams, Keep your home safe, Enhance your love life

- **THE PLANT:** The white blossoms of the Chinese Snake Gourd plant bloom at night. The plant produces gourds that make a delicious addition to the dinner table when they're young, but as they age, they become very bitter.

- **HOW TO HARNESS CHINESE SNAKE GOURD'S MAGICAL PROPERTIES:** To make your deepest dreams manifest, mindfully cut up a young Chinese Snake Gourd into small pieces as you think about your deepest dreams. Prayerfully stir-fry the gourd with your favorite spices while continuing to visualize yourself living your dreams. Silently and mindfully eat the dish, knowing your dreams will come true. You can also serve the dish to someone you care about to enhance your relationship with him or her.

  Cut up the Chinese Snake Gourd into small pieces and bury them around your property to create a circle of protection.

- **MEDICINAL USES:** Chinese Snake Gourd is rich in minerals such as magnesium, calcium, and phosphorus. The fruit is high in dietary fiber and contains many medicinal compounds that have been found useful in treating HIV. Chinese Snake Gourd is a folk cure for intestinal worms and is also used to induce vomiting after poisoning.

Marjoram *Origanum marjorana*

Brings joy and happiness into your life

- **MARJORAM WILL:** Attract love, Relieve grief, Protect your home, Repel evil

- **THE PLANT:** Marjoram is native to Portugal and is a hardy perennial. It grows up to two feet tall and is very aromatic. It has a fibrous, fleshy root. The stems are reddish, and the plant easily roots wherever it touches the ground. Marjoram blooms from June to September. The flowers vary in color from lilac to rose to white. To harvest Marjoram, cut the stem a few inches above the ground and hang the plant upside down in a shady place until it is dry. Harvest the leaves just before the flowers open for the best potency.

- **HOW TO HARNESS MARJORAM'S MAGICAL PROPERTIES:** For protection, sprinkle some of the dried leaves around your home—either inside or out. Use as many as your intuition tells you is appropriate. You can also hang a few sprigs over your front door to stop evil from entering your home.

  To attract love, wear dried leaves in an amulet.

  Adding some of the dried leaves to your bath-water will relieve grief.

- **MEDICINAL USES:** Rubbing the fresh or dried leaves on the temples and forehead will relieve tension headaches. Inhaling steam made from boiling the dried leaves is useful for treating ton-sillitis, bronchitis, asthma, and colds. An herbalist might soak two tablespoons of dried leaves in a pint of water overnight to make a mouthwash that will clear up infections. Chewing on the fresh leaves will ease the pain from a toothache.

Witch Hazel *Hamamelis virginana*

Removes the pain of loss and reminds you how to love

- **WITCH HAZEL WILL:** Provide protection, Locate lost objects, Balance emotions

- **THE PLANT:** Witch Hazel is a shrub that consists of several crooked trunks emanating from a single root. It grows ten to twelve feet high and has smooth gray bark. The leaves fall off in autumn and then yellow flowers appear in large clusters. They produce a black nut that contains oily white seeds. The seeds eject from the nuts with an explosive, loud pop when they are ripe.

- **HOW TO HARNESS WITCH HAZEL'S MAGICAL PROPERTIES:** The twigs and branches of Witch Hazel have been used to find water for centuries. They can also be used to locate lost objects. Hold a twig in your hand, focus on the object you want to find, and it will lead you to it.

  For protection, hang some Witch Hazel branches over your doorways.

If you've experienced a recent loss in your life, carry Witch Hazel leaves on your person. It will help you overcome your pain and balance emotions in general.

- **MEDICINAL USES:** The leaves and bark are wonderful pain relievers and can be used to treat external and internal bleeding. A poultice made from them will also reduce the swelling of bruises. Pond's Extract of Witch Hazel was commonly used in our grandmothers' days as a general household remedy for burns, scalds, and inflammatory conditions of the skin. To reduce the pain and swelling of mosquito bites, moisten a cotton ball with the extract and apply it to the affected spot.

Clove

Syzygium aromaticum

Brings great love and riches into your life

- **CLOVE WILL:** Attract abundance, Repel negativity, Prevent gossip, Encourage love

- **THE PLANT:** The best Cloves are grown on the Molucca Islands. Cloves grow on a small evergreen tree that is very aromatic. At the start of the rainy season, flowers appear on the end of the branches. The Cloves are the embryo of the seeds. Cloves are harvested while still embryos because if the seeds are allowed to mature, they have very little potency.

- **HOW TO HARNESS CLOVE'S MAGICAL PROPERTIES:** Burning Cloves as incense will increase the spiritual vibration of your home and dispel negativity.

  To deepen your friendship, put some Clove oil in your ritual cup, fill it with cider, and then share it with your friends. You can also use the oil as a blessing in a handfasting ceremony. (Handfasting is an ancient ritual often used in place of marriages.)

  To attract abundance, rub the oil in your wallet and on your money.

  Finally, you can use Cloves for protection. String them together on a red thread and hang it over your child's crib to protect him or her. If you hang it over your door, you will prevent people from gossiping about you.

- **MEDICINAL USES:** A few drops of Clove oil on a painful tooth will relieve the pain. You can also use it to help reduce the pain of cold sores and help them heal more rapidly. Clove oil is also a powerful antiseptic. Always keep it in a dark bottle stored in a cool place to maintain its strength.

  A tea made from ground Clove will help cure nausea and relieve gas.

Galangal Root

Alpinia officinarum

Helps you open up to limitless possibilities

- **GALANGAL ROOT WILL:** Attract abundance, Release negativity, Develop your psychic abilities

- **THE PLANT:** A native of China and Java, Galangal Root is a relative of the Ginger plant. It grows five feet tall and has long, narrow leaves. The flowers are white with deep red veins. The rhizomes are approximately three inches long and three-quarters of an inch thick. The roots are cut while fresh and have rings that are scars left from previous leaves.

- **HOW TO HARNESS GALANGAL ROOT'S MAGICAL PROPERTIES:** Galangal Root is known as a visionary herb and has a long history as a magical herb in African spirituality and voodoo. When chewed like gum, Galangal Root helps invoke visions and is often used to help contact one's spirit guides and helpers.

  In the past, it was used to break curses. To release negativity in your own home and protect the occupants, sprinkle a pinch of powdered Galangal Root around the outside of your house.

  If you wear an amulet of Galangal Root with a piece of silver or gold, it will attract abundance. To increase sexual satisfaction, place some of the root under your mattress.

- **MEDICINAL USES:** Galangal Root is a stimulant and is very useful in treating gas, vomiting, and an upset stomach. It is also a very effective treatment for seasickness. Homoeopaths use it as a stimulant and to treat fevers.

Blackberry *Rubus villosus*

Helps you connect with the goddess who lives within

- **BLACKBERRY WILL:** Ensure abundance, Attract good luck, Help you connect with loved ones who have died

- **THE PLANT:** Blackberry plants grow in the United States and Europe and may be trailing, arched, or upright. The canes (stems) are very flexible and often root where they touch the ground. When upright, they may grow to more than six feet tall. Blackberry plants bloom from mid- to late June with masses of white or pale pink flower clusters. The berries start ripening toward the middle of July. Ripe and unripe berries frequently appear on the plants at the same time.

- **HOW TO HARNESS BLACKBERRY'S MAGICAL PROPERTIES:** The five-petalled flowers are symbolic of the different stages of the goddess. The fruit, which turns from green to red to black, represents the stages of the goddess of maiden, mother, and crone.

Decorating your altar with the canes will invite abundance into your life. If you meditate underneath a Blackberry plant, you will be able to talk to the spirits of people who have passed over. Plant some in your garden to attract fairies.

To attract good luck, burn the dried leaves as incense. You can also sprinkle a small handful of the dried leaves around the outside of your home for protection.

- **MEDICINAL USES:** A tea made out of two tablespoons of dried leaves boiled in a cup of water for five minutes is a wonderful treatment for diarrhea and hemorrhoids. It can also be used as mouthwash to treat a sore throat, laryngitis, or sore gums.

A lotion made from cooled tea is useful for the treatment of acne and to help remove blackheads.

Saffron

Crocus sativus

Teaches you about true abundance

- **SAFFRON WILL:** Attract wealth, Help you see into the future, Call the wind, Invite joy and happiness

- **THE PLANT:** Saffron is a low ornamental plant with grasslike leaves and large lily-shaped flowers. It's indigenous to the Middle East and is now grown in many places around the world. The plants are grown for their yellow-orange stigmas, which are picked by hand and then dried to be used as a spice in cooking. Each flower has only three stigmas, and it takes more than fourteen thousand stigmas to produce just one ounce of Saffron, which is the reason why the spice is so expensive. It's used to season dishes such as paella, risotto, and bouillabaisse, among many others.

- **HOW TO HARNESS SAFFRON'S MAGICAL PROPERTIES:** Having Saffron in your herb collection will invite wealth and happiness into your life.

  To increase your clairvoyant abilities and help you see more clearly into your future, sprinkle a little Saffron on your tongue or drink a tea made with a small amount of it before meditating.

  If you'd like to ensure a long and happy marriage, sprinkle a little Saffron onto the sheets of your marriage bed.

  Burning Saffron as incense invites the power of the goddess into your life.

- **MEDICINAL USES:** Saffron is used to help calm jittery nerves, reduce fevers, and soothe an upset stomach.

  It will also help relieve menstrual cramps and stop excessive bleeding.

Goldenseal

Hydrastis canadensis

Brings out the best in you

- **GOLDENSEAL WILL:** Attract money, Heal your mind, body, and spirit, Release negativity

- **THE PLANT:** Goldenseal is a small perennial herb that lives in the shaded undergrowth in forested areas of Canada and the eastern United States. It is a member of the Buttercup family, and its berries resemble Raspberries. It has flowers in April, and the flower stalks appear before the leaves do. It has a fibrous rhizome that spreads horizontally. The roots are yellow and have been used by Native Americans to make dye.

- **HOW TO HARNESS GOLDENSEAL'S MAGICAL PROPERTIES:** To attract money, add a small piece of dried Goldenseal to an amulet.

    It will strengthen the effect of other herbs, and when a piece of the root is held in your right hand, it will make any magical ritual you perform more effective. You can also put a piece of the root on your altar to help you deepen your connection with your spirit.

    Sprinkle some dried Goldenseal in your mop water to purify your home and release any negativity. When burned as incense, it will deepen your meditations.

- **MEDICINAL USES:** Goldenseal root is most effective for treating a cold after your nose has become stuffy. It will help the mucus break up quickly. As a tea, it settles the stomach and aids in digestion. Goldenseal helps strengthen the immune system so the body can better fend off infections.

Mullein *Verbascum thapsus*

Helps you feel courageous and adventurous

- **MULLEIN WILL:** Protect you and your home, Enhance your curiosity, Give you courage, Help you see into the future

- **THE PLANT:** Mullein grows all over Europe, throughout the temperate regions of Asia as far as the Himalayas, and in North America. It is very abundant in the eastern United States and is often considered a weed. It is a hardy biennial that puts out bright yellow flowers in July and August of the second year. The leaves are hairy and the flowers spiral up over the plant on a single stalk that grows up to six feet tall.

- **HOW TO HARNESS MULLEIN'S MAGICAL PROPERTIES:** The leaves should be collected during the first year and the flowers when they are fully open the second year. Growing Mullein in your garden will bless your garden and home. Smoking the dried leaves in a pipe will help you connect with the ancient knowledge of the ancestors.

You can use the fresh flower stalk as a torch if you dip it in wax. You can then use it to bless outdoor rituals and call upon the spirit guides and angel helpers.

To prevent nightmares, place the stalk under your pillow.

Sprinkling a few dried Mullein leaves in your shoes will prevent you from straying off your spiritual path.

To feel stronger, have greater confidence, and make life-enriching decisions, bathe in water to which you've added some Mullein tea. To make the tea, add two tablespoons of the dried leaves to two cups of boiling water, steep for at least ten minutes, and then strain.

- **MEDICINAL USES:** A tea made from the leaves and flowers will strengthen the digestive system and stop internal bleeding. It will also help relieve congestion in the lungs and soothe a sore throat.

Adder's Tongue *Ophioglossum pusillum*

Brings love to all the shadowy areas of your life

ADDER'S TONGUE WILL: Heal emotional, spiritual, and physical wounds, Create a protective environment, Deepen your spiritual connection, Enhance your writing abilities

■ **THE PLANT:** Adder's Tongue grows in the vast carpets of leaves covering the forest floor. It is also called the Trout Lily because of its speckled leaves. It originates from a small bulb and is easily cultivated, although it is endangered in some areas.

■ **HOW TO HARNESS ADDER'S TONGUE'S MAGICAL PROPERTIES:** Adder's Tongue's dappled leaves blend into the shadows of the forest floor. Undaunted by its dark environment, the spirit of this plant is courageous and strong. Gather the leaves and flowers early in the summer and dry them for use all year long.

To harness some of Adder's Tongue's strength and courage, crush the dried leaves and put two tablespoons into a pint of cold water. Slowly bring to a boil and then allow the mixture to cool. After the herbs have settled, dip a clean washcloth into the unstrained tea, wring it out, and apply it to your forehead. It will help quiet your mind and soothe your soul. You can also strain the mixture and add it to your bathwater.

To create a ring of protection, take a few pinches of the dried leaves, put them in the palm of your hand, and sprinkle them around the outside of your home.

If you're feeling blocked mentally or just need a creative boost, place the dried flowers in your journal or hang a bunch near your computer.

■ **MEDICINAL USES:** Adder's Tongue makes a good poultice when applied to sprains and bruises. According to old legends, soaking the dried leaves in cold water, applying them directly to wounds, and then burying the leaves outside would heal wounds.

Bitter Melon *Momordica charantia*

Infuses you with the energy of creation

- **BITTER MELON WILL:** Help you create what you want, Protect your home, Create community

- **THE PLANT:** Bitter Melon is native to tropical areas including East Africa, Asia, parts of the Amazon, and the Caribbean. It is cultivated throughout South America as a food and medicine. It's an annual, climbing vine with long-stalked leaves. The fruit looks like a warty gourd and is about the size of a small cucumber. The young fruit is emerald green and turns orange-yellow when ripe.

- **HOW TO HARNESS BITTER MELON'S MAGICAL PROPERTIES:** Bitter Melon is a member of the Gourd family and as such symbolically represents the crucible that holds the creative energy of the universe.

  Place the fruit on your altar to assist you in manifesting your desires. Write your hopes, dreams, and desires on its surface. When it has dried, bury it in your garden and know your re-

quests will soon manifest. If the Bitter Melon rots while it is drying on your altar, it is an indication that you need to review your beliefs and change them so you can manifest what you want.

- **MEDICINAL USES:** Bitter Melon has been used by healers in the Amazon to treat diabetes, intestinal gas, and measles. It promotes menstruation and can also be used to topically treat sores and eczema. Indigenous healers have used it for hypertension, malaria, fevers, and headaches. A tea made from it is very bitter, but it does expel worms and parasites in adults and children.

Larch *Larix europaea*

Fills your heart with joy

- **LARCH WILL:** Protect you from evil spells, Improve your self-esteem, Assure you of success

- **THE PLANT:** : Larch is indigenous only to central Europe, although it has been cultivated throughout Europe and North America. The leaves are bright green in the spring and can be used in salads. The tree grows up to 140 feet tall and is very bushy. The pinecones ripen in the fall. The wood is highly valued for its waterproof qualities and its resistance to fire.

- **HOW TO HARNESS LARCH'S MAGICAL PROPERTIES:** Place a few Larch pinecones on your altar to enhance your self-confidence. You might also put a few drops of Larch oil in your bathwater to relieve self-doubts.

   To protect your home and fill it will love, joy, and compassion, put a few drops of the oil on a dust rag and use it to clean your house.

To create a good luck charm, put a few Larch needles in an amulet worn around your neck.

   Finally, to help you expand your ability to love yourself and have greater compassion, rub a few drops of Larch Bach Flower Remedy on your heart daily.

- **MEDICINAL USES:** Larch has been used as a stimulant and diuretic. When combined with beeswax, the oil is a useful external treatment for chronic eczema and psoriasis. Larch is used as a Bach Flower Remedy that is given to people who doubt themselves and fear failure.

Coriander

Coriandrum sativum

Fills your life with love

- **CORIANDER WILL:** Attract love, Fill your home with peace and protection, Reduce strife

- **THE PLANT:** Coriander is an annual that grows one to three feet tall with slender branches and shiny green leaves. Its flowers are pretty and delicate. They look like lacy umbrellas and are a pale mauve that is almost white. The seeds look like tiny balls and have a disagreeable scent when first harvested, but the longer they dry, the better they smell. Coriander was brought to the East by the Romans and is a very popular herb in Peru and Egypt.

- **HARNESS CORIANDER'S MAGICAL PROPERTIES:** Coriander has been used as a love potion for centuries. The ancient Chinese believed it had the power to make a person immortal, and the Egyptians used it as a funeral offering.

  If you hang a wreath of fresh Coriander leaves tied with a purple ribbon in your home, it will bring love, laughter, and peace into your house. It will also help people who have fought in the past to get along quite amicably.

  Worn as an amulet, the leaves will keep you safe and attract love. It will also help you let go of painful memories from the past.

- **MEDICINAL USES:** Coriander is mainly used as a flavoring in other medicines to make them more palatable. Tea made from the seeds is said to help relieve colic in small children.

Lemongrass

Cymbopogon citratus

Expands your horizons

- **LEMONGRASS WILL:** Chase away snakes, Enhance sexual satisfaction, Deepen your psychic abilities, Purify your home

- **THE PLANT:** Lemongrass was originally indigenous to India. It is used extensively in Thai cooking and is a very popular tea. It is cultivated all over the world but grows best in warm climates. Lemongrass is cultivated for the oil made from the grass and for the dried leaves, which are used for tea. It is a tall, clumping grass with a broad leaf. It grows about three and a half feet tall, and the leaves are rough to the touch.

- **HARNESS LEMONGRASS'S MAGICAL PROPERTIES:** To ensure that snakes don't come around, plant a clump of Lemongrass at the edge of your property.

  Drinking a tea made from a cup of dried leaves steeped in a quart of boiling water for at least ten minutes and then strained will improve your psychic abilities. Adding the tea to your bathwater before having sex will increase your sexual pleasure. Using the tea in your cleaning solution when you clean your home will purify it.

- **MEDICINAL USES:** Lemongrass is considered a diuretic. A tea made from its leaves is a wonderful tonic and stimulates the body's innate healing process. It also promotes good digestion. Lemongrass brewed with Black Pepper will relieve menstrual troubles and nausea. It can also be used as an insect repellent.

Hawthorn Berries

Crataegus oxyacantha

Shows you how to be truly happy

- **HAWTHORN BERRIES WILL:** Protect your home, Bring you happiness

- **THE PLANT:** Hawthorn is a common thorny bush that grows up to five feet tall on hillsides and in sunny wooded areas of North America, Europe, western Asia, and northern Africa. It blossoms in May, producing clusters of bright red berries. Hawthorn leaves are usually shiny but may grow in a variety of shapes and sizes. The plant is considered sacred, and it is believed it furnished the crown of thorns placed on Jesus. Hawthorns live to a very old age, some as old as hundreds of years.

- **HARNESS HAWTHORN BERRIES' MAGICAL PROPERTIES:** A tea made from Hawthorn berries and then sprinkled around the outside of your home will protect you and prevent any evil influences from entering. Using a bit of the tea in your mop water will purify your home and raise the spiritual vibration. To make the tea, add about a handful of Hawthorn berries to two cups of boiling water and allow the mixture to steep for at least ten minutes.

  Place a few of the berries on your altar as a good luck charm. Wearing a few berries in an amulet will ensure you of happiness.

- **MEDICINAL USES:** Hawthorn berries have been used since the Middle Ages to treat heart conditions. Studies have shown that the berries increase blood flow to the heart and brain, protect the heart from irregular beats, enhance the strength of the heart's contractions, and mildly lower blood pressure. A tea made from both the flowers and the berries cures sore throats.

▶ Top: Coriander, Middle: Lemongrass, Bottom: Hawthorn Berries

Deer's Tongue

Liatris odoratissima

Shows you the power of gentleness

- **DEER'S TONGUE WILL:** Attract a lover, Increase your psychic abilities, Empower you to succeed

- **THE PLANT:** Deer's Tongue is common throughout North America and grows best in Pine forests that have been kept open by fires. The leaves are long and narrow with a streak of reddish purple down the middle, making them look like a deer's tongue, hence the name. They smell like Vanilla when crushed. In August and September, small purple flowers appear in dense clusters from the base.

- **HOW TO HARNESS DEER'S TONGUE'S MAGICAL PROPERTIES:** To increase your psychic powers, crush the fresh leaves and inhale the warm vanilla scent that is released.

    Placing dried crushed leaves on your bed will ensure you of a very satisfying sexual encounter.

    To fill your home with a sense of peace, burn the leaves as incense.

    If you add a tea to your bathwater made from two tablespoons of dried leaves boiled vigorously in a quart of water for at least ten minutes and then strained, you will feel refreshed and empowered to do anything you want.

    To attract love and repel negativity, sprinkle the dried leaves around the rooms of your home.

- **MEDICINAL USES:** The plant has numerous medicinal purposes. Although bitter, a tea made from its leaves is effective in reducing fevers, soothing irritated mucous membranes, and cleansing the blood by promoting perspiration.

Amaranth

Amaranthus hydrochondriacus

Deepens your connection to spirit

- **AGARIC WILL:** Promote long life, Make you bulletproof, Deepen your connection to the gods and goddesses

- **THE PLANT:** Amaranth is also called the flower of immortality. It is an annual herb that has a cluster of flowers and blooms in August. It's also grown in Asia and the Americas as a food source. The Aztec used it in many of their ceremonies, and the Hopi Indians used it to make a dye for their ceremonial robes.

- **HOW TO HARNESS AMARANTH'S MAGICAL PROPERTIES:** Wearing a wreath made of Amaranth flowers will assist you in connecting with your spirit in a profound manner and is also said to impart invisibility. To make a wreath, you can wind the flowers around a circle made from a Willow branch or a thin piece of Bamboo.

  To mend a broken heart, place dried Amaranth flowers on your altar. Doing so will also promote long life.

  There is an old ritual you can use to protect yourself from being shot by a bullet. On a Friday night, right before a full moon, pull up an Amaranth plant, roots and all. Say a prayer of thanks to the spirit of the plant and leave some Tobacco and cornmeal as an offering. Wrap the whole plant in a white cloth and wear it near your heart. Legend says that as long as you are wearing it, you will be bulletproof.

  Sprinkling Amaranth flowers on a person's grave will help him or her pass over into the light.

- **MEDICINAL USES:** To promote healing, place a wreath of Amaranth flowers on the head of a sick person. A tea made from the Amaranth grain will settle the stomach and relieve gas.

Holly

Ilex aquifolium

Helps you plant the seeds of success in all areas of your life

■ **HOLLY WILL:** Protect your home, Bring good luck, Create balance, Enhance your dream life

■ **THE PLANT:** Holly is an evergreen shrub or tree that grows up to forty feet tall. It is native to most of the central and southern parts of Europe and also grows in North America. Its glossy green leaves and red berries have been part of the winter solstice celebration for centuries.

■ **HOW TO HARNESS HOLLY'S MAGICAL PROPERTIES:** Hang a bunch of Holly next to your bed to ensure pleasant dreams and invite visions and wisdom into your dreamscape.

To protect yourself and your home, plant Holly on your property. Hanging some Holly on a wall is believed to prevent lightning from striking your home.

Before the winter solstice, decorate your altar with Holly and set aside some time to decide what you want to create in the coming year. Then perform a ceremony to celebrate all of your gifts and invite happiness, joy, and success into the new year. You could light some candles, invite friends over for dinner, play some music, and sing and dance—whatever feels right to you.

■ **MEDICINAL USES:** When the leaves are soaked in vinegar for two days and then ground up, they can be used as a poultice for corns. Holly leaves have been used to treat fevers, bronchitis, pneumonia, influenza, pleurisy, and smallpox.

Note: The berries are very toxic and cause vomiting as soon as they are swallowed.

Fennel Seed

Foeniculum vulgare

Improves your memory

FENNEL SEED WILL: Protect your home, Purify your mind, body, and spirit, Give you courage

THE PLANT: Fennel is a hardy perennial that grows wild in most of temperate Europe and is considered indigenous to the shores of the Mediterranean. Fennel seeds are widely used in Italian cooking. Fennel has a thick, perennial rootstock that grows four to five feet long. The bright golden flowers produce thirteen to twenty rays and bloom in July and August.

HOW TO HARNESS FENNEL SEED'S MAGICAL PROPERTIES: Stuff a jar with Fennel leaves and then fill it with olive oil. Allow it to age for at least a month. Use the oil to encourage healing by rubbing it on the affected area.

To purify and protect your residence, sprinkle some of the oil around the inside of your home.

Use the seeds as incense to bless any new activities. Adding a few seeds to your bathwater will strengthen your body, help you relax, and clear your mind.

MEDICINAL USES: Fennel tea has a very calming effect and is made by pouring half a pint of boiling water on a teaspoonful of bruised Fennel seeds and steeping for approximately ten minutes before straining it. It will settle an upset stomach and relieve gas.

Balm of Gilead *Commiphora opbalasamum*

Brings a sense of wonder and ease to your life

- **BALM OF GILEAD WILL:** Attract love, Bless your home, Help heal your mind and spirit, Quiet your mind

- **THE PLANT:** The true Balm of Gilead is a rare desert shrub. A hardy evergreen that grows to four feet tall, Populus basamifera is often used as Balm of Gilead. The leaves are highly aromatic. It bears clusters of pink flowers in the late summer through the early fall. Pick the leaves before the flowers open and collect flower buds whenever they are available.

- **HOW TO HARNESS BALM OF GILEAD'S MAGICAL PROPERTIES:** Balm of Gilead is a powerful love charm. Carry it in your pocket, your wallet, or an amulet worn around your neck to attract love into your life.

  To make a love potion, fill a glass with flower buds, cover them with red wine, and allow them to stand overnight. The next day, strain the wine. You can serve it to your potential partner with a lovingly prepared dinner.

  To cleanse your home of negativity and help manifest your dreams, burn the dried leaves or flowers as incense.

  An infusion of Balm of Gilead can be made by packing a jar with dried leaves and flowers and then filling it with any cold-pressed, light-colored oil. Leave it in a warm place for two weeks and then strain. You can use the oil to anoint people during spiritual healings or sprinkle a few drops in each room to bless your home. A few drops added to your bathwater will help you relax and unwind after a long day.

- **MEDICINAL USES:** Balm of Gilead has few medical properties, but it has been used to treat urinary tract infections. A tea made from two teaspoons of the closed buds boiled in a cup of water will ease the congestion from bronchitis, soothe sore throats, and quiet coughs.

Turmeric

Curcuma longa

Purifies your heart and your mind

◀ **TURMERIC WILL:** Protect your home, Purify a sacred space, Deepen your spiritual connection

◀ **THE PLANT:** Turmeric is native to southern Asia and parts of India. It is a perennial plant with large, tuberous roots. The leaves are about two feet long. The flowers are erect and yellow. The plant is propagated by root cuttings. When the roots are dried, they can be ground into a fine lemon-yellow powder. It has a particular odor much milder than that of Ginger but somewhat similar.

It is very useful in coloring food without adding a lot of flavor.

◀ **HOW TO HARNESS TURMERIC'S MAGICAL PROPERTIES:** Place a root near your front door for protection. When placed on your altar, it will help deepen your spiritual connection.

To purify your home and impart a feeling of peace and sanctity, burn some dried Turmeric as incense. When ground up and mixed with coarse sea salt, the root can be scattered to purify and bless an area.

◀ **MEDICINAL USES:** Turmeric is seldom used in medicine today except as a coloring for other remedies. In the past, it was used to purify and cleanse the liver in people who had jaundice. Its chief use today is as an ingredient in curry powder.

Vervain

Verbena officinalis

Teaches you how to act from love

- **VERVAIN WILL:** Chase away negative spirits, Attract love, Calm emotions, Instill peace and happiness

- **THE PLANT:** Vervain is found growing by roadsides and in sunny pastures in Europe and North America. It is a perennial and has many small, pale lilac flowers. The name Vervain is derived from Celtic words that mean "to drive away." The plant has little or no smell. It must be harvested before it flowers and dried immediately because it spoils quickly.

- **HOW TO HARNESS VERVAIN'S MAGICAL PROPERTIES:** To attract love and keep yourself safe from all harm, carry a small piece of Vervain on your body or in your pocket.

  Bury some Vervain in your garden near your house and not only will your garden flourish but money will also begin to flow freely into your life in miraculous ways.

  To instill a sense of peace and well-being, scatter the dried herb around you. Rubbing it in your hands will calm your emotions and those of anyone you speak to.

  Roman priests used the herb to sanctify and cleanse their temples. Adding a small amount of Vervain to your cleaning water will purify your home and altar.

  A bunch of the herb placed over a child's bed will ensure a happy and successful life and will instill a love of learning in them.

- **MEDICINAL USES:** Vervain is said to be useful for more than thirty complaints. It helps reduce fevers, soothes ulcers, and treats pleurisy. As a poultice, it helps relieve the pain of rheumatism, headaches, earaches, and neuralgia.

Nutmeg *Myristica fragrans*

Deepens your ability to enjoy life

■ **NUTMEG WILL:** Bring you good luck, Ward off illness, Keep your joints healthy, Attract happiness, joy, and abundance

■ **THE PLANT:** The Nutmeg tree grows to about twenty-five feet tall with smooth gray-brown bark. The tree flowers three times a year, producing both male and female flowers. It takes nine years for the tree to produce its first crop. It will continue to yield a crop with little or no attention for seventy-five years. The seed, or Nutmeg, is harvested by hand using a long stick with a hook on the end. The nut and the Mace (the red, brittle covering of the nut) are separated and then dried separately.

■ **HOW TO HARNESS NUTMEG'S MAGICAL PROPERTIES:** Carrying Nutmeg in your pocket or your purse will bring you good luck, ward off negativity, and attract abundance.

To prevent negativity from entering, sprinkle ground Nutmeg around the outside of your home.

Listen to your intuition to tell you how much Nutmeg to use.

Hanging the nut over a baby's crib is said to stop teething pain.

Placing a nut under your mattress will ensure that neither partner strays.

■ **MEDICINAL USES:** Both Nutmeg and Mace are used to relieve gas and the nausea arising from other drugs. It will also stop vomiting. Grated Nutmeg mixed with beeswax makes an excellent ointment for hemorrhoids. It is said that taking a bath in tea made from boiling the nut cut in half will prevent arthritis and relieve joint pain.

Couch Grass

Agropyrum repens

Teaches you the importance of tenacity

- **COUCH GRASS WILL:** Protect your home, Assure you of success, Strengthen other magic

- **THE PLANT:** Couch Grass is a tenacious plant that isn't a favorite of farmers. It has slender, creeping underground stems, or rhizomes, that will invade an area very rapidly. It is abundant in fields and waste areas across Europe, North and South America, Asia, and Australia. Along the seashore, it is very useful in preventing sand dunes from shifting and eroding. The roots have a sweet taste and at one time were dried and ground into flour to make bread.

- **HOW TO HARNESS COUCH GRASS'S MAGICAL PROPERTIES:** Because of Couch Grass's tenacity, it is a very useful addition to any magical endeavor. Braid its roots and drape them around the edge of your altar and call upon its energy of tenacity.

    Hanging a wreath made from the roots and the grass over your front door will protect your home.

    If you have financial worries, put a few blades of this grass in your wallet to attract abundance. To attract a perfect job, put a bunch of the grass on top of your resume and place it on your altar overnight.

- **MEDICINAL USES:** The juice of the grass can be rubbed on painful joints to relieve the pain. A tea made from the roots acts as a diuretic and will purify the blood. Consumed on a daily basis, the tea acts as a wonderful tonic. Finally, dogs instinctively know to seek out this grass when they have an upset stomach.

Horehound

Marrubium vulgare

Acts as a stabilizing force in your life

■ **HOREHOUND WILL:** Bring balance, Promote creativity, Invite healing

■ **THE PLANT:** Horehound is a bushy perennial plant that lives throughout Europe and North America. The leaves are wrinkled and covered with white, fuzzy hairs, so they almost look like wool. They have a musky smell that diminishes when they're dried. Horehound is covered with white flowers from June through September.

■ **HOW TO HARNESS HOREHOUND'S MAGICAL PROPERTIES:** Horehound was once used as protection from witchcraft and magical spells. When the dried plant is used as incense, it will help you focus and remove any mental blocks you're having to access your inner wisdom and creativity.

If your home has been a place of contention lately, arrange some cut Horehound flowers around it. They will create a peaceful and loving environment and help you achieve personal balance.

When Horehound is worn in an amulet, it will facilitate healing.

■ **MEDICINAL USES:** Horehound is widely used to quiet coughs because it helps to break up congestion. It is also helpful in the treatment of asthma and bronchitis. A warm tea made from its flowers and leaves calms an upset stomach and stimulates the appetite. Combined with beeswax, it makes a wonderful treatment for eczema and psoriasis.

Bloodroot

Sanguinaria canadensis

Purifies your thoughts and expands your ability to love

- **BLOODROOT WILL:** Repel negativity, Attract love, Help you be more positive and proactive

- **THE PLANT:** Bloodroot is a perennial and one of the earliest and most beautiful of the spring flowers. It is native to North America. It has a lovely white flower and produces only a single leaf. When the leaf first appears, it is wrapped around the flower bud and is grayish green. After the plant flowers, the leaves get bigger and the undersides become paler with prominent veins. The roots are harvested in the fall and must be thoroughly dried before you store them, or they will deteriorate rapidly.

- **HARNESS BLOODROOT'S MAGICAL PROPERTIES:** Hanging a dried root over the entrance to your home will protect your house and make sure only loving, kind, and helpful people enter. Carrying a small piece of the root in your wallet will attract abundance and love.

  The dark red roots are called king roots and will give you the courage to face anything. They'll also help you release limiting beliefs. Put a dried king root under your pillow and sleep with it there for a month. At the end of the month, bury the root in your garden with the intention of letting go of anything that no longer serves you. Reaffirm that release every morning as you look in the mirror, and watch your life transform!

- **MEDICINAL USES:** Bloodroot is poisonous but can be used to topically treat ringworm. Native Americans traditionally used the root as a dye for their clothing and bodies.

Eucalyptus

Eucalyptus globules

Helps you breathe easier and release fear

- **EUCALYPTUS WILL:** Help with all forms of healing, Protect your home, Enhance your financial success

- **THE PLANT:** Eucalyptus is native to Australia, Africa, India, and southern Europe. It is a very fast-growing tree with leathery leaves that contain an aromatic oil. When the flowers bud, they're covered with a cuplike membrane, which drops off when the flowers open. The fruit are also cup shaped and contain numerous tiny seeds.

- **HARNESS EUCALYPTUS'S MAGICAL PROPERTIES:** The dried flowers make a powerful stuffing for poppets (magical dolls) to be used for healing emotional, spiritual, and physical ailments.

  Sprinkle the oil around the inside of your home to raise the spiritual vibration and dispel any residual negative energy.

  If you're feeling financially strapped, rub the oil on your money to ensure abundance.

  To ward off illness, hang the dried leaves over your front door. If you sleep with the leaves under your pillow, they will induce sweet dreams and prevent colds.

- **MEDICINAL USES:** Eucalyptus oil is one of the most powerful antiseptics. It's also believed to increase cardiac strength. When the oil is added to boiling water, the steam helps break up a chest cold.

Cardamom Seed

Elettario caramomum

Spices up your life

■ **CARDAMOM SEED WILL:** Increase libido, Deepen the passion in your relationship, Attract love

■ **THE PLANT:** Cardamom is native to southern India. It is a large perennial herb with thick, fleshy roots and silky leaves that are one to two and a half feet long. The small yellow flowers spread horizontally along the ground. The seeds of the fruit are aromatic and are collected before they're fully ripe. Once fully ripened, they are not as flavorful.

■ **HARNESS CARDAMOM SEED'S MAGICAL PROPERTIES:** Crush a few seeds and place them in your favorite bottle of wine. Then serve the wine to your beloved to increase the passion between the two of you and enhance your sexual experience.

To attract love, you can use the seeds in a love amulet or add them to a sachet you hang in your closet. The seeds are a wonderful addition to incense. You can burn the incense to fill your home with a warm feeling of love, safety, and comfort.

■ **MEDICINAL USES:** Cardamom seeds are often brewed into a tea to help relieve indigestion and alleviate gas. You can chew the seeds to get rid of bad breath. They are also thought to be useful in the treatment of colic and headaches.

Cardamom seeds are often combined with Orange zest, Cinnamon, Cloves, and Caraway and used in cooking.

▶ Top: Bloodroot, Middle: Eucalyptus, Bottom: Cardamom Seed

Star Anise *Illicium verum*

Shows you how to honor your deepest dreams

- **STAR ANISE WILL:** Bring good luck, Expand your psychic powers, Ensure a good night's sleep

- **THE PLANT:** Star Anise is an evergreen shrub native to China and Vietnam. Its seedpods are shaped like a star, having from five to ten points. The seedpods, which are hard and brownish red, are picked before the fruit ripens and then dried in the sun. Star Anise was first introduced to Europe in the seventeenth century. An oil is extracted from the seedpods using steam and is often used in beverages. In Japan, because of the symbolic nature of the star-shaped fruit, the tree is often planted near tombs and around temples.

- **HOW TO HARNESS STAR ANISE'S MAGICAL PROPERTIES:** For protection and to bring good luck, place a whole fruit in each of the four corners of your property. Placing a fruit on your altar will increase the spiritual vibrations and help spread that sacred energy to enfold your entire home.

  To ensure a good night's sleep and invite prophetic dreams, sleep with some Star Anise under your pillow.

- **MEDICINAL USES:** The fruit is used to treat colic and rheumatism. It has a calming effect and is a diuretic.

  It will relieve gas and calm an upset stomach.

Peony *Paeonia officinalis*

Shows you how to blossom fully in your own life

PEONY WILL: Protect your home, Get rid of negative spirits, Bring you good luck

■ **THE PLANT:** Peonies grow two to four feet tall and thrive in sunny locations and well-drained soil. They tolerate many types of soils, but they do best in soil rich in organic matter. They have a wonderful smell and their blooms are magnificent. They are a hardy perennial that die back each fall. Their buds for the coming year form underground on the crown in colder climates. The Peony is native to southern Europe, but it has been naturalized in the colder north.

■ **HOW TO HARNESS PEONY'S MAGICAL PROPERTIES:** For good luck, plant some Peonies in your garden. Doing so will also fill your home with happiness and protect you and your family.

To banish negative spirits from your home and ensure that they never return, place a vase of Peony flowers inside your house. You can also burn the dried root as incense to bless your home and deepen your meditations.

■ **MEDICINAL USES:** The plant is named after Paeon, the physician to the Greek gods. Hippocrates used Peony to treat epilepsy. The root is useful for encouraging menstruation and can be used to expel the placenta following childbirth. The root is also said to relieve the symptoms of menopause.

Bay Leaf

Laurus nobilis

Deepens your awareness of your divinity

■ **BAY LEAF WILL:** Enhance any magical endeavors, Strengthen your spiritual connection, Increase creativity, Bless and protect your home

■ **THE PLANT:** Bay Leaf comes from the Sweet Bay Laurel tree, which has been grown for as long as historical records have been kept. The tree grows fifteen to twenty feet tall in mild climates. It grows very slowly and does well in containers. The leaves are a vivid green and are rather stiff with a sharp point. They have a very distinctive odor.

■ **HOW TO HARNESS BAY LEAF'S MAGICAL PROPERTIES:** To increase your psychic powers, purify your home, and enhance any magical rituals you perform, burn the dried leaves as incense.

Bay Leaf can also be used to increase your imagination and creativity. Put the leaves under your pillow at night to ensure inspiration, deepen your visions, and invite powerful dreams.

Kitchen shops often sell wreaths made from Bay Leaves, and hanging one in your home will bring you wisdom and inspiration, as well as invite abundance and justice into your house.

Bay Leaf is often used during Yuletime ceremonies to bring the light of summer into the darkest time of the year. A leaf carried on your person will ward off curses and negative energy.

Finally, it's said that if you make a wish while holding a Bay Leaf, it will always come true.

■ **MEDICINAL USES:** Adding a tea made from Bay Leaves to bathwater will relieve aching limbs and can help treat sprains and rheumatic joints. An herbalist might mix Bay oil with honey and use it as a salve for itching, sprains, bruises, skin irritations, and rheumatic pain.

Sassafras *Sassafras officinale*

Ensures good health

SASSAFRAS WILL: Improve your health, Chase away the blues, Attract abundance

THE PLANT: Sassafras is a tree native to eastern North America. It grows from twenty to fifty feet tall. The bark ranges from gray to brown and orange. The leaves are oval and about five inches long. The greenish yellow flowers are small. The roots are large and woody. The bark often has a soft cork layer and beneath that there are small crystals. The bark and the roots have a very fragrant odor and a somewhat bitter and harsh taste.

■ **HOW TO HARNESS SASSAFRAS'S MAGICAL PROPERTIES:** Place a piece of Sassafras in your wallet to attract money.

When used as incense, Sassafras will infuse you with a sense of well-being.

Bathing in a tea made from the bark will improve your health. To make the tea, add two tablespoons of the bark to two cups of boiling water. Allow the mixture to steep for approximately ten minutes and then strain it.

To enhance your dreams and keep nightmares at bay, place dried Sassafras in a dream pillow. Sleeping with it will also help you make sound financial decisions.

■ **MEDICINAL USES:** When combined with Sarsaparilla, it is used to treat chronic rheumatism, syphilis, and skin diseases. Sassafras relieves the pain caused by menstrual cramps and is useful for treating gonorrhea. It makes a wonderful disinfectant and deodorizer for dentures. A tea made from the leaves makes an excellent spring tonic.

Feverfew *Chrysanthemum parthenium*

Brings passion to everything you do

- **FEVERFEW WILL:** Protect you from accidents, Create a peaceful atmosphere, Keep you healthy

- **THE PLANT:** Feverfew grows along the side of the road in hedgerows. It has small daisylike flowers with white outer rays and a yellow center that is almost flat. Feverfew grows about two feet tall with slightly hairy leaves four inches long that alternate along the stem. The leaves are a beautiful shade of green and can often be seen even in the winter. The whole plant has a strong bitter smell and is avoided by bees.

- **HOW TO HARNESS FEVERFEW'S MAGICAL PROPERTIES:** Feverfew is an herb that is most powerful around the summer solstice, so gather its leaves then. Carrying a few sprigs on your body will help you avoid accidents and stop you from getting a cold.

  When the dried leaves are burned as incense, they will fill the room with a profound sense of peace. They are excellent to burn when meditating.

- **MEDICINAL USES:** Dried Feverfew leaves can be moistened and applied directly to insect bites to relieve the pain and itching.

  Tea made from two heaping tablespoons of dried Feverfew added to a quart of boiling water, steeped for approximately ten minutes, strained, cooled, and then sweetened to taste makes a good general tonic for nervousness and depression.

Pepper Tree *Schinus molle*

Frees you from negativity

- **PEPPER TREE WILL:** Protect you, Heal your mind, body, and spirit, Purify your home

- **THE PLANT:** The Pepper Tree is indigenous to Peru. It is evergreen and rapidly grows up to forty feet in height. The branches tend to droop, the leaves are smooth, and it blooms with a profusion of small white flowers. The small fruit is a light pinkish red, feels leathery, and contains hundreds of berries. The bark, leaves, and berries are all very aromatic.

- **HOW TO HARNESS PEPPER TREE'S MAGICAL PROPERTIES:** To protect yourself from negativity and physical harm, carry the ripe berries or string them together and wear them as a bracelet.

  If you've been feeling anxious or unsettled, add a few of the dried leaves to your bathwater. They will purify you and fill you with a sense of well-being. Soaking in the bath while calling upon your spirit guides and helpers will deepen your connection to them and enhance your psychic abilities.

- **MEDICINAL USES:** Mexican curanderos (native healers) have long used the branches of the Pepper Tree as part of their healing rituals. The patient is cleansed using the branch and then the branch is burned or buried, removing the disease.

  The berries are used to make a drink that is known for its curative properties. It can be boiled down to make a gruel that will settle upset stomachs and soothe the digestive system.

PART II
Mystical Flowers

FLOWERS THAT WILL BRING PEACE AND PROSPERITY

For information on harvesting, drying, and storing herbs, plants, and flowers, see page 14.
For directions for using them to make tea and incense, see page 18.

Dandelion *Taraxacum officinale*

Reminds you of the abundance life holds

■ **DANDELION WILL:** Attract love, Grant wishes, Summon spirits, Calm the wind

■ **THE PLANT:** Dandelion is a perennial plant with a thick, long taproot. It is a very tenacious plant, and once established, it can be very hard to get rid of. It is now naturalized throughout the Northern Hemisphere. There is some debate about the origin of the plant because it is so prevalent everywhere. The leaves are long and jagged and form a rosette that grows close to the ground. A purple flower stalk grows straight up from the center of the plant. It is hollow and bears a bright yellow flower. Dandelions bloom most of the summer, and when the flowers are mature, they turn into fuzzy puffballs that carry seeds freely in the wind.

■ **HOW TO HARNESS DANDELION'S MAGICAL PROPERTIES:** The Dandelion seed head is a symbol of abundance. The small seeds of the Dandelion are carriers and messengers. Pick a mature Dandelion under the light of the full moon while focusing your attention on your deepest dream. Then face each of the four directions and blow the seeds off. Your wish will come true if you visualize each of the seeds carrying your dreams. You can also use the seeds to summon spirits and calm the wind in much the same way.

■ **MEDICINAL USES:** When applied externally, the fresh juice from a Dandelion fights bacteria and helps heal wounds. The milky sap contained in the plant can be used to remove corns and warts. A tea made from the dried root can be used to cleanse the gallbladder, kidneys, and urinary tract.

Pansy *Viola tricolor*

Reminds you just how powerful love can be

- **PANSY WILL:** Attract love, Reveal your life's purpose, Help you feel safe

- **THE PLANT:** Pansies are perennials, but they are more attractive when grown as an annual. They do well in cool weather and have cheerful, smiling faces. They are self-seeding and their flowers come in a range of colors, including yellow, gold, orange, purple, violet, red, and even black. Most have large showy face markings and many of them are bicolored.

- **HOW TO HARNESS PANSY'S MAGICAL PROPERTIES:** If you're struggling to find your purpose in life, place a bunch of Pansy flowers on your altar. Take a few moments to really look at the flowers and connect with their essence. When you meditate, ask to be shown your life's purpose.

  Pansies can also help with your love life. If you're in a relationship and you plant Pansies outside your bedroom window and they thrive, your love will deepen and grow. If you want to attract new love, plant them in the shape of a heart.

- **MEDICINAL USES:** Pansy can be used to treat eczema and other skin problems. A tea made from its flowers will relieve coughs and soothe a sore throat. The tea will also help relieve frequent urination and clear up bladder infections.

Dogwood *Pyiscidia erythrina*

Teaches you about loyalty

- **DOGWOOD WILL:** Expand your awareness of new ideas, Make wishes come true, Provide protection

- **THE PLANT:** Dogwood is a deciduous tree indigenous to Europe and North America. It grows ten to thirty feet tall and has bright green leaves. The flowers appear in clusters and are surrounded by four white bracts that make it look like the tree has large white flowers. It blooms in May and is often used as an indicator that it is time to plant Corn seeds. The oval berries are bright red, orange, or black, depending on the variety. Dogwood has a very hard, fine-grained wood that polishes to a beautiful finish. The bark can be used to make black ink.

- **HOW TO HARNESS DOGWOOD'S MAGICAL PROPERTIES:** Traditionally, Dogwood symbolizes dog magic. Dogs are loyal and can be protective friends or dangerous enemies.

Dogwood grown near your front door or a sprig hung over your door will offer protection from negative influences.

The sap from the tree will help you see life from a more expansive perspective. Place it on your altar to remind you of your limitless, spiritual nature.

If you carry a piece of fresh Dogwood on Midsummer Night's Eve and rub the sap on your hands, your wishes will come true.

- **MEDICINAL USES:** The bark from the Dogwood tree is used to treat intermittent fevers and as a weak tonic for digestive upsets. The fruit can be used to treat diarrhea.

Larkspur

Delphinum consolida

Helps you find your inner guidance

- **LARKSPUR WILL:** Repel ghosts, Remove negative energy, Inspire generosity of spirit

- **THE PLANT:** Larkspur is an old-fashioned flower that is quite spectacular. The plant grows three to four feet high with tall flower spikes. The flowers range from light blue to deep midnight blue. There are also shades of pink, ruby red, and white. Bees absolutely love the flowers, which bloom from June through September. Larkspurs do best when planted against a wall because their flowers have a hard time withstanding the wind. They have a very subtle scent and originated in the Mediterranean.

- **HOW TO HARNESS LARKSPUR'S MAGICAL PROPERTIES:** Growing Larkspur in your yard will keep ghosts away from your house.

  To help connect with your spirit, pick the flowers and place them on your altar. Doing so will also help you open up to the generosity that comes from that spiritual connection.

  Displaying Larkspur flowers in your home will fill it with love, light, and laughter.

  Finally, to invite Larkspur's guidance, take a bath with the flower petals floating on the water. Focus on their beauty, relax, and open your heart. Ask to be guided and follow through on any actions that come to mind.

- **MEDICINAL USES:** Larkspurs have a variety of medicinal uses, including helping to close wounds. A tea made from its seeds has been used to kill lice and their eggs. The plant is poisonous, so it should never be used internally.

Camellia *Camellia japonica*

Shows you the riches life can hold

- **CAMELLIA WILL:** Provide protection, Invite riches and wealth, Deepen your connection to spirit

- **THE PLANT:** Camellia is an evergreen flowering shrub that is native to Japan, Korea, and China. In its natural habitat it will grow up to thirty feet tall. It has numerous, showy, five-petalled red flowers that grow up to five inches in diameter. Over two thousand hybrids have been developed from the original plant. The flowers bloom from early spring until late fall.

- **HOW TO HARNESS CAMELLIA'S MAGICAL PROPERTIES:** Many herbs will attract abundance, but this is one of the few plants that promises riches. The blossoms themselves are very rich-looking, and planting a bush in the left corner of your property will attract great wealth into your life. That wealth may be material or spiritual.

  To help you connect with the powerful energy of gratitude, place the flowers on your altar before you meditate. Also make a list of all the things, both large and small, for which you are grateful. Read it every day and open your heart to the riches the universe has waiting for you.

- **MEDICINAL USES:** When mixed with Sesame oil, the flowers can be used to treat burns and scalds. The plant has shown some promise in the treatment of cancer.

Indian Paintbrush

Castilleja miniata

Reminds you of the importance of unconditional love

- **INDIAN PAINTBRUSH WILL:** Attract love, Deepen your spiritual connection, Repel fear

- **THE PLANT:** Indian Paintbrush is a perennial that has a cluster of stems that grow upward from the base and are about a foot tall. The leaves are long and narrow. They are pointed but don't have teeth. The tops of the leaves have fine hair, and the flowers are set in clusters. The long, tubelike, pale green flowers are partially hidden by the bright red hairy bracts. Indian Paintbrush often grows in pastures and looks very magical standing amid the grass. It blooms all summer.

- **HARNESS INDIAN PAINTBRUSH'S MAGICAL PROPERTIES:** Indian Paintbrush has a strong ability to attract love. Place the flowers on your altar to remind you of the loving nature of the universe and to help you connect with your divine nature.

  Use the flowers as a symbolic broom and "sweep" your house clean to remove negativity and fill your home with joy, happiness, and love.

  Wear a few petals in an amulet to attract love, connect with your spirit, repel fear, and release negative thinking.

- **MEDICINAL USES:** Tea made from the leaves and the flowers treats kidney diseases, stops excessive menstrual flow, and is said to prevent conception.

Woodruff

Asperula odorata

Gives you the courage to carry on

- **WOODRUFF WILL:** Ensure justice is served, Bring balance, Attract wealth, Help with divination

- **THE PLANT:** Woodruff is a hardy perennial that loves the shade of the forest's floor. It grows two to four feet tall with erect stems covered with a silvery down. The flowers are greenish yellow. It originated in the Mediterranean and blooms from July through August. The flowers are bright white and star shaped. The deep green leaves rapidly fade if exposed to full sunlight.

- **HARNESS WOODRUFF'S MAGICAL PROPERTIES:** To purify your home or other space and fill it with a sense of balance and empowerment, burn some dried Woodruff as incense.

  Woodruff is associated with attracting wealth and producing justice. Scattering it around the outside of your home will help facilitate change.

  If you have a question about the future, make some tea out of the leaves and take a bath in it before you go to bed. Think of the question as you go to sleep and then pay attention to your dreams. To make the tea, add two tablespoons of dried Woodruff leaves to two cups of boiling water, allow the mixture to steep for about ten minutes, and then strain it before pouring it into your bathwater.

- **MEDICINAL USES:** Woodruff was very popular in the Middle Ages. The leaves were crushed and applied to wounds. It was also used as a tea to cleanse the liver and used as a general tonic. The dried herb may be kept among linen to repel insects and keep it fresh smelling. It was also used for stuffing beds.

Columbine

Aquilegia canadensis

Reminds you of the futility of jealousy

- **COLUMBINE WILL:** Attract a mate, Balance emotions, Help people see the truth

- **THE PLANT:** Columbine grows well in shade or sunshine and blooms from May through July. It comes in a variety of colors, including red, white, yellow, blue, and violet as well as multicolored. It is native to large areas of the Northern Hemisphere. The leaves are blue-green with a scalloped shape.

- **HARNESS COLUMBINE'S MAGICAL PROPERTIES:** Columbine is a beautiful plant. Having one in your garden will bless your home.

  Whenever you have an important decision to make, brew the seeds into a tea and pour it into your bath-water. You will gain greater clarity. For the same reason, add a bit of the tea to other beverages and drink them while you are having an important discussion with someone. To make the tea, add two tablespoons of the seeds to two cups of boiling water, allow the mixture to steep for about ten minutes, and then strain it.

  Scatter the dried leaves and flowers around your home if jealousy has reared its ugly head. This works equally well if you're trying to get rid of your own jealous feelings or if you fear that someone is jealous of you.

- **MEDICINAL USES:** The roots and sometimes the leaves were chewed by colonists and Native Americans as a diuretic. It was also used to treat diarrhea and to settle an upset stomach. The plant can be toxic, especially to children, if taken in large quantities.

▶ Top: Indian Paintbrush, Middle: Woodruff, Bottom: Columbine

Life Everlasting *Gnaphalium uliginosum*

Enhances all areas of your life

■ **LIFE EVERLASTING WILL:** Help restore youth, Prevent illness, Rekindle your passion

■ **THE PLANT:** Life Everlasting is a small perennial plant found growing in large patches in the mountains and flatlands of both Europe and the United States. It forms a mat of rosettes with narrow, thin leaves that are dark green with wooly white undersides. It has eight-inch-tall flower stems with clusters of white, pink, or yellow flowers, which bloom from May to August. The flowers have a subtle and pleasant fragrance.

■ **HOW TO HARNESS LIFE EVERLASTING'S MAGICAL PROPERTIES:** When you're feeling as if you can't keep up with the pace of modern life, place a bunch of the flowers over your front door to remind yourself that life is a precious gift best savored in the moment.

If you've been troubled by nightmares, sleep with dried Life Everlasting under your pillow.

Before you eat anything in the morning, drink a cup of tea made from Life Everlasting to ensure a long and healthy life. To make the tea, put one teaspoon of fresh or dried flowering herb in half a cup of boiling water, steep for ten minutes, and then strain the tea before drinking.

To deepen your connection to spirit, place a few flowers in your bathwater.

■ **MEDICINAL USES:** Drinking tea made from Life Everlasting stimulates the flow of gastric juices and pancreatic secretions and is believed to settle an upset stomach. It is also recommended for dysentery.

Note: Life Everlasting can raise blood pressure, so it should be avoided by people who have high blood pressure or are taking medication to lower their blood pressure. As with any herb, use it only under the supervision of a qualified herbalist.

Snapdragon *Antirrhinum magus*

Helps you know the truth

SNAPDRAGON WILL: Protect you from negativity, Banish nightmares, Help you avoid deception

THE PLANT: Snapdragons are native to the Mediterranean. Most children like the flowers because they like to pinch the tiny individual blossoms and make the dragon's mouth open and close. Modern varieties provide large, blossom-laden flower heads, which are faintly fragrant, in a wide assortment of bright colors. The vertical flower spikes open gradually from the bottom to the top. The petals are velvety and lush. Snapdragons are perennials but are usually grown as annuals.

HOW TO HARNESS SNAPDRAGON'S MAGICAL PROPERTIES: To make sure that no one can deceive you, wear a Snapdragon on your person.

If you've been troubled by nightmares, place some Snapdragon seeds under your pillow. They will ensure you of a good night's sleep and banish the bad dreams.

Planting Snapdragon in your yard will dispel negativity and increase the spiritual vibrations.

To see the world from a new perspective, sit near some Snapdragon plants and watch them closely. Open your mind and your heart as you examine the flowers and the leaves. Imagine yourself becoming smaller and smaller until you can walk around inside the flower. How does the world look from that perspective?

- **MEDICINAL USES:** Snapdragon can be used as a poultice on tumors and ulcers. It is effective in reducing inflammation and hemorrhoids.

Passionflower *Passiflora incarnata*

Shows you how to be a friend

- **PASSIONFLOWER WILL:** Calm emotions, Fill your home with peace, Attract friends, Ensure a peaceful night's sleep

- **THE PLANT:** The Passionflower got its name because it looks similar to the Crown of Thorns and is associated with the crucifixion of Jesus. It has a perennial root and puts out shoots that bear three-lobed leaves and yellow, sweet-scented flowers that are tinged with purple. When ripe, the berries are orange and about the size of an apple. The fruits have numerous seeds. The yellow pulp is sweet and edible.

- **HOW TO HARNESS PASSIONFLOWER'S MAGICAL PROPERTIES:** Grow a Passionflower plant near your home to fill your life with a sense of peace, ease, and joy.

    To deepen your connection with your divinity, place the flowers on your altar; to ensure a peaceful night's sleep, put the dried flowers in your dream pillow.

Carrying a few petals in an amulet will attract love and friendship.

To calm your emotions and help you relax, make a tea from the flowers by adding two tablespoons of the dried flowers to two cups of boiling water. Allow the mixture to steep for about ten minutes and then strain it. Pour the tea into a clear bottle and put it outside when the moon is full. After it has absorbed the energy of the moon, add the tea to your bathwater and allow the elixir to fill you with peace and ease.

- **MEDICINAL USES:** Passionflower will lower blood pressure and increase the respiration rate. As a homeopathic medicine, it is used to treat epilepsy.

    It can also be used to treat diarrhea and dysentery, neuralgia, and insomnia.

Tulip *Tulipa vierge*

Keeps you safe always

- **TULIP WILL:** Attract love, Provide protection, Ensure abundance

- **THE PLANT:** Tulips originated in Turkey. They were highly valued there long before they were brought to Holland and are, in fact, the national flower of Turkey. There are about 150 wild Tulip species. Tulips are hardy bulbs that come in about every color of the rainbow. They come up early in the spring, and the flower petals can be either smooth or very feathery.

- **HOW TO HARNESS TULIP'S MAGICAL PROPERTIES:** If you're having problems attracting and keeping a lover, place a Tulip bulb on your altar. It will expand your ability to connect with the power of love. When you are fully aware of the sea of love you are always swimming in, fear is no longer an issue and you will be able to attract love and release fear.

  Carrying a Tulip bulb in your pocket or purse will protect you and bring you good luck.

  Placing a piece of the blossom in an amulet will ensure abundance.

  Finally, planting Tulips in your yard will fill your home with a sense of peace and ease.

- **MEDICINAL USES:** Tulips are more a food for the soul than the body.

Alyssum

Lobularia maritime

Soothes your troubled heart

- **ALYSSUM WILL:** Balance emotions, Protect you, Attract happiness and ease

- **THE PLANT:** An annual, Alyssum grows less than a foot tall. It flowers from June through October. It has numerous blossoms that can be white, red, or purple. They are showy, sweet-smelling little flowers that add a cheerful aura to any garden. Alyssum prefer light, well-drained soil and can tolerate salty air.

- **HARNESS ALYSSUM'S MAGICAL PROPERTIES:** If someone in your life is angry about an issue, give that person some Alyssum flowers, which will help calm him or her down. If your goal is to quell conflicts within your home, hang a bouquet of Alyssum upside down over your front door. In addition to bringing peace to your family, it will also bless your home.

  To keep yourself emotionally balanced as well as to attract abundance, carry a few Alyssum flowers in your wallet.

  To remove any negative energy, put a sachet of the dried flowers in your closet. They will also make your clothes smell good.

  A bouquet of Alyssum placed on your altar will help you deepen your connection to your spirit.

- **MEDICINAL USES:** Alyssum was used to treat rabies. A tea made from the flowers and leaves can be used to treat asthma and calm nervous disorders.

Chrysanthemum

Anacylus pyrethrum

Deepens your connection to the Divine

- **CHRYSANTHEMUM WILL:** Protect your home and its occupants, Release anger, Invite forgiveness

- **THE PLANT:** With both annual and perennial varieties, Chrysanthemums come in a wide variety of shapes, sizes, and colors. They have deep green leaves, and the entire plant has a very pleasant odor. The head of each branch is crowned with a showy bunch of flowers. They grow in a clump and are at their peak at the end of the summer when other flowers are starting to fade. They are often available as potted plants around the end of the year.

- **HARNESS CHRYSANTHEMUM'S MAGICAL PROPERTIES:** Chrysanthemums will bless and protect your home if you plant them around your house or place them inside as a potted plant.

  If you are feeling troubled and need help forgiving yourself and others, place a Chrysanthemum plant on your altar. It will also help you release any limiting beliefs that are holding you back.

  To evoke forgiveness and deepen your connection to your spirit, float several flower heads in your bath.

  In ancient times, carrying a Chrysanthemum flower was thought to protect you against the wrath of the gods if you had broken one of the rules.

- **MEDICINAL USES:** Chrysanthemum has been used in China as a medicinal beverage for thousands of years. The flower heads can be used to treat sore eyes. The flowers are warmed, placed over the closed eyes, and replaced when they are cool.

Nasturtium

Tropaeolum majus

Makes you pure of heart

- **NASTURTIUM WILL:** Impart strength and purity of spirit, Deepen your connection to your spirit

- **THE PLANT:** Nasturtium is a cheerful annual that has a profusion of orange, yellow, and red flowers. It is a native of Peru, although it is cultivated all over the world. The leaves are round and flat with attractive veins. They will often hold the morning dew in large droplets. The trumpetlike flowers appear from May through September.

- **HARNESS NASTURTIUM'S MAGICAL PROPERTIES:** Nasturtiums engender spiritual strength and purity. If you plant them in your garden, they will help you find and stay on your spiritual path.

  You can make a tea from the leaves and use it in a cleansing bath. To make the tea, add two tablespoons of the dried leaves to two cups of boiling water. Allow the mixture to steep for ten minutes, strain it, and then pour it into your bathwater.

  You can also dry the leaves and use them as incense to cleanse your home and raise the spiritual vibrations. Or add the flowers to other incenses to add strength and purity.

  Nasturtium flowers will help you invite the magic and power of spirit into your life. Simply allow yourself to connect with their essence by opening your heart and your mind.

- **MEDICINAL USES:** Both the flowers and the leaves are edible and have medicinal uses. The flowers can be used to treat wounds and clear up infections. The leaves and flowers can be brewed into a tea and used to quiet a cough and break up congestion. The leaves also can be used to stop the itching of insect bites.

▶ Top: Alyssum, Middle: Chrysanthemum, Bottom: Nasturtium

Bachelor's Button *Centaurea cyanus*

Fills your life with love

- **BACHELOR'S BUTTON WILL:** Attract love, Bring joy, happiness, and ease, Enhance your psychic abilities

- **THE PLANT:** Bachelor's Buttons are ragged little blossoms that grow profusely with very little care. Their nickname, Cornflower, originated because the flowers grow wild in the grain fields of southern Europe. Depending upon the variety, the plants will grow one to three feet tall. They are so abundant that they make a wonderful addition to a cutting garden. They also dry very well, so they make very attractive dried arrangements.

- **HOW TO HARNESS BACHELOR'S BUTTON'S MAGICAL PROPERTIES:** If you're trying to enhance your psychic abilities and deepen your meditations, use dried Bachelor's Buttons to decorate your altar.

  To repel negativity and fill your clothes with magic and miracles, place the dried flowers in a sachet and hang it in your closet.

  If you're looking for a mate, put some dried flowers in an amulet. They will help you attract a lover.

  Hang a bouquet of the dried flowers next to your front door to ensure your safe return and keep your home safe while you are away.

- **MEDICINAL USES:** An herbalist might recommend rubbing the cut end of a Bachelor's Button on a cut or scrape. The flowers can also be made into a tea in which a washcloth is soaked and then used as an eye compress.

Periwinkle *Vinca minor*

Fills your heart with love

◼ **PERIWINKLE WILL:** Attract abundance, Invite love, Increase psychic abilities, Enhance mental acuity

◼ **THE PLANT:** Periwinkles are evergreens that grow well in the shade. They retain their glossy leaves all winter. Their leaves always grow in pairs, and the flowers spring from the joint. The seeds seldom, if ever, ripen. Periwinkle plants spread through long, trailing roots and grow so thickly that they choke out any other plants. Each flower has five petals that open out flat. With its five petals and vibrant blue colors, Periwinkles are strongly associated with the goddess.

◼ **HOW TO HARNESS PERIWINKLE'S MAGICAL PROPERTIES:** Dried Periwinkle can be used as incense to attract abundance and love. You can also use the smoke to cleanse your home as well as yourself. Allow the smoke to wash over you, and walk through the rooms of your home to cleanse them.

To help you relax and reconnect with your essence, put a handful of Periwinkle flowers in your bathwater.

If you've been worried about your resources, put a few petals in your wallet to attract abundance.

If you're preparing for an exam, keep a bouquet near your desk while you are studying. They are said to increase your mental acuity. Take a flower with you when you take the exam to improve your test scores.

◼ **MEDICINAL USES:** A homeopathic tincture made from Periwinkle is used to treat infants having a hard time digesting milk. The tincture is also used to treat internal hemorrhages. Periwinkle is a gentle laxative for children and can be used by adults for chronic constipation.

Heather

Calluna vulgaris

Teaches you the beauty you can find in solitude

- **HEATHER WILL:** Deepen your connection with spirit guides, Bring balance to your relationships, Provide protection, Bring you good luck

- **THE PLANT:** Heather is indigenous to Europe and is the national flower of Norway. It is a short, bushy perennial that grows close to the ground on heaths, moors, and bogs. Heather has small needlelike leaves. It tolerates grazing and can regenerate after being burned. Bees are particularly fond of Heather. Its flowers are either pale pink, white, or purple. It has a subtle smell and blooms most of the summer. In the past, Heather was used to stuff mattresses. The leaves and stems were placed near the feet and the flowers near the head of the mattress.

- **HOW TO HARNESS HEATHER'S MAGICAL PROPERTIES:** To promote good luck and protect your home, grow white Heather flowers outside.

  Wear pink Heather flowers in an amulet for help when a love affair is beginning or you are about to end one.

  Having purple flowers around you can deepen your spiritual connection.

  Making a tea of the flowers and mindfully washing your body with it is a wonderful way to sanctify your mind, body, and spirit. To make the tea, add two tablespoons of dried flowers to two cups of boiling water. Allow the mixture to steep for about ten minutes before straining it.

- **MEDICINAL USES:** Heather flowers were used to treat coughs and consumption and to soothe the nerves. They were also mixed with beeswax to make an ointment that was used to treat arthritis and rheumatism.

Cyclamen

Cyclamen spp.

Helps you release the pain from the past

- **CYCLAMEN WILL:** Increase your self-esteem, Attract love, Ensure a good night's rest, Banish nightmares

- **THE PLANT:** Cyclamens grow from tubers that are round and rather flat. The plants have ivylike leaves that are very attractive because of their contrasting greens, whites, and purplish colors that form a geometric pattern. The stem is about four inches long and bare. The flowers are a variety of reds, pinks, whites, and fuchsia. They rise up over the plant and their petals fold backward, making them look like they are standing in a very strong wind. Cyclamens are dormant in the warmer summer months and grow well during the cooler fall weather.

- **HOW TO HARNESS CYCLAMEN'S MAGICAL PROPERTIES:** If you've been hard on yourself emotionally lately, grow a Cyclamen plant in your home. It will fill you with a profound sense of self-love and self-acceptance. The plant is known as a self-esteem builder.

  If you place a Cyclamen plant next to your bed, it will ensure a good night's rest and protect you from any negative influences. It will also chase away bad dreams.

  To attract true love, place the plant on the right side of your altar toward the back.

- **MEDICINAL USES:** A homeopathic tincture is made from the fresh tubers to cleanse the bowels and cause purging.

Edelweiss

Aesculus glabra

Gladdens your heart and fills you with joy

- **EDELWEISS WILL:** Help you manifest your dreams, Stop you from being stabbed

- **THE PLANT:** Edelweiss is a European mountain flower that is part of the Sunflower family. The name means "noble white" in German. Edelweiss is protected because of its rarity. It grows very low to the ground and has small, wooly, star-shaped flowers. It prefers rocky limestone found in mountainous regions. The flower is often associated with mountaineering because it often grows in inaccessible places. The flowers bloom between July and September.

- **HOW TO HARNESS EDELWEISS'S MAGICAL PROPERTIES:** Edelweiss itself is magical, with its tiny starlike flowers. You can purchase the seeds from seed catalogs, or you may just find a plant waiting for you in a gardening store. Place a plant on your altar and nurture and care for it. As you do, allow yourself to get in touch with your dreams. As the flowers open, imagine them as your dreams unfolding. The spirit of the Edelweiss plant will help make all your dreams come true.

  Legend says that if you carry an Edelweiss plant wrapped in linen, you will never get stabbed. But chances are if you are carrying a plant and you are up in the mountains, there is no one around to stab you anyway!

- **MEDICINAL USES:** Edelweiss was traditionally used to treat diarrhea. It was also cooked with butter and honey and used to treat respiratory ills. Recently, it was discovered to contain antioxidants that slow the aging process of skin, so it is used in skin care products.

▶ Top: Heather, Middle: Cyclamen, Bottom: Edelweiss

Marigold *Calendula officinalis*

Helps you use your dreams to connect with the wisdom of the ages

- **MARIGOLD WILL:** Provide protection, Chase away unwanted energies, Help your dreams come true

- **THE PLANT:** Marigolds are often associated with the Virgin Mary. They're found planted around her statues because the flowers symbolically represent Mary's radiant, spiritual glow. A favorite for home landscapes, the Marigold is an annual that blooms all summer long. Its leaves and flowers have a pungent odor.

- **HOW TO HARNESS MARIGOLD'S MAGICAL PROPERTIES:** To protect your property and attract positive energy into your home, plant Marigolds around your house; they will fill it with love and laughter.

  If you need to dispel negative energy, dry the flowers and place them in your closets. To dry Marigolds, use a needle and thread to string the flowers together. Hang the garland in a warm, dry location for several weeks until the flowers are thoroughly dry. If you want to preserve their color, avoid hanging them in the sun.

  If you add the dried flowers to your bathwater, it is said that people will respect and admire you.

  Troubled by scary dreams at night? Scattering the blossoms under your bed will protect you from nightmares and invite prophetic dreams. And to make your dreams come true, put Marigold flowers in your dream pillow. Every night for a month, before you go to sleep, focus on what you want to create.

- **MEDICINAL USES:** Marigold flowers are useful in treating chronic ulcers and varicose veins. Rubbing a Marigold flower on a bee or wasp bite is said to reduce the swelling and stop the pain. An herbalist might use a mixture of Marigold flowers and beeswax as a treatment for sprains. A remedy for soothing eye irritations involves boiling Marigold flowers in water and then using the cooled, strained water as an eyewash.

Gardenia *Gardenia jasmenoides*

Fills your life with magic and miracles

- **GARDENIA WILL:** Facilitate healing, Fill your home with peace, Uplift the spiritual vibrations of your home, Bring abundance

- **THE PLANT:** Gardenias are native to China. When they bloom, Gardenias have the most incredibly sweet smell. They can be used as screens, hedges, borders, or ground covers. If you want to enjoy the flowers' fragrance, plant Gardenias in areas with good air circulation, near patios or windows where the fragrance will be sure to come into your home. They are also sold as houseplants, and as long as you give them enough light and moisture, they will do fine.

- **HOW TO HARNESS GARDENIA'S MAGICAL PROPERTIES:** To raise the spiritual energy in your home and help you with manifestation rituals, place a bouquet of the flowers on your altar.

  If you've been worried about your financial situation, sprinkle a few flower petals in your wallet to ensure abundance. When placed near a sick person, Gardenia flowers will facilitate the person's healing.

  To raise the spiritual vibrations in your home, burn the dried petals as incense. They can also be added to other incense to increase their vibration and make them more powerful.

- **MEDICINAL USES:** Gardenia's flowers and leaves can be used to relieve abdominal pains and gas. The flowers can be soaked in water and used as an eyewash. The leaves are also said to relieve the pain of a toothache.

Elder

Sambucus canadensis

Gives you a fresh outlook on life

- **ELDER WILL:** Bring prosperity, Accelerate healing, Provide protection

- **THE PLANT:** The Elder bush is a familiar sight along many roadways in the Northern Hemisphere. It is a large bush with showy white flowers that bloom in June and July. It is hardy to zone 3. The flowers are large umbrellas of smaller white flowers that ripen into berries in September. The plant can withstand strong winds but not salt air. It can tolerate atmospheric pollution fairly well.

- **HARNESS ELDER'S MAGICAL PROPERTIES:** To clear out any negative energy and fill your home with a light, vibrant energy, sprinkle some Elder flower water around the rooms of your home. To make Elder flower water, fill a large jar with fresh Elder blossoms with all the stems removed. Press them down and then pour two quarts of boiling water over them. Cover the jar with a white cloth and let the jar stand in a warm place for eight hours. Then strain the mixture through a fine muslin cloth.

  Use a splash of Elder flower water in your bathwater to heal your mind, body, and spirit. Rinse your money in it to ensure abundance.

  You can consider Elder flower water the holy water of the herbal realm and use it to bless anything in your world. For example, sprinkling it on a new car will ensure a long and damage-free life.

- **MEDICINAL USES:** Elder flower water is wonderful for your skin. It is used as an eyewash and in skin lotions.

Carnation

Dianthus carophyllus

Helps you release anything that no longer serves you

- **CARNATION WILL:** Provide protection, Give you courage, Promote emotional and physical healing

- **THE PLANT:** Carnation's scientific name roughly translates into "flower of love" or "flower of the gods," depending on the source. Carnations have been revered for centuries. Christians believe that the first Carnation on Earth bloomed when Mary wept for Jesus as he carried his cross.

  Carnations are upright plants with feathery leaves. Each stem has a profusion of flowers that are heavily ruffled and have an earthy clovelike scent. They bloom for a very long time and are also long-lasting as a cut flower. The buds will open after cutting, and as long as the water is changed regularly, they will last for weeks. They come in a very large variety of colors.

- **HARNESS CARNATION'S MAGICAL PROPERTIES:** To protect your house and all the occupants, place a bouquet of the flowers near your front door. To invite abundance, place some on your dining room table.

  Put some of the flowers in an amulet for protection and healing, and to attract love.

  Each color has a slightly different energy, so use your favorite color. Red is said to be best for healing, so place some red Carnations on your altar before you perform any healing rituals.

- **MEDICINAL USES:** Carnation flowers are an aromatic that can be used to treat fevers. A tea made from the flowers will relax the nervous system and help in the healing process.

Hibiscus

Hibiscus sabdariffa

Helps you live your life from a place of love

- **HIBISCUS WILL:** Open your heart to love, Help you see into the future, Help you to relax and let go of your fears

- **THE PLANT:** Hibiscus is the name given to more than 250 species of herbs, shrubs, and trees of the Mallow family. These shrubs are native to tropical climates but are now grown around the world. The flowers are large and showy and have a pronounced stamen that is very decorative. Hibiscus comes in a variety of colors, with red being the most common.

- **HARNESS HIBISCUS'S MAGICAL PROPERTIES:** Hibiscus tea is a very powerful spiritual tool. You can drink it to remind yourself to savor all of life. To make Hibiscus tea, add two tablespoons of dried Hibiscus to two cups of boiling water. Allow the mixture to steep for about ten minutes before straining it.

  For protection, sprinkle the tea around the outside of your home. To reconnect with your spiritual essence, add some of the tea to your bathwater.

  Hibiscus can also help you make decisions about your future. Hold a Hibiscus flower in your hand while you are meditating and look closely at its leaves. Feel its presence and see what sort of insights it brings to you.

- **MEDICINAL USES:** It is believed that Hibiscus flowers will help hair grow. The juice from the leaves and flowers will regulate menstrual cycles. When eaten raw, the flowers will improve digestion and relieve gas.

▶ Top: Elder, Middle: Carnation, Bottom: Hibiscus

Milkweed *Asclepias curassavica*

Helps you transform your life

- **MILKWEED WILL:** Provide protection, Grant wishes, Invite prophetic dreams

- **THE PLANT:** As its name implies, Milkweed emits a milky sap when the plant is cut or bruised. It is native to North America, but there are varieties indigenous to most parts of the world. Milkweed grows from a thick rhizome, and the stems and the leaves are hairy. The flowers are a tight grouping of small pink blossoms that have a rich scent. The seeds are attached to a silky down, which was used in the past to stuff mattresses and pillows. The fibers of the stem produce a long, fine white thread much like Hemp and Flax.

- **HOW TO HARNESS MILKWEED'S MAGICAL PROPERTIES:** Milkweed attracts butterflies, which are the symbol of transformation. Place some of the down from the seedpods on your altar. Then sprinkle some of your favorite essential oil on it and allow the scent to fill your mind and your heart before you meditate. The Milkweed will enhance the oil's property and infuse it with the energy of transformation.

  To enliven your dream life, stuff your dream pillow with the down.

  To enhance a child's creativity and imagination, rub a small amount of the juice from a Milkweed leaf on a child's third eye. Doing so will also deepen the child's spiritual connection.

- **MEDICINAL USES:** The root can be used to treat asthma, colds, and fevers. A tea made from the root will ease a persistent cough and relieve the aches and pains of a fever.

Oregon Grape *Mahonia aquifolia*

Helps you show off your awesome talents

- **OREGON GRAPE WILL:** Help you be more popular, Attract money, Invite ease

- **THE PLANT:** Oregon Grape is an evergreen shrub that isn't related to grapes. It gets its name from the clusters of purple berries it has in the fall. Oregon Grape is native to the West Coast of North America and considered an invasive species in other areas. Its leaves look a lot like Holly. The flowers are bright yellow. Oregon Grape is resistant to drought and makes an attractive hedge. The fruits are bitter with large seeds. They are often added to other fruit when making jelly for their rich purple color.

- **HOW TO HARNESS OREGON GRAPE'S MAGICAL PROPERTIES:** The root of the Oregon Grape plant can be used to attract abundance. Simply carry the root or grind it up and sprinkle the powder in your wallet. Carrying the root will also help you be more popular.

Oregon Grape can also help you reach your dreams. First write all your hopes and dreams down in a letter. If you'd like, you can address the letter to God or the universe. Then wrap several Oregon Grape leaves around the letter. Place the letter on your altar and visualize enjoying yourself as you live your dreams.

- **MEDICINAL USES:** Oregon Grape can be used as an anti-inflammatory and antibacterial. It will speed recovery from candida and diarrhea. A tea made from the berries is useful in the treatment of eczema and psoriasis.

Note: Oregon Grape should not be used by women who are pregnant or breast-feeding.

Buttercup *Ranunculus bulbosus*

Teaches you ancient wisdoms if you come to it with an open and pure heart

- **BUTTERCUP WILL:** Attract abundance, Help with divination, Invite ancient wisdom

- **THE PLANT:** Buttercups have bright yellow or white flowers. The white flowers have a bright yellow center. Buttercups usually flower in May and June but may occasionally be found throughout the summer. They spread very easily and can become a pesky weed.

  The leaves can raise blisters, so wear gloves when you're picking them.

- **HOW TO HARNESS BUTTERCUP'S MAGICAL PROPERTIES:** Buttercup is an ancient medicine best approached with care.

  To help deepen your spiritual connection, place the petals in a bowl on your altar. Ask the spirit of the flowers to help deepen your connection to spirit and see into the future. If you do so with a pure heart, the spirit of the Buttercups will help you manifest your deepest dreams and desires.

  For protection, hang a bunch of the flowers over your front door.

- **MEDICINAL USES:** Buttercup leaves, flowers, and roots are known to raise blisters when applied to the skin. Occasionally, Buttercup is used to treat arthritis and rheumatism. Years ago beggars were known to use the plant to raise blisters to help elicit sympathy.

Jasmine

Jasminum officinale

Helps you let go of your fears and create balance

- **JASMINE WILL:** Attract abundance, Deepen your spiritual connection, Help you feel loved

- **THE PLANT:** Jasmine is a vine with small, heavenly scented flowers. It originated in Persia and is a perennial. The flowers are usually yellow, but occasionally they are pink. They are heavily scented, so plant them near a window. Jasmine will also do well as a houseplant and will fill your home with their scent. Keep them trimmed to ensure continuous flowering.

- **HOW TO HARNESS JASMINE'S MAGICAL PROPERTIES:** Plant Jasmine on the south side of your property to provide protection for your home and your family. The smell from the flowers will enhance your dream life and help you develop new ideas. It will also deepen your meditations and your spiritual connection.

   Growing Jasmine in your home will not only fill your house with a wonderful smell but will also attract abundance and fill your life with a sense of peace and love.

- **MEDICINAL USES:** Jasmine is used to balance both male and female reproductive conditions. It is said to help prevent infertility and postnatal depression. It has a calming effect and can help relieve stress and bring you back into balance. Jasmine can also help stop muscle spasms.

Goldenrod

Solidago virgaurea

Guides you to your inner treasure

- **GOLDENROD WILL:** Attract money and guide you to hidden treasure, Bring good luck, Lift your mood

- **THE PLANT:** Goldenrod is native to Europe but has spread to Asia, the Azores, and both North and South America. It has the unusual ability to cross-pollinate with other plants, so there are more than 130 species of Goldenrod in the United States alone. It is a perennial that grows three to seven feet tall. It has large clusters of yellow flowers, which appear in August and September.

  Goldenrod's leaves alternate between smooth and saw-toothed edges. It is frequently blamed for allergies, but its pollen is too heavy to be carried by the wind, so it is often one of the other plants that bloom at the same time that is the culprit.

- **HOW TO HARNESS GOLDENROD'S MAGICAL PROPERTIES:** Goldenrod will act as a divining rod, leading you to hidden treasure, or at least so the story goes.

  For help deepening your meditations and connecting with your inner wisdom, place Goldenrod on your altar. It will help you remember that loving yourself releases the greatest gifts you have.

  Growing Goldenrod near your front door will bring you magical blessings.

  To attract money, rub some of the leaves on your wallet and carry a few petals from the flowers inside.

- **MEDICINAL USES:** Goldenrod has been used historically to heal wounds. Its Latin name, solidago, means "to make whole." Studies have found that Goldenrod can help reduce inflammation, relieve muscle spasms, fight infections and cancer, and lower blood pressure.

Lilac

Syringa vulgaris

Reminds you of the power of magic and a life well lived

- **LILAC WILL:** Remind you of the beauty of your soul, Attract love, Banish negative spirits

- **THE PLANT:** The only drawback to Lilacs is that they bloom only for a few weeks each spring. They have a lovely fragrance that will fill your home. Allow yourself to fully enjoy them when they are in blossom because you will have to wait fifty more weeks to smell them again. Lilacs are a perennial bush that grows from eight to fifteen feet tall. The classic Lilac is a beautiful shade of purple. There are now more than five hundred varieties, and they vary in color from deep purple to white. There are even shades of red and pink. Lilac trees are very long lived, often living for more than a hundred years, so if you plant a bush, it will be there long after you have passed from this world.

- **HOW TO HARNESS LILAC'S MAGICAL PROPERTIES:** Just standing downwind from a Lilac bush in blossom will help you connect with the beauty and wonder of divinity.

  To attract love and dispel negativity, wear a few petals in an amulet. If you sprinkle some petals around your property, they will chase negative spirits from your home.

  If you'd like to deepen your meditations or your ability to love, burn dried Lilac flowers as incense.

- **MEDICINAL USES:** This plant has a history of herbal use going back more than 3,500 years. It is considered one of the fifty fundamental herbs of Chinese medicine. The flower can be made into a tea to control coughs. The buds are an anticoagulant and antiseptic. They can also be used to treat constipation.

Geranium

Pelargonium maculatum

Encourages you to see life's beauty

- **GERANIUM WILL:** Invite protection, Help you conceive a child, Encourage love, Attract abundance

- **THE PLANT:** The term Geraniums is often confusing because what most people think of as Geraniums are not Geraniums at all but rather Pelargonium, which are a relative of the perennial Geranium. They have beautiful feathery and showy leaves. They are easy to cultivate and have a distinct, pleasant odor. They are an annual and are deep red, pink, white, and shades of fuchsia.

- **HOW TO HARNESS GERANIUM'S MAGICAL PROPERTIES:** Planting Geraniums around your home will protect it from negative energies and unwanted visitors. Red Geraniums will invite love and abundance, while pink ones will attract friendship and love. White Geraniums will raise the spiritual vibrations.

    If you want to conceive a child, place a Geranium in your bedroom and allow yourself to connect with it as it grows. As you watch it bloom, invite life to grow within you as well.

    Finally, to relieve stress, make a bath with Geranium by putting the leaves and flowers in a mesh bag (or something similar) and hanging it under the faucet as you fill your bathtub.

- **MEDICINAL USES:** A tea can be made out of the leaves and used to wash the face.

▶ Top: Goldenrod, Middle: Lilac, Bottom: Geranium

Aster

Callistephus chinesis

Helps you balance the light and dark sides

- **ASTER WILL:** Attract love, Sanctify your altar and your home, Deepen your connection to the power of the divine feminine

- **THE PLANT:** Asters are native to northern China, Siberia, and Japan. They are perennials with a hairy stem and daisylike flowers. They are often found in meadows and along riverbanks. The flowers range from pale pink to deep purple to blue to white, and they generally have a yellow center. They bloom from August through October. They have a pungent odor and have been considered sacred to the gods since the early Greeks. The ability to grow Asters was thought to symbolize a person's knowledge of the darker side of magic.

- **HOW TO HARNESS ASTER'S MAGICAL PROPERTIES:** Use Asters to decorate your altar. This flower is of particular significance to the divine feminine, so when you place it on your altar, you can call upon the goddess Venus or Hecate.

  At least once a year, make a tea from Aster and use it to clean your altar and your home. You can make the tea by adding two tablespoons of dried Aster leaves and flowers to two cups of boiling water. Allow the mixture to steep for at least ten minutes before straining it.

  To make sure your home is protected from negative influences, hang a dried bouquet in your attic.

- **MEDICINAL USES:** Asters are used in Chinese medicine to treat hemorrhages, malaria, and pulmonary ailments.

Evening Primrose

Oenothera biennis

Helps you feel safe

- **EVENING PRIMROSE WILL:** Ensure successful hunting, Provide protection, Attract love, Invite a profound feeling of safety

- **THE PLANT:** Evening Primrose is native to North America. These biennial plants are tall, often growing more than five feet high. The stem is erect and stout with soft hairs. The plants are reddish brown and branch to form a shrub. The leaves are lemon scented. The taproot is long and fibrous. The flowers are about two and a half inches across. They open at night and close up during the day. They are very fragrant, have only four petals, and are bright yellow.

- **HOW TO HARNESS EVENING PRIMROSE'S MAGICAL PROPERTIES:** Traditionally, Evening Primrose was used in rituals to ensure good hunting. Though few people actually hunt for their food today, you can still use this herb to help you hunt for a job, relationship, happiness, lover, etc. Place the petals on your altar while clearly stating what you want. After you state your intent, sprinkle the leaves into the wind and allow them to be carried away. Do this in each of the four directions, leaving a few petals on your altar to remind you of your intent.

- **MEDICINAL USES:** Evening Primrose is both edible and medicinal. Evening Primrose oil helps relieve pain and inflammation and has a positive effect on the uterine muscles, nervous system, and metabolism. A tea made from the roots is used in the treatment of obesity.

Persimmon

Diospyros virginiana

Fills your heart with gratitude

■ **PERSIMMON WILL:** Bring good luck, Attract abundance, Sweeten your attitude toward life

■ **THE PLANT:** Persimmon is native to China, where it has been cultivated for centuries. It spread to Korea and Japan and was introduced to California in the mid-1800s. It is a deciduous tree that grows up to twenty-five feet in height. The leaves droop and are a very rich deep green. The leaves look like those on a Mango tree, giving it its tropical appearance.

In the fall, the leaves often turn dramatic shades of yellow, orange, and red. Tea can be made from both the fresh and the dried leaves. The fruits are very sweet and when ripe are a deep orange that looks almost red.

■ **HOW TO HARNESS PERSIMMON'S MAGICAL PROPERTIES:** Eat fully ripe Persimmons to help you feel grateful for life's many gifts.

To ensure good luck in the coming year, bury a green Persimmon in your backyard on New Year's Eve.

■ **MEDICINAL USES:** The leaves and fruit are rich in vitamin C and have been used to treat scurvy. The ripe fruit is useful for treating bloody stools. Externally, the fruit is used as a poultice to treat warts.

▶ Top: Aster, Middle: Evening Primrose, Bottom: Persimmon

Roses

N.O. rosaceae

Fills your life with romance

- **ROSES WILL:** Bring peace, Attract love, Mend the pain of loss, Empower you

- **THE PLANT:** Roses are one of the oldest known perennial shrubs. They probably originated in northern Persia but are now grown around the globe. There are more than ten thousand varieties and colors. The Rose is closely associated with the Virgin Mary, who is considered a Rose without thorns. Roses bloom between May and September.

- **HOW TO HARNESS ROSES'S MAGICAL PROPERTIES:** Rose is the master herb of love. Placing a bouquet of Roses on your altar will deepen your experience of divine love.

  To balance your emotions and enhance self-love and acceptance, bathe with some Rose petals floating on the water. Doing so will also help you relax and become more centered. If you're hoping to attract love, put some Rose petals in an amulet.

  The plant is considered good luck, and planting one in your yard will ensure you of abundance as well as good fortune.

  It was once the custom to suspend a Rose over the dinner table as a sign that all confidences were to be held sacred.

- **MEDICINAL USES:** Rose hips, the fruit of the Rose, have a high vitamin C content and can be used to make jellies. The deepest red petals are most desirable for medicinal purposes. Rose water works simultaneously on the physical, emotional, mental, and spiritual bodies. It will cleanse and purify the liver and ease depression and nervous tension. It will also soothe a headache, relieve shock, calm nausea, and enhance the immune system.

Dock

Rumex obtusifolius

Reminds you of the sweetness of life

- **DOCK WILL:** Attract money, Facilitate healing, Increase fertility

- **THE PLANT:** Dock is easy to recognize because it has large, leathery leaves. The lower leaves have red stems and the edges of the leaves are wavy. Dock grows about eighteen inches in height. The large clusters of green flowers turn red as they mature. Dock produces reddish brown seeds in late September.

- **HOW TO HARNESS DOCK'S MAGICAL PROPERTIES:** To cleanse and purify your mind, body, and spirit, make a tea out of the seeds and use it in a ceremonial bath. Bathing in Dock is particularly useful if you wish to conceive a child. To make the tea, add two tablespoons of Dock seeds to two cups of boiling water. Allow the mixture to steep for about ten minutes before straining it and adding it to your bathwater.

  For protection and to attract abundance, sprinkle a handful or two of the seeds around the outside of your home. You can also sprinkle them under your bed to protect you while you sleep. If you own a business, sprinkle the seeds around your establishment to attract new customers.

  If your goal is to attract a new lover, place some seeds in an amulet and wear it. You can also use the amulet to increase your fertility.

- **MEDICINAL USES:** Rubbing the milk from the leaves of a Dock plant on the affected area can relieve the pain from Stinging Nettles and insect bites. The root helps cleanse the liver and the skin.

Lavender

Lavandula angustifolia

Gives you a fresh spiritual outlook

- **LAVENDER WILL:** Infuse you with peace, joy, and a sense of connection, Control anger, Deepen your spiritual awareness, Repel negativity

- **THE PLANT:** Lavender is classified as an evergreen shrub. Lavender plants grow from two to three feet tall. They have lilac blue flowers that grow on tall spikes. The leaves are narrow and grayish green. The plants spread out and have a wonderful odor. The flowers dry easily and retain their scent and color for a long time. Lavender flowers from June through September.

- **HOW TO HARNESS LAVENDER'S MAGICAL PROPERTIES:** Place a bouquet of dried Lavender flowers on your altar to deepen your spiritual connection and expand your awareness.

  If your home hasn't been a place of peace lately, hang a bunch of Lavender flowers over your front door. It will repel negativity and fill your home with love.

  Similarly, you can soak away your fears in a warm bath by floating Lavender flowers on the surface.

  Use dried Lavender anytime as incense to deepen your meditations and fill your home with the magic of Midsummer Night's Eve.

  Put dried Lavender flowers in your drawers and closets to repel negative energy and refresh you wardrobe without spending a cent!

- **MEDICINAL USES:** Lavender has been used for centuries as an herbal remedy. It's useful as an antiseptic, antibacterial, antifungal, anti-inflammatory, anticonvulsive, and antidepressant. The flowers make a relaxing tea, but the oil should be used only in small doses due to its strong scent.

▶ Top: Roses, Middle: Dock, Bottom: Lavender

African Violet *Saintpaulia ionantha*

Shows you how to be happy no matter what

- **AFRICAN VIOLET WILL:** Bless your home, Deepen your spiritual connection, Fill your home with lighthearted energy

- **THE PLANT:** There are thousands of varieties of African Violet with different colored blossoms with different shaped flowers. The plants themselves also come in different shapes and sizes. There are even some that are only the size of your thumb. Generally they have dark green hairy leaves and bloom profusely. A cluster of flowers emanates from the center of the crown of leaves. Placed on an east-facing window, they will bloom most of the year, sharing their cheerful countenance freely with you. African Violets are native to South Africa.

- **HOW TO HARNESS AFRICAN VIOLET'S MAGICAL PROPERTIES:** Growing African Violets will promote spirituality. If you want to deepen your connection to your spirit, place a deep purple African Violet on your altar. When grown on your windowsills, they will bless your home and fill it with cheerful and loving energy.

  African Violets make a wonderful housewarming gift. Learning to care for them and getting them to bloom will help you connect with Earth-based energies. The patience and attention you give to your plants will come back to you multiplied.

- **MEDICINAL USES:** The fresh flowers can be added to Peppermint tea to calm an upset stomach, improve the appetite, and improve digestion.

Venus Fly Trap *Dionaea muscipula*

Shows you how to "catch" the energy of creation

- **VENUS FLY TRAP WILL:** Attract love, Provide protection, Help you manifest your dreams

- **THE PLANT:** Venus Fly Trap is a carnivorous plant that catches insects for food. At the end of each leaf there is a trap capable of telling the difference between living and nonliving stimuli. It takes the trap only a tenth of a second to close. The plant will reopen within twelve hours if it was just a raindrop or a bug too small to be worth eating. Venus Fly Trap is a small herb that has a rosette of four to seven leaves and a bulbous rhizome root system. The plant's name refers to the Roman goddess of love, Venus.

- **HOW TO HARNESS VENUS FLY TRAP'S MAGICAL PROPERTIES:** If you want to attract love, grow some Venus Fly Traps. Place one on your altar in the right back corner. Nurture it, care for it, and make sure it flourishes.

  Place another Venus Fly Trap plant near your front door to provide protection for your entire home. As you care for the plant, call upon the goddess Venus and allow her love and guidance to fill your heart, your mind, and your home.

- **MEDICINAL USES:** Some people believe Venus Fly Trap has the ability to cure skin cancer and is more effective than radiation therapy and chemotherapy. Supporters believe using the enzyme produced by the Venus Fly Trap can lead to the total reversal of skin and other forms of cancer.

Poppy *Papaver rhoeas*

Helps you manifest your dreams

- **POPPY WILL:** Increase fertility, Attract abundance, Help you overcome grief

- **THE PLANT:** There are more than a hundred species of Poppy. The flower petals look like crepe paper. The foliage is a deep, dark green, and the flowers open wide, revealing a black center. The most common color is bright red. Poppy grows well in areas that have been freshly cultivated. The flowers produce seedpods that hold hundreds of tiny seeds, so they easily reseed themselves. The flowers have a rich opium scent when they are freshly picked, but they lose the smell as they dry. The flower petals can be used to make ink, but it takes a lot of petals to make a small amount of ink. The flowers fade immediately after they are picked.

- **HOW TO HARNESS POPPY'S MAGICAL PROPERTIES:** Poppies represent both death and rebirth. Romans placed Poppies on graves, yet Poppies are said to grant immortality.

To provide protection and attract love, sprinkle the seeds around the outside of your home. If the seeds grow and blossom, you can expect tremendous success in your life.

Eating the seeds in baked goods will increase fertility.

Bathing in a tea made from Poppies will deepen your connection with your spirit and help you overcome grief. To make the tea, add two tablespoons of the flower petals and the seeds to two cups of boiling water. Allow the mixture to steep for about ten minutes and then strain it before adding it to your bathwater.

- **MEDICINAL USES:** Opium can be made from some varieties. The juice from the stems of the leaves can be used to treat insect bites. A tea made from the flower petals can be used as a face wash. It will soothe the skin and help clear up the complexion.

Hyacinth *Hyacinthus oriental*

Helps you relax and trust the process called life

- **HYACINTH WILL:** Fill your home with a sense of peace and joy, Relieve the pain of grief, Protect you spiritually, Banish nightmares

- **THE PLANT:** Hyacinth is native to southwestern Asia and Turkey. It is a bulb that produces beautiful, highly scented flowers. The leaves are long, about two inches across, and light green. The flower stalks come up from the center of the bulb and often have forty to a hundred small blossoms. Hyacinths flower early in the spring and will appear year after year as long as the winters allow the bulb a period of dormancy and the leaves are allowed to feed the bulb. For this reason, after the flower dies, the leaves shouldn't be cut back for six to eight weeks. The vibrantly colored flowers can be deep purple, pink, white, yellow, or red.

- **HOW TO HARNESS HYACINTH'S MAGICAL PROPERTIES:** It is said that the scent will ease the pain of grief.

  If you put a Hyacinth plant on your nightstand, it will protect you spiritually, ensure a good night's sleep, and prevent nightmares.

  To attract love and abundance, wear dried Hyacinth petals in an amulet.

  The smell of the flowers will fill your home with happiness, joy, and a sense of peace. Placing one on your altar will help you remember that all of life is sacred.

- **MEDICINAL USES:** Hyacinth bulbs are poisonous. The flowers can be made into a tea and used to wash the face and scent soap and bathwater. Perfume made from the flowers is highly prized. The plants are most useful for their beauty, which will soothe the heart and feed the soul.

Sunflower *Helianthus annus*

Shows you how to tap into your inner wisdom

- **SUNFLOWER WILL:** Make wishes come true, Deepen your integrity, Bring you good luck, Provide protection

- **THE PLANT:** Sunflowers are native to Peru, where they were revered by the Aztecs. Aztec priestesses were crowned with Sunflowers and carried them in their hands.

  Sunflowers are an annual that grow three to twelve feet tall. The plant has a hairy stem, large rough leaves, and a large flower head made up of numerous tubular flowers on a flat disk. The individual flowers produce meaty, individual striped seeds. The flower heads follow the sun throughout the day. The head always faces the sun, turning toward the east overnight so it can catch the first rays of the rising sun.

- **HOW TO HARNESS SUNFLOWER'S MAGICAL PROPERTIES:** Sunflowers have often been used to represent devotion because they follow the sun. Planting them in your yard will fill your property with good luck and fill your home with a profound sense of safety and protection.

  To expand your sense of integrity, place a flower head on your altar.

  Eating the seeds is said to increase fertility and bring good luck. Sleeping with them under your pillow will ensure you of always knowing the truth.

  Finally, taking time to watch Sunflowers follow the sun will remind you of the magical nature of life.

- **MEDICINAL USES:** The seeds will help strengthen the immune system. A tea made from the seeds will help treat bronchitis and asthma and ease coughs from colds.

Cardinal Flower

Lobelia cardinalis

Brings you great joy

- **CARDINAL FLOWER WILL:** Invite great happiness and joy, Attract abundance, Repel negativity

- **THE PLANT:** Cardinal Flowers are bright red and extremely showy. Flashes of the flowers are visible from marshes, stream banks, and low woods in the late summer. Few native North American plants have flowers of such intense color as this perennial. The blossoms are delicate and open slowly from the bottom to the top on two- to four-foot spikes. The plant has numerous dark green leaves that are tapered on both ends. Hummingbirds love its sweet nectar. It produces numerous seeds in two-celled pods that open from the top.

- **HOW TO HARNESS CARDINAL FLOWER'S MAGICAL PROPERTIES:** Hang a bunch of the fresh flowers over your front door to protect your home, its occupants, and all those who enter. These flowers will also fill your home with a light, joyous energy.

  To make sure you stay healthy all winter, put a few of the seeds in a bowl in the center of your altar each autumn.

  If you need to visit a sick friend, wear a few seeds in an amulet to avoid getting sick. The amulet will also attract joy and happiness into your life.

- **MEDICINAL USES:** Native Americans used the roots to treat worms, stomach problems, and syphilis. This plant is poisonous, and extracts of the leaves and fruit produce vomiting, sweating, pain, and finally death.

Daisy

Bellis perennis

Helps you fill your life with love

- **DAISY WILL:** Attract love, Protect children, Enhance feelings of safety, happiness, and joy

- **THE PLANT:** The common Daisy is a perennial, but it is often grown as an annual. The flower head is actually made up of a group of tiny flowers that grow in a disc shape, making it look like a much bigger flower. The flowers close up at night and open again in the daytime. The Daisy family has lots of members. The plant has a subtle, fresh smell and flowers from May until September.

- **HOW TO HARNESS DAISY'S MAGICAL PROPERTIES:** Most people are familiar with the charming old practice of picking a Daisy and then individually pulling out the petals while saying, "He loves me, he loves me not," until the final petal is removed, thus determining your fate.

  When placed in an amulet and hung over their beds, Daisies will protect babies and children.

  Put a bouquet of Daisies on your altar to renew your interest in a project.

  Placed around the house, Daisies will emanate a feeling of safety and joy.

  To inspire an old love to return, place some Daisy petals under your pillow. Doing so will also enhance your dream life.

- **MEDICINAL USES:** Centuries ago, Daisies were often used in medicine. A tea made from the flowers was used as a healing tonic. The sticky leaves were used to help wounds heal.

Violet

Viola odorata

Helps you connect with the ancient power of love

- **VIOLET WILL:** Attract love, Surround you with supportive people and spirits, Remind you of the importance of dedication, Fill your life with joy

- **THE PLANT:** Violets have a sweet scent and arrive early in the spring. The leaves are heart shaped and slightly downy. The flowers are full of nectar, but they bloom before bees are fully active. They are predominately purple or white. Violets rarely set seed. There are more than two hundred species that live all over this beautiful planet.

- **HOW TO HARNESS VIOLET'S MAGICAL PROPERTIES:** Violets have a rich, mystical past. They have long been associated with love, attracting helpful and loving spiritual beings, and pulling in powerful healing vibrations. For such a small flower, they are very powerful.

  The white Violet is the symbol of innocence and humility, while the blue Violet represents loyalty and consistency. Most of all, Violets generate the energy of steadfastness. If you want your spiritual practices to bear fruit, you must be consistent. So surround yourself with Violets to remind you to be true to yourself and follow through on all of your commitments. Wear them in an amulet, place them on your altar, or put them around your home.

- **MEDICINAL USES:** Violet flowers make a very gentle laxative that also has healing properties. The old herbalists believed Violets could ease inflammation, calm a sore throat, comfort the heart, and quiet the mind to allow a restful and healing night's sleep. Violets were sold by most druggists as an all-around tonic.

Morning Glory

Convolvulus sepium

Brings you peace, joy, and happiness

■ **MORNING GLORY WILL:** Stop nightmares, Provide protection and peace, Attract money, Deepen your connection to spirit

■ **THE PLANT:** Morning Glory is a vine with leaves that are shaped like arrows. They are somewhat thin and delicate in texture. The plant has very showy bell-shaped flowers that blossom from July to September. As long as it is sunny, the flowers open in the morning and close at night. The plants are indeed a glory to behold when the morning dew glistens on the newly open flowers.

■ **HOW TO HARNESS MORNING GLORY'S MAGI-CAL PROPERTIES:** Growing Morning Glory near your home will bring peace, joy, and happiness to you and all who enter your home. It also repels negativity, including thieves.

If you've been troubled by insomnia or night-mares, fill a sachet with the seeds and place it under your pillow to ensure a good night's sleep and to chase away bad dreams.

To deepen your connection to your spiritual side, sit beside the plant when the flowers are fully open and do an open eye meditation while really allowing yourself to connect with the flower. Let yourself feel the magic and hear the whispers of your innate inner wisdom.

You can also soak the seeds in olive oil for a month and then rub the oil on your money to ensure abundance.

■ **MEDICINAL USES:** Native Americans used a tea made from the roots as a diuretic, a laxative, an expectorant, and a cough suppressant. A tea made from the leaves can be used to cure headaches and indigestion.

▶ Top: Daisy, Middle: Violet, Bottom: Morning Glory

Yarrow *Achillea millefolium*

Helps you create the future of your dreams

- **YARROW WILL:** Give you the courage to change, Attract love, Increase psychic power, Release negative energy

- **THE PLANT:** Yarrow originated in Asia and Europe but is now common over much of the world. It flowers from June through September. The flowers are white or pale lilac and look like miniature daisies. The entire plant has a strong semisweet smell. The leaves are pleasantly aromatic when crushed and have a feathery appearance. Yarrow grows about two and a half feet tall and is erect. It can become a pest because its roots creep and the seeds spread quite easily.

- **HOW TO HARNESS YARROW'S MAGICAL PROPERTIES:** Yarrow has been found in Neanderthal graves, attesting to its long use as a sacred herb. When you carry Yarrow, it will banish fear and infuse you with the courage to face whatever issues are holding you back.

Placed under your pillow, dried Yarrow will protect you as you sleep and invite prophetic dreams.

To deepen your spiritual connection and expand your psychic awareness, add Yarrow tea to your bathwater. To make the tea, add two tablespoons of dried leaves and flowers to two cups of boiling water. Allow the mixture to steep for about ten minutes before straining it and pouring it into your bathwater.

Finally, to fill your home with love, happiness, and ease, burn some dried Yarrow as incense.

- **MEDICINAL USES:** A tea made out of Yarrow is a wonderful remedy for severe colds and will relieve the aches and pains of the flu. Some herbalists recommend adding a pinch of Cayenne Pepper to each cup. Drinking this tea makes a big difference very quickly.

Honeysuckle *Lonicera caprifolium*

Brings balance back into your life

- **HONEYSUCKLE WILL:** Deepen your spiritual connection, Protect your home, Enhance the effectiveness of other herbs

- **THE PLANT:** The Honeysuckle family includes almost two hundred species of shrubs and climbing vines that grow in varied habitats ranging from woodlands to rocky places. They are deciduous or evergreen bushes ranging from two to thirty feet in height. They have a fruity, sweet fragrance. The flowers are one to two inches in length, and they are white or red and shaped like a bell. The berries will cause mild stomach distress. Honeysuckle is a very low-maintenance plant that is seldom bothered by pests.

- **HOW TO HARNESS HONEYSUCKLE'S MAGICAL PROPERTIES:** Honeysuckle is an herb that works well with others. When you use it with other herbs, it brings balance and adds to their effectiveness.

  Before meditating, rub the leaves on your forehead to deepen your meditation and help you connect with the spirit realms. This will also remind you of the importance of being mindful no matter what you are doing.

  Decorate your altar with the sweet flowers to help generate a sense of gratitude and joy.

- **MEDICINAL USES:** Traditional Chinese medicine considers Honeysuckle one of the most important herbs for releasing toxins from the body. The flowers can be used to make a syrup that is an expectorant for bad coughs, asthma, and allergies. Honeysuckle can also be used to soothe minor skin irritations and to clear up infections in wounds.

Crocus

Crocus vernus

Teaches you about making the unseen seen

- **CROCUS WILL:** Attract love, Bless your home, Create visions

- **THE PLANT:** Crocus grow wherever there are cold winters with snow. Their natural habitat is woodland clearings and subalpine meadows. They are a bulb and are usually the first flower visible in the spring. The flowers are various shades of purple, yellow, and white. They are harbingers of spring and will often bloom while there are still patches of snow on the ground.

- **HOW TO HARNESS CROCUS'S MAGICAL PROPERTIES:** Growing Crocus plants around your home will attract love. Put a pot of Crocus near your front door and they will fill your home with happiness, joy, and, above all else, hope.

  By their very presence, Crocus plants remind each of us that even at the darkest points in life, the seeds of happiness and joy live within our hearts. If you are going through a rough time in your life, hold a Crocus flower or an image of one in your hand while you are meditating. Then simply open your heart and your mind to visions of what you can create.

- **MEDICINAL USES:** The pollen from the flowers was used to stop the pain of toothaches and to prevent tooth decay. It was also used to treat headaches, dysentery, measles, fever, jaundice, cholera, diabetes, urinary tract infections, and skin diseases.

Sweet Pea

Lathyrus odoratus

Brings you courage and deepens your wisdom

- **SWEET PEA WILL:** Attract new friendships, Increase your courage, Provide spiritual energy and strength

- **THE PLANT:** As the name implies, Sweet Peas are sweet-smelling flowers that come in a wide range of colors. They are a climbing plant that grows from six to nine feet tall. The dwarf varieties are only eight to twenty inches high. They do well in colder climates but can grow in warm places. They need full sun and rich, well-drained soil. The seeds should be sown directly where you would like the plants to grow. Unlike other peas, these are poisonous.

- **HOW TO HARNESS SWEET PEA'S MAGICAL PROPERTIES:** Planting Sweet Peas in your yard will fill it and your home with peace, love, and joy. Sweet Peas attract people and will encourage new friendships.

  Carrying the flowers will cause you to tell the truth.

  If you wear the flowers, they will give you additional physical and spiritual strength. They will also help deepen your connection with your spirit and expand your ability to access ancient wisdoms.

- **MEDICINAL USES:** None; flowering ornamental Sweet Peas are poisonous.

Lily of the Valley

Convallaria magalis

Surrounds your life with joy and ease

- **LILY OF THE VALLEY WILL:** Attract happiness, joy, and success, Deepen your spiritual connection, Lift your spirits

- **THE PLANT:** Lily of the Valley has broad leaves with small, fragrant, bell-shaped flowers. Early in the spring the rhizomes send up small, thin shoots. First, two leaves unfurl one within the other. One leaf is always bigger than the other, and at the back of the leaves, in the same sheath, there is a flower stalk. The flowers begin greenish, and as they open, they hang downward like pure white fairy bells with six scallops. By September the flowers turn into hard red berries. Lilies of the Valley are native to Europe but are distributed throughout North America and Asia.

- **HOW TO HARNESS LILY OF THE VALLEY'S MAGICAL PROPERTIES:** If you've been feeling out of sorts lately, add the flowers to your bathwater to cleanse your energy and raise your spiritual vibration.

  To invite happiness, joy, and success into your life, plant Lily of the Valley near your home.

  Place a bouquet of the flowers on your altar to remind you just how magical life really can be.

- **MEDICINAL USES:** Lily of the Valley is a wonderful tonic for the heart. It will slow irregular heartbeats while increasing the heart's ability to pump. A tea made from the flowers will help clear up a urinary tract infection.

▶ Top: Crocus, Middle: Sweat Pea,
Bottom: Lily of the Valley

PART III
Other Magical Plants
OTHER PLANTS THAT WILL IMPROVE YOUR LIFE

For information on harvesting, drying, and storing herbs, plants, and flowers, see page 14.
For directions for using them to make tea and incense, see page 18.

Corn

Zea mays

Teaches you about the energy of creation

- **CORN WILL:** Attract abundance, Bring good luck, Repel negativity

- **THE PLANT:** Corn is native to South America but cultivated throughout much of the world. The top of each plant produces a flower that fertilizes the silk of the individual ears of Corn. The ears form at various levels from the ground and are enclosed by several thin layers to form a husk. From the husk hang pale yellow silk filaments. Once the silk is fertilized, seeds, or kernels, form within the husk. The kernels are usually yellow but can be red, blue, black, pure white, or any combination of these colors.

- **HOW TO HARNESS CORN'S MAGICAL PROPERTIES:** Corn was considered sacred by the Aztec and Mayan people. It is symbolic of fertility and is closely aligned with the energy of the goddess and Earth Mother.

    To bring good luck to all members of your household and attract abundance, hang dried Corn in your home with the husks folded back. It will protect your home from negativity.

    Whenever you harvest anything, leave a pinch of cornmeal behind. It is a sign of respect and ensures that you will always have more than enough.

    Seeking guidance? Placing cornmeal and Tobacco on your altar will invite the wisdom of the ancestors and deepen your connection to your spirit.

- **MEDICINAL USES:** Corn silk is an excellent diuretic and mild stimulant that will help cleanse the body.

    When mixed with beeswax or lard, it can be used as a poultice for skin ulcers, swellings, and rheumatic pains. Cornmeal makes a nutritious gruel that is good for convalescents.

Spider Wort

Tradescantia ohiensis

Deepens your connection with spirit

- **SPIDER WORT WILL:** Attract love, Repel negativity, Enhance your inner beauty

- **THE PLANT:** Spider Wort is also called Spider Lily. It is a perennial that will bloom most of the summer. The flowers vary from deep purple to violet to occasionally a yellowish white. The common name Spider Wort is thought to come from the way the flowers hang like spiders from a web off the main stem. Spider Wort requires no special care. In some areas it can spread and become a noxious weed, while in other areas it is easily overrun by other plants.

- **HARNESS SPIDER WORT'S MAGICAL PROPERTIES:** Its three-petalled flower reminds many people of the trinity of body, mind, and soul. In many traditions the trinity plays an important role, and Spider Wort will deepen your understanding of the importance of that connection.

  If you're hoping to attract greater abundance into your life, carry the dried flowers in your wallet.

  To help you relax and connect with your innate inner beauty, float a handful of the flowers in your bathwater.

  Scatter the flowers around your home to chase away negativity and attract the blessings of love.

- **MEDICINAL USES:** Spider Wort was once believed to cure spider bites. The plant is very sensitive to pollutants and radiation. The flowers make a wonderful measure of the amount of pollutants present. They will rapidly turn from blue to pink in the presence of toxins.

Barley

Hordeum distichon

Fills your home with love

- **BARLEY WILL:** Protect your home and the occupants, Heal your mind and body, Invite abundance

- **THE PLANT:** Barley is a grain that looks very similar to wheat. A ripe field of Barley on a sunny day is a sight to behold. Watching the wind as it moves through a ripe field can remind you of the magic and wonder of Mother Nature. Pearl Barley is the grain without the skin. It is rounded and polished. Milled barley, also known as pot barley, is the grain with the husks partially removed. Barley is widely used in the production of malt extract, which is needed for the production of all alcoholic malt beverages.

- **HARNESS BARLEY'S MAGICAL PROPERTIES:** To attract abundance and create a circle of protection, soak some Barley overnight in water and then sprinkle the water around your property. Adding the water to your bath will give you a youthful glow and rejuvenate your mind and your body.

  To deepen your connection to the great Earth Mother, place a jar of Barley on your altar.

- **MEDICINAL USES:** Barley water is used to dilute cows' milk for young infants and prevents upset stomach. Malt vinegar is the only vinegar that should be used medicinally. Malt has wonderful nutritional benefits and, when taken on a daily basis, can be used to hasten recovery from most illnesses.

Cypress

Cupressus sempervirens

Brings you comfort and joy

- **CYPRESS WILL:** Encourage longevity, Provide comfort, Help heal the mind and body, Provide protection

- **THE PLANT:** The Cypress tree is native to the Mediterranean and grows well over a hundred feet tall. It is an evergreen with a conical shape. It is very long lived, with numerous trees reported to be more than a thousand years old. The seed cones are oval with ten to fourteen scales. They are green when they first appear and turn brown after they are pollinated. They mature after about two years.

- **HARNESS CYPRESS'S MAGICAL PROPERTIES:** Cypress will help you overcome the pain of loss. Wear a sprig of it to a funeral to help release your grief.

  Plant a Cypress tree near your home for protection.

  To deepen your connection to spirit, place a Cypress branch on your altar.

  When Cypress is used for healing purposes, it is very important that it be harvested properly. Pick a branch and make a small notch near the base. Slowly, over a period of three to four months, cut the branch from the tree, allowing each cut to heal before deepening the notch. When it is finally removed from the tree, it will be a very powerful wand useful expressly for healing.

- **MEDICINAL USES:** Cypress can be used to treat swelling. A salve made from the bark removes scabs, helps ease the pain of menstruation, and can be used to treat ear infections.

▶ Top: Spider Wort, Middle: Barley, Bottom: Cypress

Horseradish *Cochlearia armoracia*

Gives you the strength to accomplish your goals

- **HORSERADISH WILL:** Purify your mind, body, and spirit, Remove negative energy, Protect you from negative spirits

- **THE PLANT:** Horseradish is a perennial plant that is primarily used for its root. It is a member of the mustard family, along with Cauliflower and Brussels Sprouts. In the Middle Ages, Horseradish roots were believed to be an aphrodisiac and thought to be the cure for almost everything. Perhaps the first person to grind Horseradish for a profit was Henry J. Heinz in 1844.

- **HOW TO HARNESS HORSERADISH'S MAGICAL PROPERTIES:** Place the root over your door to protect your home from negativity and to repel negative hexes.

  To attract good luck and abundance, place a small piece of the root in the four corners of your property.

  If you feel you need help with your meditations, place a piece of Horseradish root on your altar. It will deepen your meditations and assist you in connecting with your ancestral knowledge.

- **MEDICINAL USES:** Horseradish can be made into a syrup and used as cough medicine. It acts as a stimulant for the digestive system. It is also a diuretic and can be used as a poultice to help relieve the pain of arthritis. It is one of the five bitter herbs traditionally served at Passover.

Elm

Ulmus campestris

Expands your ability to love

- **ELM WILL:** Attract good luck, Bless your home, Expand your capacity to love

- **THE PLANT:** Elm grows throughout much of the temperate regions of the Northern Hemisphere. It is a graceful tree capable of attaining heights of more than 150 feet. It was planted in cities throughout Europe and the United States during the 1800s because it was able to grow well in air polluted by numerous coal furnaces. It has a distinctive canopy that creates an inverted triangle of leaves.

- **HOW TO HARNESS ELM'S MAGICAL PROPERTIES:** If you're hoping to attract love, wear a small piece of Elm wood around your neck.

  To protect your property from negative energy, plant an Elm tree near your home. Place a branch over your front door to attract good luck.

  To increase your ability to love, place some Elm branches on your altar and meditate on your heart. Imagine it opening wider and wider until it has the capacity to allow love to flow freely.

- **MEDICINAL USES:** A poultice made from Elm bark can be used to treat ringworm and leprosy. A tonic can be made from Elm flowers to cleanse and strengthen the body.

Poke

Phytolacca decandra

Eases your burdens and shows you how to dance through life

- **POKE WILL:** Impart courage, Break negative spells, Help you find lost objects, Enhance beauty

- **THE PLANT:** Poke is indigenous to North America and is now common in Mediterranean countries. It is a perennial with a large fleshy root and hollow stem. The flowers are white and the berries are a deep purple and look similar to Blackberries. The young shoots of the plant taste a lot like asparagus, and the berries are flavorful and can be used as a dye.

- **HOW TO HARNESS POKE'S MAGICAL PROPERTIES:** To help you feel safe and to give you the courage to face anything, carry some Poke root with you.

  To help you relax and feel beautiful, make a tea out of the leaves and add it to your bathwater. It will also help you release any negative energy. To make the tea, add two tablespoons of dried Poke leaves to two cups of boiling water. Allow the mixture to steep for about ten minutes before straining it and adding it to your bathwater.

  To open your mind and your heart to limitless possibilities, place some of the berries on your altar.

  If you've lost something and can't seem to find it anywhere, mix some dried Poke leaves with flowers from a Violet plant and sprinkle the mixture around your home. You will soon find the object you've been looking for.

- **MEDICINAL USES:** Poke can be made into a poultice to treat sprains and bruises. A salve made by grinding the plant and mixing it with lard or beeswax is a powerful treatment for arthritis and rheumatism. It will sting at first but then produce a soothing feeling of the heart.

Sea Buckthorn

Hippophae rhamnoides

Helps you surrender to and flow with life

- **SEA BUCKTHORN WILL:** Attract love, Invite abundance, Enhance health

- **THE PLANT:** Sea Buckthorn is a beautiful plant that is hardy and able to survive temperatures of -50°F. It is disease resistant and grows easily in a variety of regions. Native to Russia, it grows from six to ten feet tall with narrow silver leaves. The female plant produces numerous orange-yellow fruits. The branches are often used in flower arrangements, and the fruit is high in vitamin C. In Europe, the fruit are used to make jelly and juice. The fruit is tart, but when combined with other fruit, it makes a delicious and healthy dietary addition.

- **HOW TO HARNESS SEA BUCKTHORN'S MAGICAL PROPERTIES:** If you've had a stressful day or are feeling worn out, make a tea from the leaves and cut-up fruit by boiling one-quarter cup of the mix in a quart of water for about ten minutes. After straining the tea, add a small amount of it to your bath. It will relax you and leave you radiant.

  To attract love and dispel negativity, place several branches over your front door.

  To ensure abundance, place a few leaves in your wallet and in your checkbook.

  Rubbing some of the leaves against your forehead before you meditate will deepen your meditation.

- **MEDICINAL USES:** The fruit and its seeds are the main components with medicinal value. Sea Buckthorn's high rate of absorption when applied topically is very useful in smoothing fine wrinkles, healing festering wounds and abrasions, and rejuvenating aging skin. This quality also makes Sea Buckthorn a good lotion for use after exposure to the sun.

Manzanita

Arctostaphylos

Helps you find your true path

- **MANZANITA NUT WILL:** Help you stop smoking, Banish negative energy, Deepen your spiritual connection

- **THE PLANT:** Manzanita are small evergreen trees or bushes that are highly drought tolerant and produce attractive flowers and berries. They have crinkled bark with deep grooves that make it seem as if you can see images in it. The wood has a nice, woodsy aroma.

- **HOW TO HARNESS MANZANITA'S MAGICAL PROPERTIES:** Drinking Manzanita tea on a daily basis will help activate your gift to heal others. To make the tea, add two tablespoons of dried Manzanita to two cups of boiling water. Allow the mixture to steep for approximately ten minutes before straining it.

  To provide protection, dispel negative energy, and fill your home with love, hang a branch over your door.

  To deepen your connection to spirit, find a piece of the wood for your altar that really speaks to you. Place it in the center of your altar with a candle. If you focus your attention on it before you meditate, you will find that your connection to spirit strengthens and expands.

  Ready to quit smoking? Chew on a twig. Get a new one each day until you are finished with the habit.

- **MEDICINAL USES:** Manzanita bark can be brewed into a tea to treat nausea and settle upset stomachs. Chewing on the young leaves can relieve thirst. The berries make a tea that is an overall tonic for the body. Chewing on the leaves will also help prevent tooth decay.

▶ Top: Poke, Middle: Sea Buckthorn, Bottom: Manzanita

Cotton *Gossypium barbadense*

Helps purify your thoughts

- **COTTON WILL:** Bring good luck, Repel negativity, Help with healing

- **THE PLANT:** Cotton is native to Asia Minor and cultivated in the United States, Egypt, India, and the Mediterranean. The seeds are wooly and yield copious amounts of cotton. The plant grows two to six feet tall and has yellow flowers with a purple spot in the center. The seed capsule splits open when ripe, showing a white tuft adhering firmly to the outer coating. The plant is quite spiny, and picking cotton is difficult and strenuous work.

- **HOW TO HARNESS COTTON'S MAGICAL PROPERTIES:** Cotton is the ideal cloth for making amulets, poppets (magical dolls), and other magical items. It is always helpful to have a large piece of good-quality unbleached white muslin on hand.

You can put a few drops of your favorite essential oil on Cotton balls and then place them on your altar or in your closet, or carry them around on your person.

Placing sugar on a Cotton ball will bring you good luck, and sprinkling Pepper on one will encourage a lost love to return.

To repel negativity, place Cotton balls soaked in water and sea salt over your doorways and windows.

- **MEDICINAL USES:** Cotton root is the main part of the plant used in healing. It will increase the contractions during childbirth. A tea made from the seeds will increase the milk production of nursing mothers.

Ti

Cordyline fruitcosa

Helps you rejoice in the magic of your life

TI WILL: Bless and protect your home, Invite happiness and joy into your life, Heal all aspects of your life

THE PLANT: Polynesians introduced Ti plants to Hawai'i, where it is used in sacred rites. The leaves of the Ti plant grow up to two feet long. It is a member of the Lily family and is a fast-growing plant that can reach up to twelve feet high.

HOW TO HARNESS TI'S MAGICAL PROPERTIES: To repel negativity and bless your home and everyone in it, hang two Ti leaves over your front door. Change the leaves every few days to keep them fresh and green.

If you've been troubled by ill health, wave a Ti leaf over the part of your body in need of healing.

Wrap Ti leaves around a vase of flowers and place it on your altar as you say a prayer of thanks. It will help serve as a reminder of the sacred nature of life.

To bless the water as you bathe, hang a Ti leaf over your bathtub.

MEDICINAL USES: The boiled roots can be brewed into a tea and used to settle an upset stomach. The leaves can be used to wrap warm rocks to serve as hot packs. The leaves are also used in poultices and applied to sprains and bruises. The steam from boiled young shoots and leaves makes an effective decongestant.

Henna

Lawsonia alba

Reminds you of your inner beauty

- **HENNA WILL:** Enhance your inner beauty, Invite romance, Heal your mind and body, Deepen your connection to your spiritual essence

- **THE PLANT:** Henna is native to Egypt, India, Kurdistan, Levant, Persia, and Syria. It is a shrub that grows eight to ten feet tall. It has small yellow and white flowers that are very fragrant and sweet smelling. The powdered leaves are used to dye the hair. A dye for the skin can be created by making a paste out of the leaves and combining it with cat-echu. The paste is spread on the skin and allowed to remain overnight.

- **HOW TO HARNESS HENNA'S MAGICAL PROP-ERTIES:** If you've been tossing and turning at night, place the leaves under your pillow to ensure a good night's sleep. You can also do this to attract love into your life.

  Combine the powder with water and use it to write down all your deepest desires. Place the note in a red envelope on your altar to help them manifest.

  To deepen your connection to your spiritual essence, use Henna to draw a small heart on your forehead over your third eye (found in the middle of your forehead).

- **MEDICINAL USES:** Henna can be used to treat jaundice, leprosy, smallpox, and other skin problems. A poultice made from the flowers helps make the limbs supple.

Prayer Plant

Maranta leuconeura

Reminds you that all of life is a sacred act

- **PRAYER PLANT WILL:** Protect your home, Attract abundance, Bless your home

- **THE PLANT:** The Prayer Plant gets its name from the fact that its leaves fold up at night. It is a native of Brazil and has beautiful large oval leaves that are dark green with lovely lighter green geometric patterns. It is a small plant that makes an excellent housewarming gift. A Prayer Plant is happy in low light, but does enjoy a bit of morning sun.

- **HOW TO HARNESS PRAYER PLANT'S MAGICAL PROPERTIES:** Place a Prayer Plant on your altar or near your bed. Then use it as a reminder to take time during the day to deepen your connection to your spirit.

  To protect your family and home, place a few dried leaves under the welcome mat by your front door. They will ensure that negativity does not cross the threshold and enter your home.

  To attract abundance, place some dried leaves in the rear in the left-hand corner of your altar. If you want to attract more love, place the leaves in the rear in the right-hand corner instead.

- **MEDICINAL USES:** A poultice made from the new shoots will soothe the pain of sprains and bruises. It will also help clear up infections in small cuts.

Banana

Musa sapientum

Teaches you about ease and joy

BANANA WILL: Attract abundance, Increase fertility, Protect your property, Enhance your ability to experience joy

THE PLANT: In the tropics, Bananas are as important to the inhabitants as a food source as grain plants are to people living in cooler regions. Bananas yield one bunch of fruit and then die. The leaves are quite broad and are used to wrap food in prior to roasting. The plant produces a large purple bulb at the end of a long stem and then the bunch of bananas forms behind it. The roots of the plants are very tenacious, so once a banana patch is established, it is hard to get rid of.

HOW TO HARNESS BANANA'S MAGICAL PROPERTIES: Sitting under a Banana tree when you meditate will dispel negative thinking and increase your ability to experience joy. If they don't grow in your area, imagine yourself sitting under one, with warm trade winds blowing and the smell of fresh tropical flowers embracing you.

Place the leaves over your door for protection.

A marriage ceremony performed under a Banana tree will ensure the couple of a long and happy union.

Eating the fruit on a regular basis will increase fertility.

MEDICINAL USES: The Banana is of more interest for its nutrients, which include high levels of potassium and vitamin C, than for its medicinal properties. When juiced, Banana roots are effective in treating snake bite.

▶ Top: Henna, Middle: Prayer Plant, Bottom: Banana

Alder

Alnus Serrulata

Helps you resolve issues you have been avoiding

- **ALDER WILL:** Attract fairies, helping you recover lost items, Help you attract success in business, Blend courage with compassion and strength with generosity of spirit

- **THE PLANT:** The Alder family is indigenous to almost every country and continent. It is the common name that refers to a tree with over thirty species. It is part of the birch family and ranges in height from a few feet to over 40 feet (12 m) tall. To prepare Alder wood for use, beat the bark away with a willow stick while projecting your wishes into it.

- **HOW TO HARNESS ALDER'S MAGICAL PROPERTIES:** Alder leaves or twigs can be sewed into a pillow or small charm to act as a protection charm. Fairies are very protective of the tree so it is important to ask permission before using the tree and to leave a gift behind for the fairies. You can use a bookmark made out of the bark to aid in your studies. A whistle made from its wood will allow you to clear spaces of negative energies or to call for a lost love (or find a new one).

- **MEDICINAL USES:** Alder is part of the hazelnut family. A tea can be made from the bark. Drink it to treat diarrhea, coughs, tooth aches, and to ease the discomfort of childbirth. The tea can also be used externally as an eye wash or to ease the discomfort of poison ivy as well as lessening the swelling from sprains.

Oleander

Nerium oleander

Reminds you about your shadow self

- **OLEANDER WILL:** Attract love, Repel negativity, Dispel shame

- **THE PLANT:** Oleander is an evergreen shrub that grows up to twelve feet high and is just as wide. It has white, pink, or red flowers in the spring and summer. They have five petals and resemble tiny roses. The leaves resemble those of Olive and Bay trees. Oleander thrives in hot, mild climates and tolerates considerable drought, poor drainage, and high salt content in the soil. Because deer will not eat this plant and it is so tolerant of a variety of poor soils, it is commonly used as a decorative freeway median in California and other regions in the United States that have mild winters.

  All parts of the plant are poisonous to humans and animals. Children should be cautioned against eating it. The wood should not be used for barbecue fires or skewers. The smoke can cause severe irritation.

- **HOW TO HARNESS OLEANDER'S MAGICAL PROPERTIES:** Oleander is very poisonous, so use it with care.

  To bring good luck and attract love, hang a branch of Oleander over your front door. Planting a bush near the border of your property will chase away negativity.

  If you have been troubled by feelings of shame or regret, write a letter listing your judgments about yourself and anything you feel ashamed of and bury it under an Oleander shrub. As you bury it, say a prayer asking for forgiveness. Stand near the spot until you feel the wind begin to stir. Walk away, leaving the baggage behind.

- **MEDICINAL USES:** None; it is poisonous.

Yew

Taxus baccata

Reminds you just how precious life is

- **YEW WILL:** Bring about rebirth, Help you let go of outdated beliefs

- **THE PLANT:** A Yew tree will grow forty to fifty feet tall and is indigenous to England and much of northern Europe. Its broad trunk is covered with reddish brown peeling bark. The tree forms with lots of twists and turns. The branches create a fascinating canopy, and the lower branches often curve down, offering a wonderful place to sit curled up while watching the world go by. The female flowers produce a red, sometimes yellow, berry that encloses a seed. The tree was considered very sacred by the Druids, and the association of the tree with places of worship still prevails.

HOW TO HARNESS YEW'S MAGICAL PROPER-TIES: Yew has long been associated with death, but in that death is the promise of rebirth. Place some needles from a Yew tree on your altar. Ask for assistance in letting go of all the old beliefs that no longer serve you.

If you can, spend some time meditating under a Yew tree. As you sit in its shade, allow your shadow self to rise to the surface and allow the wind to carry it away. Know that as you die to old ideas, you are reborn into greater freedom and joy.

MEDICINAL USES: The Yew tree is highly poisonous. In homeopathy, a tincture of the young shoots and berries is used to treat cystitis, headaches, neuralgia, heart and kidney problems, dimness of vision, gout, and rheumatism.

▶ Top: Alder, Middle: Oleander, Bottom: Yew

Grape

Vitis vinifera

Infuses your life with joy

- **GRAPE WILL:** Invite joy, happiness, and ease, Inspire you to greatness, Attract prosperity, Increase fertility

- **THE PLANT:** Grape is a deciduous vine with heart-shaped leaves. The flowers are small and barely noticeable. The vine grows up to twenty feet tall. It blooms in the spring, producing a bunch of Grapes late in the summer. Indigenous to the Mediterranean, the vines are grown in many temperate areas. Grapes are best picked close to the full moon.

- **HOW TO HARNESS GRAPE'S MAGICAL PROPERTIES:** The allure of good wine often overshadows the magical properties of the Grape vine itself. Write your hopes, dreams, and desires on a piece of paper and then wrap the paper in a Grape leaf. Bury it in the west corner of your property to ensure that what you have written will come to fruition.

  To attract abundance, hang Grape vines in your kitchen.

  If you'd like to conceive a child, place a wreath made from the vine over your bed. Before your child's first birthday, decorate your home with Grape leaves to ensure a long and prosperous life.

- **MEDICINAL USES:** Drinking Grape juice daily is said to help treat psoriasis, syphilis, and conditions related to the blood. It also improves digestion and absorption of nutrients.

Peyote

Lophophora williamsii

Shows you the great mysteries

- **PEYOTE WILL:** Deepen your spiritual connection, Enhance your meditations, Expand your ability to heal others

- **THE PLANT:** Peyote is also called the Divine Cactus or Mescal Button. It is native to central Mexico and portions of Texas. It is a small, spineless cactus and is well known for its mind-altering properties. The pink flowers emerge between March and May. They produce a fruit called a button. The buttons have been used by shamans and indigenous healers for thousands of years as part of rituals and healing ceremonies.

- **HOW TO HARNESS PEYOTE'S MAGICAL PROPERTIES:** Peyote is mind-altering. When consumed in a sacred manner, it will help you connect with your spirit and expand your ability to tap into your innate wisdom and healing abilities. It is best to use it only under the direction of a shaman or healer who is well versed in its use.

- **MEDICINAL USES:** Peyote is used to treat nervous disorders, high blood pressure, and cardiac diseases.

Apple

Pyrus malus

Teaches you about the power of Earth magic

APPLE WILL: Attract love, Deepen your spiritual connection, Teach you about Earth magic

THE PLANT: The Apple tree has been cultivated for at least three thousand years. The trees blossom in the early spring, putting out a profusion of wonderful-smelling blossoms before the first leaves appear. The blossoms are white with pink veins.

HOW TO HARNESS APPLE'S MAGICAL PROPERTIES: When an Apple is cut crosswise, it reveals a pentagram, which is an ancient symbol of magic. The Apple has also long represented immortality.

Besides making your house smell wonderful, placing a bouquet of the blossoms in your home will attract love or enhance the relationship you are already in.

To expand your ability to see into the future and deepen your connection to all Earth magic, place an Apple branch on your altar. Eating an Apple before you meditate will increase your ability to access ancient wisdom.

If you've found someone special and you're hoping that this person fall in love with you, take an Apple and fill it with your desire for a partner by holding it in the palms of your hands and visualizing a loving relationship. Then give the person the Apple.

MEDICINAL USES: "An Apple a day keeps the doctor away" is a respectable old rhyme that has validity behind it. The acids of the Apple not only make the fruit itself digestible, but are also helpful in digesting other foods. Apple juice will settle the stomach, and eating Apples will help clean the teeth and relieve constipation.

▶ Top: Grape, Middle: Peyote,
Bottom: Apple

San Pedro Cactus

Trichocereus pachanoi

Helps you see the magic in everything

- **SAN PEDRO CACTUS WILL:** Remind you of the divine presence in everything, Help you heal your mind, body, and spirit connection, Bring good luck, Attract abundance

- **THE PLANT:** San Pedro Cactus is a fast-growing columnar cactus native to the Andes Mountains. It has been used in traditional medicine and divination for more than three thousand years in the region. The plant has between four and eight ribs. It usually grows in groups and can grow up to fifteen feet tall. It can have multiple branches emanating from the base.

- **HOW TO HARNESS SAN PEDRO CACTUS'S MAGICAL PROPERTIES:** San Pedro Cactus grows fairly easily in many locations. To deepen your connection to spirit, grow a small plant in your yard or in your home. Remembering the sacred nature of the plant and having reverence for its sacred healing ability will help you invite healing, wisdom, and a profound sacred connection into your own life.

  To attract abundance, place a San Pedro Cactus plant on your altar on the left side near the wall.

- **MEDICINAL USES:** San Pedro Cactus is used to treat nervous conditions, cardiac disease, and high blood pressure. A poultice made from the cactus can be used to treat wounds and clear up infections.

Wax Plant

Hoya camosa

Protects you

- **WAX PLANT WILL:** Provide protection, Attract success and love, Repel negativity

- **THE PLANT:** Wax Plant is a thick succulent with heavy waxy leaves alternating on opposite sides of the stem. It has variegated foliage. The long vines have numerous flowers, which look like clusters of stars. The Wax Plant is a rain forest climber from eastern Australia. It is native also to Tonga and Samoa and has been found on the Fiji Islands and in Southeast Asia. It is very easy to grow in most homes and is a nice addition to your sunnier windows.

- **HOW TO HARNESS WAX PLANT'S MAGICAL PROPERTIES:** Looking for a partner? Hang a Wax Plant in your bedroom to attract love and banish any negative energy.

   To attract abundance, place a dried flower in your wallet.

   Grow a Wax Plant in your living room to bless all your visitors and provide protection for your entire home. When the plant blooms, save all the flowers, place them in a sunny place to dry, and then put them in all of your drawers and closets to attract love and abundance while dispelling any unwanted negative energies.

   When you give a gift away, put a Wax Plant flower on the package as an extra bonus.

- **MEDICINAL USES:** A poultice made from the leaves of the Wax Plant will soothe insect bites as well as minor scrapes and burns.

Heliotrope *Heliotropium Peruviana*

Reminds you of the romance around you

- **HELIOTROPE WILL:** Expand your dream life, Deepen your connection to spirit, Remove negativity, Heal your emotional wounds

- **THE PLANT:** Heliotrope is a sweet-smelling plant that follows the course of the sun. In the morning after opening, it gradually turns from the east to the west. During the night, it turns back toward the east to meet the rising sun. The ancients recognized this characteristic of the plant and applied it to mythology. Just as the plant follows the sun, mortals have fastened their eyes on the gods. Heliotrope is a wonderfully exotic plant with dark green, heavily veined leaves. The deep violet flowers are honey-vanilla scented and are four to six inches wide. They appear in clusters. The flowers open on alternate sides of the plant, first on the left, then the right. They have a wonderful, exotic scent and will transform any area into a romantic retreat.

- **HOW TO HARNESS HELIOTROPE'S MAGICAL PROPERTIES:** If you're interested in exploring the power of your dreams, place the flowers next to your bed. You will have many profound and prophetic dreams.

   To deepen your connection to your spiritual essence, place the flowers on your altar or where you meditate.

   To dispel negativity, sprinkle the blossoms around your home. Breathe in their sweet smell and mentally forgive everyone you have ever felt hurt by while in your heart asking anyone you may have harmed for forgiveness. Do this once a day for a month and you'll be amazed by how much better your life becomes.

- **MEDICINAL USES:** In homoeopathic medicine, Heliotrope was used to treat sore throats. It was also used to treat uterine displacement. In small doses it is useful as a cardiac stimulant and diuretic. In large doses it is a powerful poison. Death occurs from muscular spasms and exhaustion.

Blueberry

Vaccinum frodosum

Improves your ability to see your limitless nature

■ **BLUEBERRY WILL:** Provide protection, Enhance your psychic abilities, Refresh your memory, Help you feel happy and free

■ **THE PLANT:** Blueberries grow on bushes that vary in height from one to ten feet tall. Most blueberries grow on the lower bush variety. Some bushes are evergreen while others drop their leaves in the fall. July is the peak of Blueberry season, although the fruit is available from May through October. The flowers are bell shaped and range from pale pink to deep red. The berry has a flared crown and is deep purplish blue. Blueberries can be eaten fresh or used for jelly, jam, pies, pastries, or juice.

■ **HOW TO HARNESS BLUEBERRY'S MAGICAL PROPERTIES:** For protection, place some Blueberries around your front door. You can also pour Blueberry juice around the perimeter of your property to repel negativity and to stop jealousy and gossip.

　To improve your memory, eat a bowl of Blueberries regularly. They will also expand your spiritual awareness. If you eat them before bed, they will invite pleasant dreams and assure you of a restful night's sleep.

■ **MEDICINAL USES:** Blueberries have a long history of use for medicinal purposes. Their high pectin content has been proven to lower blood cholesterol. Blueberry juice prevents urinary tract infections. They are also good for inducing menstruation. During World War II, the English Royal Air Force reported having improved night vision after eating Blueberry jam.

Leek

Allium porrum

Shows you how sweet life can be

- **LEEK WILL:** Attract love, Evoke protection, Repel negativity

- **THE PLANT:** The Leek is a member of the Onion family. The flavor is more subtle and is sweeter than the standard Onion. The leaves are somewhat flat, and the bulb is long, slender, and oval rather than round like most Onions. Leeks are thought to be native to the Mediterranean. They have been cultivated for more than three thousand years and have long been popular in Europe for soups and other dishes. Leeks were mentioned in the Bible as one of the foods most missed by the Children of Israel when they left Egypt.

- **HARNESS LEEK'S MAGICAL PROPERTIES:** To bless your home and prevent negative influences from coming into your house, plant Leeks in your garden.

  To attract love, hang a Leek over your front door. You can also use a Leek made out of pottery and hang it in your kitchen to attract abundance. It is said that if two people take a bite from the same Leek, they will fall in love.

- **MEDICINAL USES:** Leeks have many similar healing properties to those of Garlic, although Leeks aren't as strong. Eating Leeks on a daily basis will lower blood pressure and reduce cholesterol. Crushed Leeks can be used to make a wonderful poultice for skin abrasions and to relieve the pain of bruises.

Thistle

Carduus nutans

Makes you feel really alive

- **THISTLE WILL:** Deepen your spiritual connection, Invite spiritual helpers, Stop thieves from coming onto your property, Help with healing

- **THE PLANT:** Thistle grows two to three feet tall. The flowers are numerous and are a very deep, crimson purple. They often have a musky smell, and the down around the flowers can be used to make paper.

  Both the leaves and the flowers have sharp edges and prickles.

- **HARNESS THISTLE'S MAGICAL PROPERTIES:** Hoping to attract loving spirit guides and helpers? Gather a bunch of Thistle flowers and place them in an attractive bowl on your altar. Thistle will also help deepen your connection to your spirit.

  To prevent thieves from entering your home, collect the down from the Thistle and put it under your welcome mat.

  If a friend or family member is ill, place Thistle flowers in his or her room. They will help the person heal more rapidly.

- **MEDICINAL USES:** Thistle can be used to treat intermittent fevers. In small doses it is a general tonic and a stimulant. In larger doses it causes nausea and vomiting.

Sacred Mushrooms

Psilocybe mexicana

Invites you to see beyond what you believe is life

- **SACRED MUSHROOMS WILL:** Expand your awareness, Deepen your connection to your spiritual essence, Release limiting beliefs

- **THE PLANT:** Sacred Mushrooms are small mushrooms with gray caps and purple gills underneath. Identifying mushrooms properly is extremely important because similar-looking mushrooms can be extremely toxic. Make sure an expert verifies the type of mushroom you've picked before you use it. Sacred Mushrooms are also considered illegal in many countries.

- **HARNESS SACRED MUSHROOMS' MAGICAL PROPERTIES:** Sacred Mushrooms are used in ceremonies to help heal the mind-body-spirit connection. They create profound altered states of consciousness. They are best used under the supervision of a shaman who has mastered the spiritual uses of the Sacred Mushroom. They induce a deep trance state that can be very disconcerting if you aren't properly guided.

  The connection to one's spiritual essence can be extremely healing and revitalizing to the soul. Sacred Mushrooms are great teachers and advisors and, when used mindfully with a spiritual discipline, bring forth very deep insights into human nature and illumination of the soul.

- **MEDICINAL USES:** Sacred Mushrooms have been used by shamans and healers for centuries in healing ceremonies. The mushrooms help them access spiritual realms so they can remove the blockages in a person's energy body.

▶ Top: Leek, Middle: Thistle, Bottom: Sacred Mushrooms

May Apple *Popophyllum peltatum*

Helps you create abundance

- **MAY APPLE WILL:** Attract abundance, Repel negative energy, Promote a sense of well-being

- **THE PLANT:** The May Apple is also known as Devil's Apple, Hog Apple, Indian Apple, and Wild Lemon. It is a perennial plant that grows six to eighteen inches high. It produces a single white flower in May. The flower turns into a pulpy, lemon-yellow berry that ripens late in the summer. It is the only part of the plant that isn't poisonous.

- **HOW TO HARNESS MAY APPLE'S MAGICAL PROPERTIES:** Hang the root over your front door to protect your home and fill it with a feeling of peace and well-being.

    To help attract abundance, place the root on your altar. Placing small pieces of the root on all of your windowsills will repel negative energy.

    Write your deepest hopes, dreams, and desires on the root and bury it on the night of a new moon in a sacred location. Your requests will be granted if you believe.

- **MEDICINAL USES:** The fleshy rhizomes can be dried and ground into a fine powder, which can be used as a poultice to treat warts and tumors on the skin. The roots are poisonous, so they should never be ingested.

Ground Ivy

Glechoma hederacea

Expands your capacity to love

- **GROUND IVY WILL:** Help you see into the future, Open your mind and heart to love

- **THE PLANT:** The root of the Ground Ivy plant is a perennial, and it has long trailing branches. Ground Ivy has kidney-shaped leaves and will send down roots wherever a branch touches the ground. The leaves stand up several inches from the stem and grow opposite one another. The flowers have a purplish tint and open in early April. The plant blooms through much of the summer and often into the fall.

- **HOW TO HARNESS GROUND IVY'S MAGICAL PROPERTIES:** Place a small pot of Ground Ivy on your altar to remind you of the true nature of love: it takes root wherever it touches a receptive surface.

  To bless your home and fill it with love and abundance, make a wreath of Ground Ivy vines and place it over your front door.

  It is said that if you wind Ground Ivy around a blue candle, it will help you see into the future.

- **MEDICINAL USES:** Ground Ivy is a popular remedy for coughs and headaches. An herbalist might recommend a beverage known as Gill Tea, which is made by taking an ounce of the leaves and infusing them with a pint of boiling water. It is then sweetened with honey, and a bit of Licorice Root is added. It can be consumed several times a day as a tonic and to stop a pesky cough.

  As with all herbs, contact an herbalist before using Ground Ivy.

Vetch

Vicia sativa

Shows you all about freedom

- **VETCH WILL:** Encourage fidelity, Open your heart and mind to love, Repel negativity

- **THE PLANT:** Vetch is a perennial. It climbs about eighteen to twenty-four inches tall. It flowers from May until August with beautiful purple flowers that look a lot like a Pea flower. Vetch fixes nitrogen in the soil. Its leaves are a rich dark green and the plant is hardy to zone 5.

- **HOW TO HARNESS VETCH'S MAGICAL PROP-ERTIES:** Pick a bouquet of the flowers and put them on your dinner table to brighten your home and fill it with love and joy.

  To make sure your partner doesn't stray, put some Vetch flowers under your pillow. To open your mind and heart to your inner beauty and perfection, place some of the flowers in your bathwater.

  If your goal is to deepen your connection to your spirit, put some of the flowers on your altar.

- **MEDICINAL USES:** The leaves and flowers are edible and will settle an upset stomach.

Bamboo

Bambusa vulgaris

Shows you the power of patience

- **BAMBOO WILL:** Bring good luck, Protect your home, Help you manifest your wishes

- **THE PLANT:** Bamboos are fast-growing, giant grasses that have woody stems. The woody, hollow culms (branches) of Bamboo grow in clusters from a thick underground stem (rhizome).

  The culms are often so dense they exclude other plants. Bamboo can grow to more than 150 feet tall and range in diameter from the size of a blade of grass to ten inches. Most Bamboos flower only once in sixty to 120 years. They have large heads much like sugar cane. After blooming, all of the Bamboo plants of the same species die back. This is said to happen worldwide at the same time! The sound of Bamboo rustling in the wind is very soothing to some and annoying to others.

- **HOW TO HARNESS BAMBOO'S MAGICAL PROPERTIES:** Bamboo sticks have been used for centuries in Chinese temples for divination. A person poses a question and throws the sticks. The priest will interpret the pattern they create and reveal the answer to his or her question.

  Grown near your house, they will provide protection and fill your home with a sense of peace and sanctity.

  To ward off evil spirits, carry a piece of Bamboo.

  Writing your dreams and desires on a piece of Bamboo and then launching it on a moving body of water will ensure you of success.

- **MEDICINAL USES:** Bamboo has a variety of med-ical uses depending on the species of the plant. Bamboo is used to treat diarrhea and to control ticks and fleas.

Plantain

Plantago major

Helps you feel grounded

- **PLANTAIN WILL:** Heal your mind and body, Protect you and your home, Dispel fatigue, Give you extra strength

- **THE PLANT:** Plantain grows from a short rhizome that has a number of short yellow roots. It is often found growing along roadsides in warmer, frost-free climates around the world. The leaves are blunt and taper rapidly into the base. The flowers are erect and form at the end of a long spike. They are purplish green. The fruit is two-celled and contains a number of seeds.

- **HOW TO HARNESS PLANTAIN'S MAGICAL PROPERTIES:** Starting to lag? Rubbing the bottom of your feet with a Plantain leaf will dispel fatigue and give you a burst of energy.

    To protect yourself from negativity, carry a piece of the root in your pocket. Similarly, you can hang a root over your front door to make sure only supportive and loving people enter your home.

    To banish illness, sleep with a Plantain root under your bed.

    Finally, if you're feeling anxious or afraid, take a bath with several pieces of the root. They will relax you and give you the courage to face anything.

- **MEDICINAL USES:** The Plantain fruit can be rubbed into the skin to help clear up sores and acne. The leaves can be rubbed on insect bites and burns for pain relief. The leaves will also stop the bleeding of minor wounds.

▶ Top: Vetch, Middle: Bamboo, Bottom: Plantain

Nettle

Urtica dioica

Helps you transform your life with love

- **NETTLE WILL:** Help you release old beliefs that cause stress, Nurture a new project, Show you your worth

- **THE PLANT:** The most common form of Nettles is Stinging Nettles, which feature stinging hairs along the stems and leaves. Traditionally, the leaves were used to wrap arthritic joints to help alleviate the pain and swelling of arthritis. Nettles species can be annuals or perennials. The leaves are elliptical and usually have three to five veins. The leaves are usually serrated and course-toothed.

- **HOW TO HARNESS NETTLE'S MAGICAL PROPERTIES:** The adjectives most used to describe the magic of Nettles are nurturing and mothering. Sprinkle Nettles around your home to fill your life with love. Drink Nettle tea to help release limiting thinking and repel negativity. Wrap a fresh leaf in a piece of purple cloth (use gloves to avoid touching the leaf) and place it in your wallet to attract abundance.

  Sprinkle dried leaves around the foundation of your home to fill your home with love and to make sure unwanted energies don't enter within.

- **MEDICINAL USES:** Nettles are primarily used to relive joint pain. The person's joints are wrapped with stinging Nettles. The stinging pain of the skin actually cancels out the pain in the arthritic joints. A tea of Nettles cleanses the kidneys and purify the bladder.

Wild Plum

Prunus americana

Deepens your spiritual connections

- **WILD PLUM WILL:** Remove all negativity, Attract love and abundance, Help you deepen your connection with the Divine

- **THE PLANT:** The Wild Plum is one of nature's rarest and most unique fruits. Wild Plum grows in the high desert at altitudes between four and six thousand feet at the edges of Oregon, California, and Nevada. It tolerates great extremes of heat, cold, alkaline soils, and drought. The Wild Plum grows on a large bush that is five to six feet tall. The fruit is about the size of a cherry and has a distinctive tart flavor. The Native American tribes of the area gathered the ripe fruit and dried it for winter to garnish their wild fowl and game.

- **HOW TO HARNESS WILD PLUM'S MAGICAL PROPERTIES:** If you're hoping to attract love and abundance, put a few Wild Plums in a bowl on your altar.

  To banish all negativity, hang a branch over your front door. You can also use a branch to symbolically sweep your house clean and raise the spiritual vibrations. Start at the point farthest from your front door, leave the door open, and systematically sweep toward the front of the house. When you are done, throw the branch outside and close the door.

- **MEDICINAL USES:** The bark can be applied to skin abrasions to accelerate healing and can also be used as a gargle to heal mouth ulcers. The crushed roots are used to treat diarrhea.

Shamrock

Oxalis acetosella

Allows joy to fill your entire being

- **SHAMROCK WILL:** Attract love, Increase your abundance, Bring you good luck

- **THE PLANT:** The Shamrock is the unofficial symbol of Ireland. It is a small clover plant with tiny white flowers. Shamrocks have three leaves that are shaped like a heart. They have long been the symbol of good luck.

- **HOW TO HARNESS SHAMROCK'S MAGICAL PROPERTIES:** Having a Shamrock plant in your house will ensure you of good luck. To attract abundance into your life, place a Shamrock leaf in your wallet.

  Giving a Shamrock plant to the person you are interested in romantically is sure to open the door to a long and loving relationship. It also makes an excellent housewarming gift. If a friend is sick or in the hospital, give her a Shamrock plant for her room. It will help her heal quicker and brighten her spirits.

- **MEDICINAL USES:** The Shamrock is touted for its ability to heal sores, especially of the mouth. It is also used to cool fevers and treat urinary problems.

▶ Top: Nettle, Middle: Wild Plum, Bottom: Shamrock

Devil's Weed

Datura stramonium

Helps you connect with the angelic realms

- **DEVIL'S WEED WILL:** Protect you from evil, Deepen your connection to your spirit, Invite beings of light into your life

- **THE PLANT:** Devil's Weed is an annual with erect purple stems that fork. It grows one to five feet tall and has large leaves that look similar to oak leaves. The flowers are trumpet shaped and range from white to deep purple. They open and close throughout the evening. The plant's nickname is Moonflower. The fruit is walnut sized and covered with prickles.

- **HOW TO HARNESS DEVIL'S WEED'S MAGICAL PROPERTIES:** Despite its name, this plant is useful for inviting angelic beings of light. Place a leaf on your altar in the front right-hand corner and call upon the angels. They will immediately fill your home with a sense of well-being. And when you meditate, your ability to connect with high levels of spiritual consciousness will be enhanced.

- **MEDICINAL USES:** Devil's Weed is extremely toxic and can cause severe hallucinations. A trained herbalist might use the plant and roots to help relieve an asthma attack. A poultice made from the crushed seeds and roots can be applied to joints to relieve the pain of arthritis and rheumatism.

Pineapple

Ananas comusus

Welcomes others into your life

- **PINEAPPLE WILL:** Attract good luck, Invite prosperity, Bless your home

- **THE PLANT:** The Pineapple is native to Brazil. Columbus is responsible for spreading it to the rest of the world. Pineapples are a tropical plant but will survive brief periods of freezing weather. It is a perennial plant with long, pointed leaves. The leaves have a needle-sharp end and arise from a central core, forming a rosette. Pineapples bear fruit on a long stalk after a year and a half. They produce small red or pink flowers that turn into a miniature version of a large pineapple that matures over a period of several months.

- **HOW TO HARNESS PINEAPPLE'S MAGICAL PROPERTIES:** Pineapples are a symbol of hospitality. When given as a present, they will bless both the giver and the receiver.

    To attract abundance into your life, place a Pineapple near your front door. Using a symbol of a Pineapple as your door knocker will ensure that only supportive and loving people enter your home.

    To make sure you always have lots of food, grow a Pineapple plant indoors in or near your kitchen.

    If you place a Pineapple on your dining room table, it will impart a feeling of goodwill to all who sit around your table.

- **MEDICINAL USES:** Poultices made from Pineapple can reduce inflammation in wounds and other skin injuries. The juice aids in digestion and will cure stomachaches.

Hemp

Cannabis sativa

Reminds you of your inner wisdom and strength

- **HEMP WILL:** Attract love, Enhance your psychic abilities, Deepen your meditations, Heal your mind-body connection

- **THE PLANT:** Hemp is an annual that grows between three and twelve feet tall. The leaves, which are feathery and have grayish green hairs, are small and appear in clusters. The seeds are smooth and light brown. Hemp grows naturally in Persia, northern India, southern Siberia, and parts of China. Hemp is illegal in many countries and heavily taxed in others.

- **HARNESS HEMP'S MAGICAL PROPERTIES:** When burned as incense with Mugwort, Hemp will induce profound spiritual experiences. The incense will deepen your connection to spirit and remove any imbalances in your mind-body connection.

  When used to smudge your home, Hemp will remove any negative energy and increase the spiritual vibrations. (For more on smudging, see "Making Herbal Tea and using Incense" on page 13.)

  Hemp has the most magical powers when it is grown in the south corner of your garden.

- **MEDICINAL USES:** Hemp will ease pain and induce sleep. It has a soothing influence on nervous disorders. It is useful for treating neuralgia, gout, rheumatism, delirium tremens, insanity, and infantile convulsions.

  A tea made from the seeds will ease the discomfort of menstrual pain.

Rosary Vine

Ceropegia linearis woddii

Reminds you of the magic of the Divine

- **ROSARY VINE WILL:** Bring you good luck, Bless your home, Help you manifest your dreams, Open your heart to love

- **THE PLANT:** Rosary Vine was originally from Africa. The vines look like thin wires with heart-shaped leaves that are silvery and marbled. They grow well as a houseplant. The vines will grow two to four feet in length. It is best to put the plant in a sunny window on a pedestal so the vines can hang freely. It has slender pink flowers that look like an inverted vase. Hummingbirds are very attracted to the flowers. If you place your plant outside for the summer, the flowers will turn into small beads that can be replanted later.

- **HARNESS ROSARY VINE'S MAGICAL PROPERTIES:** Having a plant in your home will bring many blessings to you, your family, and any visitors. Place it near your altar to open your heart to the power of unconditional love.

  To help you achieve what you desire in life, write down all your wishes, hopes, dreams, and desires on a piece of paper and place it under the plant. Each day as you tend to the plant, affirm your intent to allow those blessings into your life.

  To help bring blessings into the lives of others, make cuttings from your plant and give them to your friends.

- **MEDICINAL USES:** A poultice made from the leaves makes a good treatment for rheumatism. The leaves can be applied to the forehead to treat neuralgia and headaches. The juice from the plant makes an excellent treatment to get rid of ringworm.

Cherry

Prunus avium

Teaches you how to be young at heart

- **CHERRY WILL:** Attract love, Expand your spiritual awareness, Increase fertility

- **THE PLANT:** Cherries belong to the same family as Almonds, Peaches, Plums, and Apricots. The word Cherry refers to the tree as well as to the fleshy fruit of the tree that has one seed, or stone. The tree has long, curved, deep green leaves and blooms profusely in the spring. It grows up to ninety feet tall. Cherry blossoms are very showy and sweet smelling. The fruit is sweet and demands a high price because of the high cost of production.

- **HARNESS CHERRY'S MAGICAL PROPERTIES:** Cherries are symbolic of youth and fertility. Carrying Cherry blossoms in your bridal bouquet will ensure a long, happy, and prosperous marriage.

  When you want to deepen your meditations and see into the future, burn the bark as incense.

  Place a Cherry branch over your front door to provide protection for your home, but make sure you put a new one up each year.

- **MEDICINAL USES:** Cherries have several health benefits. The chemicals that give cherries their red color, known as anthocyanins, reduce pain and inflammation. Cherries also contain high levels of melatonin, which helps improve sleep, builds up the immune system, and helps improve the functioning of the heart.

▶ Top: Hemp, Middle: Rosary Vine,
Bottom: Cherry

Norfolk Island Pine *Araucaria heterophylla*

Makes sure you always feel safe

- **NORFOLK ISLAND PINE WILL:** Protect your home and all who enter, Dispel negativity, Attract abundance

- **THE PLANT:** Norfolk Island Pine is a conifer native to the Southern Hemisphere, primarily the Norfolk Islands and Australia. It is one of the few Pine trees able to adapt to interior environments. In its native habitat, the tree may reach two hundred feet in height and grows in full sun. Norfolk Island Pine is salt tolerant, so it can live along the coast. It has long, graceful branches and is commonly sold as a living Christmas tree.

- **HOW TO HARNESS NORFOLK ISLAND PINE'S MAGICAL PROPERTIES:** To provide an aura of protection, plant a Norfolk Island Pine near your home or purchase a potted one for the inside of your house. As long as you are living near one, you will always have enough food to eat and all your basic needs will be met.

  To ensure that more happiness and joy will come your way, place a branch on your altar and spend a few minutes every day thinking of all the things you have to be grateful for.

- **MEDICINAL USES:** The resin from the tree is often mixed with other herbs to make salves. When ground and dusted on a wound, the bark can prevent infection. When the bark is combined with beeswax, it helps reduce the swelling in sprains and bruises.

Palm Date

Phoenix dactylifera

Shows you how to share

- **PALM DATE WILL:** Attract abundance, Increase fertility, Bring good luck

- **THE PLANT:** The Palm Date originated in the lands around the Persian Gulf and in ancient times was especially abundant between the Nile and Euphrates rivers. The Palm Date is erect and grows 100 to 125 feet tall. The trunk is covered by the woody remains of the old leaves. The leaves are feathery and up to twenty feet long. A large spindle emerges from the tree and can be covered with more than six thousand blossoms. As the fruit matures, the stalk will bend over from the weight. The dates are one to three inches long and dark brown or reddish when ripe.

- **HOW TO HARNESS PALM DATE'S MAGICAL PROPERTIES:** Palm Dates produce so many dates that they have long been considered a symbol of abundance and fertility.

  Keep a bowl of the dates on your altar and offer them to all of your guests. Giving your friends dried dates will not only deepen your friendship, but it will also bring good fortune to you.

- **MEDICINAL USES:** Dates can be made into a syrup and used to treat sore throats and intestinal problems. When the seeds are ground up finely, the powder can be made into a poultice to treat wounds and soothe sprains and bruises.

Wheat *Triticum sativum*

Teaches you how to harvest all of life's blessings

- **WHEAT WILL:** Attract success, Help you reap the rewards of your labors, Repel negativity, Increase abundance

- **THE PLANT:** Wheat has been cultivated for more than ten thousand years and probably originates from the Nile River's fertile valley. It is a type of grass grown all over the world. A highly nutritious grain, Wheat has been used for eons as the main food source in most agricultural countries. Wheat grows one and a half to three feet tall and turns golden when ripe. It is an annual, so it must be replanted each year.

- **HOW TO HARNESS WHEAT'S MAGICAL PROPERTIES:** Wheat has long been the symbol of long life, happiness, and abundance. Putting a bundle of ripe Wheat in a vase near your front door will repel any negative influences and attract abundance, love, and happiness.

  Wheat can also help you realize your dreams. Find a picture of fully ripe Wheat and write all your hopes and dreams on the back of it. Fold the picture neatly, put it in a bright red envelope, and put it on your altar. After a month, burn it outside during a full moon.

- **MEDICINAL USES:** Wheat grass juice is believed by many to cure almost everything. The sprouted seeds will fortify a weak digestive system, help stop night sweats, and relieve constipation.

Hemlock *Conium maculatum*

Reminds you what a gift life really is

- **HEMLOCK WILL:** Stop sexual desire, Induce astral travel

- **THE PLANT:** Hemlock grows in most areas of the world. It is native to Europe, Asia, and northern Africa. It is a biennial plant that grows up to seven feet tall. Hemlock has a long tapering root that is forked and pale yellow. The stem is smooth and mottled with deep purple spots. It is also covered with a white fuzz that easily rubs off. The leaves can grow to as much as two feet in length. It has clusters of small white flowers that turn into oval-shaped ridged seeds. The whole plant has a foul smell.

- **HOW TO HARNESS HEMLOCK'S MAGICAL PROPERTIES:** The plant was historically given to initiates into the secret mystery schools to induce a deep trance. If they survived the experience, they were deemed worthy to go on to the next level. The tea was said to allow the student to travel to the home of the gods, where they would be given ancient wisdom and the blessings of the gods.

  In small doses Hemlock was said to remove any sexual desire.

- **MEDICINAL USES:** Hemlock is known as a very potent poison. In medieval times Hemlock mixed with Betony and Fennel Seed was considered a cure for the bite of a mad dog. Socrates ended his life with a cup of Hemlock.

Radish

Raphanus sativus

Teaches you to laugh

- **RADISH WILL:** Protect you, Dispel negativity, Invite happiness and joy

- **THE PLANT:** The Radish is unknown in a wild state, but it's thought to have originated in southern Asia. During the time of the pharaohs, the Radish was extensively cultivated in Egypt. It reached Europe sometime in the 1500s. The leaves are dark green and rough; the roots are swollen bulbs that look similar to turnips. The most common variety is red on the outside with white flesh that is crisp and tender. The flower stem grows to about three feet in height and has medium-size flowers that vary from white to pale violet.

- **HOW TO HARNESS RADISH'S MAGICAL PROPERTIES:** Radish seeds sprout very rapidly. If you are going through a difficult time, plant a few seeds in a pot and place it on your windowsill. Mentally place your cares in the seeds and watch Mother Nature transform them into new life. Also plant a few seeds with the intent of inviting joy, happiness, and laughter into your life.

  Carrying a Radish will protect you from evil.

- **MEDICINAL USES:** Radish juice is excellent for gallstones and kidney stones. An herbalist might prescribe that patients drink the juice to improve their overall health and the effectiveness of their digestive system.

Carrot

Dancus carota

Helps you see the truth

- **CARROT WILL:** Help you conceive a child, Increase your sexual pleasure, Deepen your connection to your spirit

- **THE PLANT:** Wild Carrots are small and woody; the quality of the plant has vastly improved through cultivation. The stems are erect and the leaves are very feathery and deep green. The lowest leaves are larger than the upper ones, and the plant makes a nice border to a flower garden.

- **HOW TO HARNESS CARROT'S MAGICAL PROPERTIES:** Carrot brings hidden things to light, so place one on your altar or bedside when confused or trying to understand events in your life.

  Hoping to get pregnant? Eating the seeds will increase a woman's ability to conceive. Eating Carrots on a regular basis will improve sexual performance and enhance pleasure.

  Taking a bath in a tea made from the seeds will help you relax and deepen your connection with the spirit world. To make the tea, add two tablespoons of the seeds to two cups of boiling water. Allow it to steep for about ten minutes before straining the tea and adding it to your bathwater.

- **MEDICINAL USES:** A poultice made of Carrot roots will ease the pain of cancerous ulcers and help relieve the pain of breast cancer when applied frequently with a cool compress. When applied with honey, the leaves are useful for healing sores and ulcers of the skin. It is believed that eating Carrots regularly will detoxify the kidneys and the bladder. Carrot juice will tone the entire body and improve eyesight. Drinking too much of it will turn the skin yellow, although it has no harmful effects.

Pomegranate

Punica granatum

Helps you plant the seeds for your future

- **POMEGRANATE WILL:** Encourage success, Bring good fortune, Increase fertility, Expand your capacity to love

- **THE PLANT:** The Pomegranate tree grows widely in the Mediterranean, China, and Japan, and the smaller ornamental variety is easy to grow almost anywhere. The tree rarely grows more than fifteen feet tall and has pale brown bark. The new buds are bright green, and the flowers are large and crimson. The fruit is the size of a large orange and is filled with a reddish pulpy flesh and a large quantity of seeds. The outside of the fruit is a pinky red.

- **HOW TO HARNESS POMEGRANATE'S MAGICAL PROPERTIES:** Pomegranate is said to represent the generosity of God's love. The seeds are also symbolic of fertility. If you want to get pregnant, eat the seeds every day for a month or place the seeds in a bowl under your bed.

  Pomegranate is considered good luck, so place a beautiful piece of the fruit in your kitchen windowsill to attract abundance. Given as a gift, Pomegranates bring good fortune.

- **MEDICINAL USES:** Pomegranate seeds will help break up chest congestion. The fruit will reduce fevers, and the bark is used to get rid of tapeworms. The rind can be used to treat diarrhea.

▶ Top: Radish, Middle: Carrot, Bottom: Pomegranate

Ash

Fraxinus excelsior

Teaches you about the right use of power

- **ASH WILL:** Invite prosperity, Dispel negativity, Improve health, Keep you safe at sea

- **THE PLANT:** Ash is a tall, handsome tree that is distinguished by its light gray bark that is smooth in younger trees and rough and scaly in older specimens. It has large compound leaves that impart a light, feathery arrangement to the foliage. The leaves appear in April or May, and the black flower buds from the previous year expand into dense clusters of greenish white or purple flowers.

- **HOW TO HARNESS ASH'S MAGICAL PROPERTIES:** To protect your home and all who enter, scatter the leaves from an Ash tree around your property. To drive away negative energy, place a piece of Ash wood or bark over your front door. Finally, placing a cross carved from Ash on your altar will be beneficial to all who occupy the house and will ensure everyone of good health.

    To deepen your connection to spirit, make a wand out of an Ash branch and use it while you meditate.

    If you'll be traveling on water, make an amulet out of a carved piece of Ash and carry it with you to ensure your safe return.

    Sleeping with some Ash leaves under your pillow will enhance your dreaming and aid you in having prophetic dreams.

- **MEDICINAL USES:** Ash makes a good treatment for intermittent fevers. Tea made from the bark will cleanse the liver and spleen. A poultice made from the leaves and bark relieves the pain of arthritis.

Grass

Bromus hordeaceus

Helps you be flexible and have gratitude for all of life

- **GRASS WILL:** Provide protection, Deepen your spiritual connection, Attract abundance

- **THE PLANT:** There are hundreds of different types of Grass. When many people think of summer, they think of the smell of freshly cut Grass. Years ago, in the country the aroma of freshly cut hay drying in the sun was a familiar smell. Bromus hordeaceus blooms in July. It is also called Bull Grass or Soft Chess.

    Grass is an unusual plant. Each area of this planet has Grass species that are indigenous to it. Yet when a new type of Grass is introduced into an area, it is often considered invasive and at times wipes out the original Grasses and wildflowers. The family of Grasses is the most important group of plants to mankind. The seeds provide food, while the stems are used for roofing and making mats to sleep on.

- **HOW TO HARNESS GRASS'S MAGICAL PROPERTIES:** To repel negativity and invite the blessings of earth spirits, braid some of the stems into a circle and hang it over your front door.

    If your goal is to deepen your spiritual connection, make a cross out of braided Grass and place it on your altar.

    To attract abundance, sprinkle Grass cuttings around your property while saying a prayer of thanks.

- **MEDICINAL USES:** Grass was often brewed into a tea and given as a tonic to cleanse the digestive system and strengthen the body.

Cedar

Cedrus libani

Cocoons you with your spiritual essence

- **CEDAR WILL:** Dispel negative energy, Open you up to higher levels of spiritual consciousness, Chase away nightmares, Attract love

- **THE PLANT:** Cedar trees are one of the tallest species of conifer, but they rarely grow above thirty feet. They have a graceful, conical shape and make a wonderful windbreak. The flowers are very small. The tree is fragrant and the wood is very durable, making it perfect for fencing.

- **HOW TO HARNESS CEDAR'S MAGICAL PROPERTIES:** To banish negative energy, burn some Cedar wood as incense. It will also raise the spiritual vibration of the area where it is burned. If you burn it while meditating, it will help you open up to higher levels of consciousness.

  To prevent nightmares and get a good night's sleep, sleep on a pillow filled with Cedar shavings.

  For protection, keep Cedar wood or a box of Cedar chips in your home, or carry a small piece of the wood carved in your favorite animal's form as a powerful amulet.

  To attract love, carve a small piece of Cedar wood into the shape of a heart.

  Make your altar out of Cedar wood if you want to deepen your connection to your spiritual side and to spirit in general.

- **MEDICINAL USES:** Cedar has a very strong aroma that is very soothing. An herbalist might combine the oil from the leaves with beeswax to make a treatment for rheumatism and arthritis. The salve is also useful on bruises and sprains.

▶ Top: Ash, Middle: Grass, Bottom: Cedar

Bodhi Tree

Ficus religiosa

Invites you to connect to your godlike nature

- **BODHI TREE WILL:** Expand your meditations, Deepen your connection to your spirit, Extend a sense of peace and safety, Attract abundance

- **THE PLANT:** The Bodhi Tree is a variety of the Fig tree. It was already known as the Bodhi Tree before Gautama Buddha sat under its branches while meditating and achieved enlightenment. It is a sacred tree to both Hindus and Buddhists. It is the oldest tree depicted in Indian art and literature and is often depicted as the Tree of Life. The plant was sacred to the Hindu god Vishnu, who was said to be born beneath its branches. It is a beautiful tree, and when the wind whispers through its branches, the sound is quite enchanting.

- **HOW TO HARNESS BODHI TREE's MAGICAL PROPERTIES:** Place a branch from the Bodhi Tree on your altar before you meditate to expand your awareness and deepen your spiritual connection.

  To fill your home with a sense of peace, safety, and joy, hang a small branch over your front door.

  To attract abundance, sprinkle a few of the leaves around the outside of your home.

  If you have the opportunity, sit under a Bodhi Tree and listen to the wind as you pray and meditate.

- **MEDICINAL USES:** The bark can be used to treat infections and inflammations in the neck and glandular system. Made into a poultice, it can be used to treat gonorrhea and various skin diseases. The leaves and bark are used to stop nausea, relieve diarrhea and dysentery, and treat stubborn cases of the hiccups.

Peach

Prunus persica

Reminds you about loyalty and kindness

- **PEACH WILL:** Attract love, Invite good luck, Repel negativity, Grant wishes

- **THE PLANT:** The Peach tree is of such antiquity it is not recognized anywhere in its wild state. Peach is a medium-size tree that lives only about twenty to thirty years. Its leaves are lance shaped and about four inches long. The blossoms appear in groups of two or three along the previous year's growth. They are a beautiful pink and appear before the leaves have fully opened. At the center of the fruit there is a deeply furrowed stone that encases a single seed.

- **HOW TO HARNESS PEACH's MAGICAL PROPERTIES:** To bring good luck and make sure only loving and expansive energy enters your home, hang a branch from a Peach tree over your front door.

  If you feel that a person, place, or thing is surrounded by negative energy, use a branch as a symbolic broom to "sweep" away the troublesome energy.

  If you've recently found a new love, sharing a ripe Peach with the person will cement your relationship and deepen feelings of attraction.

  Carving amulets out of Peach wood and placing them in your children's rooms will ensure them that they are loved and cared for all their lives.

- **MEDICINAL USES:** Peach leaves and bark can be brewed into a tea and used to treat whooping cough and bronchitis. The fresh leaves will expel intestinal worms if applied externally as a poultice.

Orchids

Orchis maculata

Reminds you of the power of love

- **ORCHIDS WILL:** Attract love, Nurture your soul, Deepen friendships, Remind you of your godlike nature

- **THE PLANT:** Orchis maculata is only one of hundreds of varieties of Orchids. It is known as the Spotted Orchid and is indigenous to England and Europe. Orchids are air plants. Their roots are used mainly to anchor the plant, and they get their nutrients primarily from the air and water. They have beautiful flowers that range in color from white to vivid purples, reds, and greens. Some are even brown and smell like chocolate. Vanilla beans come from Orchids. Orchids have been a symbol for many things over the ages, including retirement; friendship; perfection; numerous progeny; all things feminine, noble, and elegant; and magical connections to the ethereal realms— to mention a few!

- **HOW TO HARNESS ORCHIDS' MAGICAL PROP-ERTIES:** To feed your spirit and remind yourself of your amazing godlike nature, place an Orchid plant on your altar.

    To attract love and abundance, hang an Orchid blossom over your front door.

    If you live in a warm climate, place an Orchid plant in the tree closest to your front door to ensure that negativity stays away from your home.

- **MEDICINAL USES:** Depending on the variety, Orchids have numerous properties. They are used to ease coughs, heal skin lesions, and cure fevers. Some of the varieties are poisonous, so talk to a knowledgeable health professional before you use Orchids or any herbs.

▶ Top: Bohdi Tree, Middle: Peach, Bottom: Orchids

Beech *Fagus sylvatica*

Expands your way of thinking

- **BEECH WILL:** Expand your spiritual awareness, Help with divination, Grant wishes

- **THE PLANT:** Beech is a very tall tree, often growing more than 140 feet tall. It can be well over twenty-one feet in diameter. Its root system helps circulate air, and the amount of potash in its leaves keeps the soil around the tree very productive, improving the growing capacity of trees planted near it. The nuts of the Beech tree are called masts. The masts are allowed to ripen and then pressed to make oil. The remaining cakes are used to feed animals.

- **HOW TO HARNESS BEECH'S MAGICAL PROPERTIES:** Beech is an excellent wood for the construction of altars and for the making of runes. The runes will help you see into the future. An altar made of Beech will ensure you of a deep and abiding spiritual connection.

If you want to manifest something, write your desire on a piece of Beech and then burn it on the night of the new moon.

Use the wood to carve amulets to ensure their magical power.

Sit under a Beech tree if you are getting too rigid in your thinking. Lean against it while you meditate to open your mind to the limitless possibilities life holds.

- **MEDICINAL USES:** The bark is rendered into tar that is used internally as a stimulating expectorant in chronic bronchitis or externally as an application to treat various skin diseases. The oil can be combined with other herbs to treat a variety of arthritic diseases and skin problems.

Poplar

Populus tremuloides

Teaches you the proper use of empathy

■ **POPLAR WILL:** Invite inspiration, Expand your knowledge and wisdom, Bring success, Dispel depression

■ **THE PLANT:** Poplar trees grow quite well in North America and areas of Asia and Africa. They reach up to one hundred feet tall and have pale yellow bark. The leaves are slightly oval with fine teeth along the edge. They are generally around one to two and a half inches in diameter. They are one of the first leaves to appear in the spring, and they give off a fresh woodsy smell. Poplar's leaves turn vibrant colors in the fall.

■ **HOW TO HARNESS POPLAR'S MAGICAL PROPERTIES:** The roots of all the trees are interconnected throughout the planet by the earth. Trees are the keepers of the wisdom of the ages. Poplar trees are particularly effective for connecting with that wisdom. You can burn the bark as incense to deepen your connection to your spirit and ancient wisdom.

To invite success into your endeavors, place some Poplar leaves on your altar.

If you're feeling depressed, add a tea made from Poplar to your bathwater to chase the blues away. To prepare the tea, add two tablespoons of the dried bark and leaves to two cups of boiling water. Allow the mixture to steep for approximately ten minutes before straining it and adding it to your bathwater.

When you are in need of inspiration, spend some time meditating in a grove of Poplars.

■ **MEDICINAL USES:** The bark can be brewed into a tea and used to reduce fevers and clear up urinary tract infections.

Cucumber

Cucumis sativus

Helps you see from a more expansive perspective

- **CUCUMBER WILL:** Increase fertility, Facilitate healing, Deepen your spiritual connection

- **THE PLANT:** Cucumber is a native of the East Indies and has been cultivated for at least three thousand years. In Britain, it was first cultivated around 1573. It is a long, trailing plant that has numerous yellow flowers that produce long, deep green fruits that contain hundreds of seeds. The original Cucumber was rather small, like our modern-day gherkins.

- **HOW TO HARNESS CUCUMBER'S MAGICAL PROPERTIES:** If you're hoping to have a child, eat the seeds of the Cucumber. It will increase your fertility.

  Putting fresh Cucumber peels on your altar before you meditate will deepen your meditation.

  To remove negative energy in a room, place several cups of fresh peels in a muslin bag and swing it around the room.

- **MEDICINAL USES:** Cucumber seeds make an excellent diuretic. An herbalist might grind the dried seeds and mix them with water to help cleanse the body of a fasting patient. Fresh seeds can be pounded into a paste and eaten to soothe the intestines and urinary tract.

Orange

Citrus auranthium

Shows you how to find true happiness

- **ORANGE WILL:** Attract love, Dispel negativity, Encourage prosperity

- **THE PLANT:** Orange is indigenous to India and China. It is now cultivated in most warmer climates. It is a small tree with smooth branches and oval evergreen leaves. The tree blossoms and bares fruit at the same time. The flowers are white with a purple tinge, and they curl backward. The blossoms are extremely fragrant and sweet smelling. The fruit turns bright orange when ripe.

- **HOW TO HARNESS ORANGE'S MAGICAL PROPERTIES:** To attract love, add Orange seeds to an amulet.

  Feeling gloomy? Scatter some Orange blossoms around your house to chase away negativity and improve your state of mind. You might also try floating some Orange blossoms in your bathwater, which is very emotionally uplifting and will deepen your connection to your spirit.

  Placing a bowl of Oranges on your altar will invite abundance, and sharing them with others will ensure prosperity.

  To invite happiness and joy and dispel any negative energy you may have brought home with you, place Orange peels in all of your drawers and hang them in your closets.

- **MEDICINAL USES:** Oranges are full of vitamin C, so when eaten regularly, they can help prevent colds. The rind can be used topically on cuts and scrapes.

Daffodil

Narcissus pseudo

Shows you how to harness the energy of rebirth

- **DAFFODIL WILL:** Provide powerful protection, Banish evil spirits, Remove negative spells

- **THE PLANT:** According to mythology, the Daffodil was created when the Greek Narcissus drowned himself after he became enamored by his beautiful reflection in the water. Daffodils are native to Europe, North Africa, and Asia. It is a bulb and a perennial that flowers in the spring. It appears each spring yielding bright yellow flowers. The leaves recharge the bulb and must not be cut back for at least six to eight weeks.

- **HOW TO HARNESS DAFFODIL'S MAGICAL PROPERTIES:** Daffodils symbolically represent the energy of rebirth. Planting them in your yard provides powerful protection. A large bunch of Daffodils is effective in banishing negative energy and removing negative spells.

    A bouquet of Daffodils brings very good luck into the home as long as the bouquet contains more than thirteen flowers.

    To increase the energy and bless your home, place a pot of Daffodils on your altar.

- **MEDICINAL USES:** Daffodil bulbs are poisonous. In an ancient Roman herbal book the roots were said to have the power to disperse whatever had collected in the body, thus allowing the body to cleanse and heal itself.

▶ Top: Cucumber, Middle: Orange, Bottom: Daffodil

Fig *Ficus carica*

Helps you see into the future

- **FIG WILL:** Help you see into the future, Increase fertility, Attract love

- **THE PLANT:** Originally native to the Middle East, the Fig is a bush or small tree that rarely grows more than eighteen to twenty feet tall. It has large, heavily lobed leaves. What we refer to as its fruit is quite remarkable—it is actually neither a fruit nor a flower. It is a hollow, fleshy receptacle that encloses a multitude of flowers that never see the light of day. The seeds ripen, forming the "fruit." In a sense, a Fig is an inside-out strawberry. Figs form at the junction between the stem and the leaves.

- **HOW TO HARNESS FIG'S MAGICAL PROPERTIES:** To ensure abundance and attract many blessings, grow a Fig in or near your home. It will also prevent negative influences in your life. If you grow the Fig near your bedroom, you will always sleep well. If you grow it near your kitchen, you will always have more than enough food.

  Before you leave on a trip, place Fig leaves on your altar to ensure a safe return.

  Figs are a symbol of fertility, so eating them daily when you want to conceive a child will bring success.

- **MEDICINAL USES:** Figs can be used as a mild laxative. The soft pulp of a roasted Fig can be used as a poultice to treat dental diseases and tumors on the skin. The milky sap from a freshly broken Fig stalk can remove warts.

Mulberry *Morus nigra*

Brings you the ancient wisdom of the ages

MULBERRY WILL: Provide protection for the young, Impart wisdom, Deepen your connection to the goddess

THE PLANT: The Mulberry tree is indigenous to Asia Minor but is now widely cultivated throughout the world. It can grow twenty to thirty feet tall and form a dense spreading hedge usually wider than it is high. It has blossoms all over the tree that look more like a fuzzy mass than a flower. They rapidly turn green and then ripen into a deep purple, almost black, berry. The oblong fruit is extremely juicy and has a refreshing taste.

- **HOW TO HARNESS MULBERRY'S MAGICAL PROPERTIES:** Planting a Mulberry bush near your home will bring blessings to you and your family. An amulet made from its wood will provide protection to young children.

   To help access the wisdom of the ancients, weave Mulberry branches into a circle and place it on your altar.

   Eating the berries before you meditate will deepen your meditations and help you connect with the divine feminine.

- **MEDICINAL USES:** Mulberries are often used to make syrup to use with less flavorful herbs. It can also be used to relieve constipation. When used as a gargle, it can soothe a sore throat.

Almond

Prunus dulcis

Teaches you about wisdom

- **ALMOND WILL:** Attract abundance, Deepen your connection to spirit, Bring deeper understanding to complex issues

- **THE PLANT:** Though a native of the warmer parts of western Asia and of northern Africa, the Almond tree has been introduced to much of the world. Almond belongs to the same family as Roses, Plums, Cherries, and Peaches. The tree grows from twenty to thirty feet high and blooms in the early spring. The flowers appear on the young wood from the previous year. The fruit is greenish red and has no juice. It splits open when ripe, revealing the shell of the Almond nut.

- **HOW TO HARNESS ALMOND'S MAGICAL PROPERTIES:** To attract abundance, grind up some Almonds, place them in an amulet, and wear it around your neck. You can also attract abundance by putting a bowl of the nuts on your altar.

  Almond oil will deepen your connection to spirit and help bring understanding to complex issues. Rub a little on your forehead and temples or sprinkle it around the room.

  When you are having a hard time making a decision, place a few Almonds under your pillow and think about the issue before going to sleep. You will get an answer in your dreams.

- **MEDICINAL USES:** When the nuts are ground into a paste and used as a facial scrub, they will improve the complexion. Eating the nuts will cleanse the colon and help prevent colon cancer. Almonds will also lower cholesterol if eaten on a regular basis. They also boost the immune system and act as an anti-inflammatory.

Sugar Cane

Glycyrrhiza echinata

Shows you how sweet life is when you're smart enough to be flexible

- **SUGAR CANE WILL:** Invite love, Encourage wisdom and grace

- **THE PLANT:** Sugar Cane grows in warm regions throughout the world. It has a thick fibrous stalk that is several inches in diameter. The cane has numerous joints and grows six to twelve feet tall. The plant has long narrow leaves and the flowers shoot up from the top of the plant, creating a feathery flower that looks like a large plume. Most of the sweetness is in the root, so Sugar Cane fields are burned before harvesting.

- **HOW TO HARNESS SUGAR CANE'S MAGICAL PROPERTIES:** To invite loving influences into your life, place a short piece of Sugar Cane over your front door. Place a small piece in each of the four corners of your altar to invite love, prosperity, wisdom, and supportive people into your life.

  Before you meditate, eat a small piece of the root to help you let go of your old, limiting beliefs and see life from a more expansive perspective.

- **MEDICINAL USES:** Sugar Cane juice can be poured on deep cuts and wounds to help with the healing process. The juice is used with other plants to sweeten some of the more bitter remedies.

Chinaberry

Melia azederach

Shows you how to embrace change

- **CHINABERRY WILL:** Bring good luck, Attract supportive people, Facilitate change

- **THE PLANT:** Chinaberry trees are native to most warm temperate regions. Unlike most deciduous trees, they are never completely bare. In the winter the branches are full of bunches of pale yellow berries. The Chinaberry is a fast-growing umbrella-shaped tree that usually has only one trunk. Its lowest branches begin six to eight feet above the roots. Its lilac-colored flowers are profuse and smell like chocolate.

- **HOW TO HARNESS CHINABERRY'S MAGICAL PROPERTIES:** To attract supportive people who will help you begin a new endeavor, sprinkle the flowers over your altar.

    Carrying the seeds in your wallet will attract good luck and abundance.

    If you are going through a period of change, place some of the berries on your altar and under your bed to make the transition smoother.

    When you meditate, hold the seeds and ask for guidance.

    Planting a Chinaberry tree on your property will not only assure you of good luck, but it will also protect your home. Plus, you'll have a beautiful tree to enjoy!

- **MEDICINAL USES:** The fruit is poisonous to people, although loved by pigeons. The leaves are used as a diuretic.

▶ Top: Almond, Middle: Sugar
Cane, Bottom: Chinaberry

Glossary

Altar A table or small area that is dedicated to your spiritual practices. It can help you focus and is also a place where you can put candles, amulets, crystals, etc.

Amulet An object that is worn for protection and to attract certain vibrations.

Annual A plant that grows for only one season.

Anointing oil You can make anointing oil by combining herbs with olive oil and placing the mixture outside in the light of the moon undisturbed for a month. At the end of the month strain it through a clean piece of muslin and then store it in a dark place in a blue or brown glass bottle. You can use it in ceremonies and to bless people, places, and things.

Astral projection The ability to project your consciousness beyond the limits of your body.

Banish To permanently chase away energies.

Biennial A plant that grows during its first year but doesn't fruit or flower until the second year, then dies.

Bracts A modified leaf growing directly below a flower stem.

Censer An object in which to burn incense.

Clairaudience The ability to hear spiritual guidance.

Clairvoyant The ability to see images and visually receive spiritual guidance.

Corollas The petals of a flower that are considered a group and collectively form an inner floral layer.

Curandero A Mexican spiritual healer.

Curse A prayer or an invocation intended to do harm to another person.

Deciduous A tree that loses its leaves in the fall.

Divination The ability to gather information about people, places, events, and the future by means other than the five senses.

Dream pillow A small pillow that is made with the intent to work with your dreams; it is stuffed with specific herbs and then placed near your head before you go to sleep.

Enchantment This state is created through focused attention, prayer, and meditation. It will increase the ability of herbs to assist your magical intent.

Equinox The day each spring and fall when the sun is over the equator.

Fruit The ripe seedpods of a plant.

Handfasting An ancient and spiritual form of marriage.

Hecate Goddess of magic.

Hex A form of a curse.

Infusion A tea made by placing an herb in boiling water and then cooling it without it being boiled again.

Magic The ability to harness spiritual energy to manifest physical results.

Meditation Relaxing the mind in order to achieve an altered state of consciousness.

Midsummer Night's Eve The longest day of the year, when the sun has traveled the farthest away from the equator.

Pendulum A weighted object hanging from a string that can be used as a tool for divination. By paying attention to the movement of the object, you can get answers to your questions.

Pentagram A five-sided star that is an ancient symbol used in magical rituals.

Perennial A plant that comes up year after year.

Poppet A small doll made specifically for magical purposes. It can be made either from cloth and herbs or carved from wood.

Potion A mixture of herbs used for magical purposes.

Poultice A damp cloth filled with herbal mixtures and placed on the body for specific healing practices.

Power hand The hand you use to write with, which is also the hand you use to perform magic.

Purification The process of purifying an object, a place, or things through spiritual means.

Resin A sticky juice from a plant.

Rhizome The horizontal stem of a plant that is found underground as part of the root.

Sachet A porous bag of herbs often hung in a closet or placed in drawers or under pillows.

Samhain A holy day also called Halloween.

Scry To gaze into a dark bowl of liquid, a dark mirror, or a crystal bowl to harness your psychic abilities.

Solstice The longest or shortest day of the year when the sun is at the farthest point from the equator.

Spell A magical ritual in which you evoke the power of magic.

Talisman An object that is used to evoke a certain energy, such as love or abundance.

Tea Tea is made by placing herbs in a pot of boiling water and then allowing it to simmer or simply steep for anywhere from five minutes to a half hour. You can use a piece of muslin or a fine bamboo or stainless steel strainer to strain out the herbs before using it.

Umbel A cluster of flowers with stalks of nearly equal length that grow from the same place on the plant and look like an umbrella.

Variegated Leaves that are both light and dark colored.

Wicca The spiritual practice of witchcraft as a religion.

Yule The celebration of winter solstice or Christmas, when a Yule log is burned.

Author's Note

It has been an incredible honor and privilege to write this book. I anticipate you will enjoy reading this book as much as I have enjoyed writing it. I hope you allow yourself to really benefit from all the love and wisdom contained within its pages.

I always love hearing from my readers. If you have any questions or you'd like to contact me, just go to my website, susangregg.com.

With lots of love and aloha,

Susan

Acknowledgments

Writing this book was a wonderful adventure. I have always loved flowers and herbs. Magic has long been a part of my life. What a gift combining the two has been. I'd like to thank my wonderful agents, Sheree and Janet, for making it possible and my editor, Jill. I have enjoyed deepening my knowledge and understanding of the magical workings of the plant kingdom. I am fortunate enough to live on the Big Island of Hawaii, so I can play with plants all year round.

A special thanks to all of my supportive family and friends. Without all of them, this book wouldn't have been possible. I'd like to thank Bea for her love, patience, and endless edits.

And I'd like to thank the world for herbs, rainbows, and all the sweet-smelling flowers.

About the Author

Susan Gregg is the author of seven books, including *The Encyclopedia of Angels, Spirit Guides & Ascended Masters, The Toltec Way*, and *The Complete Idiot's Guide to Short Meditations*. Her podcast, "Food for the Soul," has earned a loyal following of thousands of listeners. She teaches Internet-based classes, as well as teleclasses, and was a speaker at The Whole Life Expo in Los Angeles and Boston. She also teaches classes at The Learning Annex, First Class in Washington, D.C., The Boston Learning Society, and the Discovery Center in Chicago. She lives in Hawaii.

Index

Page numbers in *italics* indicate photographs.